Teaching Media in the English Curriculum

Andrew Hart and Alun Hicks

Trentham Books

Stoke on Trent, UK and Sterling, USA

Trentham Books Limited

Westview House
734 London Road
Oakhill
Stoke on Trent
Staffordshire
England ST4 5NP

22883 Quicksilver Drive
Sterling
VA 20166-2012
USA

First published 2002

UNIVERSITY OF CHICHESTER

British Library Cataloguing-in-Publication Data
A catalogue record for this book is available from the
British Library

ISBN 1 85856 260 0

Designed and typeset by Trentham Print Design Ltd., Chester and
printed in Great Britain by Cromwell Press Ltd., Wiltshire.

Contents

Acknowledgements

We are very grateful to the eleven teachers who allowed us into their classrooms and were so generous in giving up their own time to be interviewed. It says much for them that, while under constant pressure in a culture of inspection and targets they remain dedicated to their own professional development and to the development of English and Media teaching.

The names used in this book are not the names of the teachers who participated.

1

Introduction: Media in the curriculum for English

Media Studies has become the most rapidly growing academic discipline at all levels of education in the UK. Over ten years in the 1990s, the number of students taking General Certificate of Secondary Education (GCSE) courses in Media, Film and Television Studies increased by 72 per cent, while the number of Advanced level (A level) students increased 20-fold over that same period of time. Undergraduate degree courses showed the highest year-on-year growth in demand (17.3 per cent) of all applications in 2000. Three new A level syllabuses in Media Studies and Film Studies, and three new General Media syllabuses, have recently been approved. According to the latest Department for Education and Employment (DfEE) official figures, there are now around 25,000 teachers in UK secondary schools who will in future be teaching about the media within the English curriculum. Yet despite the obvious strength in and importance of the subject, its position within the English curriculum remains confused.

The English teacher can hardly be blamed for being more than a little uncertain about how to approach Media Education. Society is confused about its attitudes towards new media technology, especially in relation to the young; the ambiguous position of Media Education in the English curriculum reflects the ambivalent attitude of government agencies towards it. It is left to the largely unsupported teacher of English to resolve these social and pedagogical dilemmas.

In very recent times our moral and social preoccupations were about young people's apparently addictive use of violent video games. Now, it seems, we are more likely to be concerned with how young people themselves are used and abused via Internet pornography. Yet, at the same time, we recognise the entrepreneurial spirit of slightly older teenagers who start up their own Internet companies, or, more commonly, develop innovative forms of communication via telephone text messaging. Historically, in schools it is only the English curriculum that has had the will or the capacity to deal with the creative, moral and social implications of new media. But the teacher of English is also the consumer (or not) of the new media and the parent of the young people towards whom society feels so protective. It would be understandable if, in these circumstances, many English teachers found themselves addressing an aspect of the curriculum about which they were themselves ambivalent and tentative, and within which they were inexperienced or even, compared to the young students in their classroom, naïve.

This tentativeness is represented in the following view expressed by Chris Richards. Note how the language he uses reflects the uncertainty of the English teacher's position. He writes of *conflicts, tensions, struggle* and of curriculum and culture being *unsettled, uncertain and disparate*:

> The practice of media education moves teachers into a more radically unsettled curricular space than that provided by most English teaching. The tensions and conflicts between popular discourses and between discourses arising from media education itself are productive of an uncertain, uneven, but also potentially innovative, struggle. The struggle is to conceive of a more flexible practice, attentive to the forms and the detail of the emergent and disparate cultures in which school students locate themselves. The effort of teaching, and of sustaining the discursive coherence and credibility of media education, involves teachers in some work upon themselves, drawing on experiences of change and possibility in the past, but also necessarily rethinking the more settled features of their own formation as teachers of English. (Richards, 1998, p. 50)

Teachers involved in the sort of struggle described by Richards clearly need support. Potential sources of such support must include the sort of empirical evidence produced by our research. How are teachers to draw on 'experiences of change and possibility in the past' if they do not have access to the thoughts and practices of other teachers in similar positions? The British Film Institute's (BFI) *Curriculum Statements* (Bazalgette, 1989; Bowker, 1991) provide some detailed examples of classroom work that teachers might follow. But these are all limited in value by the fact that they are uncritical accounts of teachers' own practice written by themselves and by the fact that they are cross-curricular in emphasis rather than focused within a specialised English or Media curriculum. These 'case studies' are examples of practice and reflections on forms of practice, but they do not provide any kind of critical framework through which qualitative judgements can be made. They lack the essential dimension of controlled and systematic enquiry that is implicit in a research process conducted by external observers and interviewers. Although the accounts provided by Buckingham and colleagues are much richer and focused within a specialist curriculum, they also lack this dimension of a controlled research process (see Chapter 2).

The role of research in helping Media teachers draw on the experience of others is developed later in this chapter and throughout this book. But first, we shall consider the curriculum frameworks within which teachers of English who teach Media are likely to be working.

Curriculum guidance
It might be reasonable to assume that the teachers referred to by Richards could turn to National Curriculum documents for guidance. Indeed, in the third version of the National Curriculum for English in the past ten years (Qualifications and Curriculum Authority (QCA), 1999), the position of Media Education is clearer than ever. Teachers of English are now required to include the moving image as part of Media Education and to teach students about how meaning is conveyed; how purpose, form and presentation affect meaning; and how audiences choose and respond to media. Ironically, as QCA officers themselves acknowledge, this new clarity potentially increases the gap between what many

teachers know about Media Education and what they are required to teach. But even if the problems of teacher subject knowledge and professional development could be addressed, this would not deal with the fundamental problem: historically, there have been, and still remain, significant tensions related to the position of Media Education within the curriculum for English. Some of those tensions and their impact on teaching Media in English have been explored in a number of articles by Buckingham (1990b, 1990c) and Hart (1992).

The English curriculum is an uncomfortable host for Media Education because of essential differences related to subject theory, medium and mode of communication, and attitudes towards fiction and those who 'create' it. Some of the sources of the discomfort are summarised in the table below:

English	Media Education
Has no clearly articulated 'theory' of English teaching	Depends very strongly on a set of commonly accepted Media 'concepts'
Favours print as a medium of communication	Favours sound and the moving image
Tends to regard 'production' (i.e. writing) for its own sake as an essentially personal, creative process	Tends to regard practical production as an avenue to a better understanding of theory
Values student production (writing) on its own merits with criteria drawn from a literacy paradigm	Values students' ability to pastiche and parody
Assumes that the theory of writing is implicit in the students' practice	Calls on students to articulate the theory behind their practical productions
Favours fiction	Favours non-fiction
Tends to study narrative and drama as the products of creative, influential individuals whose work is to be revered	Tends to study narrative and drama as the collaborative products of institutionalised and professional practices

4

These are, of course, broad generalisations, but the essential truth of the tensions between Media and English teaching remains. Looking to the future, one can speculate on two important curriculum developments likely to affect the situation. The first is that, from September 2001 onwards, the government's Literacy Strategy moves from the primary phase, Key Stage 2, to the secondary phase, Key Stage 3. This move coincides with the publication by QCA of a number of significant publications calling on teachers to concentrate more strongly on a grammatical approach to texts and to writing. While these developments are welcomed by many teachers, particularly those experienced in teaching A level English Language, a 'creativity' backlash has already begun. The next few years are likely to see workshops, debates and publications on 'creative' approaches to writing. If such a debate helps clarify exactly what English as a subject is, then the impact on Media Education is likely to be beneficial. If the debate leads to further curricular tensions, then a clear position for Media in English seems less likely.

But the more significant development on the horizon is the possible division of English at GCSE level into English Language and English Literature. If, as seems likely, this happens, then what will happen to the assessment of Media learning? Will it be firmly rooted in the identification of bias in and deconstruction of non-fiction texts? And if it does, then what will happen to students' response to film versions of Shakespeare and those many other adaptations that fill every English department stock cupboard? Over 60 per cent of English teachers surveyed by the British Film Institute (Barratt, 1998) regularly study film adaptations of literary texts. If the practice is to be more than a revision tool, then student response to such adaptations needs to be acknowledged and credited.

Research evidence

The sort of evidence offered by the recent BFI survey points the way towards a source of enlightenment and support for teachers in the midst of these curricular tensions. That is, one might reasonably expect that English teachers could turn to educational research to find out more about what is happening and how to respond. The Barratt report, like other BFI reports before it, does offer a usefully broad view of Media Education in English, but, from the perspective of the classroom teacher of English, has two weaknesses. The first is that its questionnaire-based approach tends to add to the confusion about Media in English, since it is not easy in such a survey to ensure that all teachers mean the same thing when they say they are 'teaching Media'. The second is that the BFI's understandable keenness to promote film and the moving image sometimes leads to the writers of such reports ignoring statistics that reveal teacher dependence on advertising and newspapers. This report will be discussed in more detail in a review of Media Education research in Chapter 2.

Also discussed in Chapter 2 is an approach to Media Education research with rather more promise for the classroom teacher, the type carried out by David Buckingham and colleagues. The fundamental theme of Buckingham's research is that one should acknowledge that the reader brings to any text a given set of experiences that significantly affect any reading of that text. He also argues that the reading of any text is strongly dependent on the social circumstances in which the text is experienced or consumed, and that reflecting on that text is as much a social activity as a cognitive one. Buckingham thus provides evidence for the teacher of the importance of paying as much attention to readers and viewers as to the texts themselves. This will have significant implications for classroom teaching and learning.

Equally important, Buckingham's research offers teachers of Media in English helpful models whereby they might conduct their own, similar investigations of their own teaching practice. But it does not offer theorised accounts of teachers' work by other teachers, accounts that offer hard-pressed teachers research findings that might inform their own curriculum organisation, planning and teaching strategies. Above all, it does not take into account the institutional constraints faced by every teacher of English, from the limitations of the chosen GCSE examination syllabus to the school's curricular priorities as reflected in its development plan. In short, there is a dearth of research that tells teachers, in terms of Media Education in English, what other teachers think, say and do in the real context of the pressurised curriculum in the new millennium.

The research in this book offers to fill that vacuum. It:

- examines in detail a range of approaches to Media teaching currently used in secondary schools at Key Stage 4 by talking to individual teachers in depth about their work

- investigates the forms and purposes of Media teaching in English in secondary schools by observing actual lessons in detail and analysing how they work

- provides an account of the role of Information and Communication Technology (ICT) in Media in English

- provides extracts from actual lessons recorded by observers

- shows how teachers deal with key concepts like representation, audience and agency

The sort of evidence and detail provided in this book will allow the teacher of Media in English to:

- plan for changing curricular needs by drawing on the experience of other successful English teachers

- lobby strongly for appropriate resources and in-service support

- analyse their own curriculum organisation in relation to the experiences and practice of others

- reflect on their own understanding of Media Education concepts by comparing it to the understanding of others

- reflect on their own teaching strategies by matching them against the strategies used by other teachers

Strategies for Survival
The status of Media Education

Although the teachers we interviewed were sometimes confused about the position of Media within English, they were agreed that the status of Media Education had risen in the past ten years. The National Curriculum revisions made since (QCA, 1999) have confirmed and enhanced that status. Those teachers who assume that their task is to teach English **through** Media Education are mistaken. It is clear from the statutory requirements that English

7

teachers are required to teach Media **in** English. This is not some semantic pedantry. The moving image, now at the heart of the National Curriculum for English, has never before been the responsibility of English teachers. But English teachers would be misled if they thought that the inclusion of film and television in the curriculum would be enough. There are three clear new elements of student experience and progress that have to be planned for, taught and recorded. The first element is the explicit study of how sound and image contribute to textual meaning. The second is how the nature and purpose of the media product influences its meaning. In effect, this means, for example, that students have to study news as a genre rather than in the form of literary newspaper articles. This entails, at the very least, explicit teaching about news values (what determines what gets into the news and the priorities given to news items) and news media ownership. The third element is the study of audience choices and audience response. The notion of audience has long been important in the teaching of writing, but it is less common to find it addressed as an element of textual understanding. Indeed, in a literature-centred curriculum, the issue of audience choice has largely been redundant, given that novels, plays and poems selected for study have, in the majority of cases, been chosen by Examination Board and teacher.

Departmental planning

We found that English departmental planning was well advanced and very influential in determining the nature of Media Education in a given school. But usually, the head of department was reluctant to be overly prescriptive in applying departmental policies. In practice, there was often scope for the individual teacher, if she or he wanted, to select their own path through the agreed Media policy. Though this allowed the sort of professional responsibility that is integral to teaching, it did raise questions about the head of department's ability to provide students with their curriculum entitlement. The broad planning implications, however, are not especially complex. As implied in the previous paragraph, to meet the requirements of the National Curriculum, the head of department needs to ensure, through collaborative or individual planning, that each teacher can answer three curriculum questions:

1. Where in the curriculum is the moving image the focus of study?

2. What explicit teaching is there about form, presentation and layout?

3. What account is taken of how readers, viewers and listeners choose and respond to the texts they read, watch and listen to?

Understandably, heads of department, when reviewing planning and policies, will often have the OFSTED inspector in mind. Our research suggests that where Media Education is concerned, most heads of English are several steps ahead of OFSTED.

Choice of Examination Board

Detailed study of examination papers, coupled with the responses of the teachers we interviewed, reveals just how significant is choice of examination syllabus. The evidence shows that, at best, the Examination Boards' interpretation of Media Education in English has led to a narrow Media curriculum, largely rooted in the study of newspaper articles. At worst, there was evidence of one Board failing to understand important distinctions between study of the media and the simple retrieval of information from non-fiction texts. GCSE syllabuses taking account of the new curriculum emphases need to address the thorny issue of *assessing* study of the moving image. A careful reading of Chapter 4 of this book will provide English teachers with a model on which to base their own judgement of the new syllabuses. Teachers need to think very carefully about how each Examination Board, via its syllabuses and, even more significantly, its examination papers, interprets the new Media demands.

Moving image teaching

We have already outlined the new significance attached to the moving image in Media within English. Our research offers very detailed analysis of three typical moving image lessons, including Shakespeare adaptations, David Lean's *Great Expectations*, and use of the very popular Levi advertisements from the English and Media Centre's *Advertising Pack*. The accounts of these well-constructed lessons provide every English teacher with touchstones to reflect on their own experiences of teaching literature on film and advertising (probably the two most common approaches to the moving image in English). However, the recurrent absences in what was seen in the research are equally important. As with the BFI report (Barratt, 1998) there was no evidence in the lessons seen, or in conversations with teachers, of contemporary television drama being a part of the school curriculum. Equally important, there was no evidence of teaching about images, moving or still, as they appear on the Internet. One could reasonably argue that the Internet is a technology developing too quickly for national curricula and examination syllabuses to cope with. Once again, it is only teachers of English who will be in a position to support young people in their response to and interpretation of the new media.

Media concepts

As outlined earlier, Media Education sometimes sits uneasily in the English curriculum because its clear conceptual framework is at odds with its relatively untheorised host. But the tension is exacerbated by the fact that interpretation and application of such concepts among English teachers is not entirely consistent. Our research shows that English teachers were most likely, in their teaching, to address *representation* and *media language*, and least likely to address *institutions* or *agencies*. When teachers talked about media language they tended to think in terms of literary rhetoric and conventions rather than the presentational codes of the moving image such as *shot, lighting* or *colour.* Quite often, the original BFI concepts (Bazalgette, 1989) had been hybridised so that they resided somewhere between Literature and the mass media. For example, *style* was a concept sometimes used to address presentational issues in the moving image and print. The need for all teachers within a given institution to have a clear and consistent view of Media concepts is very evident from this research.

Media principles

It is just as important that each department of English teachers has a debate about some of the main principles of Media Education, about what teachers think Media Education is for. In the hectic reality of day-to-day teaching, it is understandable if philosophical issues are sometimes left unaddressed. But our research shows clearly that teachers need to make explicit their sometimes unspoken attitudes to and assumptions about the media. Typically, when interviewed, teachers would declare a desire to help students **discriminate** in their choice of media or of media texts. Some teachers went further and expressed a desire to help pupils resist media manipulation. Such positions are entirely understandable, but they do need to be deconstructed. Teachers need to ask themselves how successful they think they are likely to be in this ambitious project. And how are English teachers to take account of the very substantial pleasures that young people quite reasonably find in their media consumption? Buckingham (e.g. 1993a) in particular has argued strongly that a demystification model of Media Education is seriously flawed since it mistakenly sees audiences as passive victims of a dominant ideology and fails to validate children's own culture. As many Media practitioners have demonstrated, it is possible to support students in their critical thinking without necessarily seeing the media as 'the enemy'.

Media across the curriculum

Our research found no evidence that Media Education was flourishing in any school outside the English department, beyond actual GCSE Media Studies courses. Ordinarily, this might be a message for English teachers to concentrate their Media efforts on English rather than on cross-curricular Media projects. However, it is clear that at the heart of the government's literacy strategy, now moving to Key Stage 3, is the notion of literacy across the curriculum, with the Education Authority's literacy consultant and the school's literacy co-ordinator at the heart of the development. Teachers of English will need to have a very clear view on whether they see 'Media Literacy' as part of this development, and whether they have any particular role to play in relation to it.

Professional development and Media resources

The teachers we observed were unlikely to have experienced any recent specialist Media training, unless it had been provided by the Examination Board and related directly to syllabus requirements.

Four implications are clear. Firstly, the role of the Examination Board in such training has become increasingly influential. It is essential that English teachers lobby their Board to ensure that Media understandings in the syllabus and examination paper accurately reflect the new National Curriculum syllabus. Secondly, heads of English need to use the sort of evidence we have provided to lobby school senior management to ensure that Media Education becomes some part of the school development plan. Its absence from planning at this level appeared to be one of the major reasons why Media in-service training was not often funded. Thirdly, where GCSE Media Studies existed as a discrete course, the expertise of the teachers involved in it often proved an invaluable source of internal in-service training for English teachers. Lastly, teachers whose schools were near recognised centres of Media Education were more likely to be in touch with contemporary Media developments. (Such sources of training in this research were Southampton University and the very influential English and Media Centre in London.)

The English and Media Centre proved equally significant as a provider of Media resources. When English teachers used commercially produced resources, the English and Media Centre was mostly likely to be the source. There was, however, some evidence of teacher over-reliance on the very good but overused activities related to the Levi Jeans advertisements from *The Advertising Pack*. It seems likely that this reflects the tendency of the less experienced teacher of Media to reuse well-rehearsed analysis of one particular media text or group of texts. There would seem to be some value in English departments reviewing the resources they actually use (rather than the ones they buy) to ensure that students' Media experience does not come via a too narrow range of media texts.

For some time it has been common in health care for best practice to be 'evidence-based'. Education is moving swiftly in the same direction. In 1996 the UK Teacher Training Agency (TTA) began a low-key scheme, awarding research grants to 26 projects that entailed 'classroom-based research carried out by teachers, to raise other teachers' interest in research and evidence'. By 2001 the scheme had grown, with the TTA receiving over 100 collaborative bids for this type of research funding. In relation to English teaching, the pre-occupations are unsurprising, including, for example, research into the under-achievement of boys, spelling and writing strategies. This type of funding for teacher-led classroom research is also available from the DfEE who, in 2001, offered 1000 Best Practice Research Scholarships. The designated research topics do not directly mention Media Education, but one related area is 'information technology and its impact on learning', and potential applicants are encouraged that the list is 'not prescriptive' and applications will be 'considered on their merits'.

It is hoped that this book will encourage teachers to conduct their own research into Media teaching, and contact the DfEE or TTA to see what support remains available. The research design in this book has already been adapted in 14 other European countries as well as by colleagues in South Africa, Western Australia, the USA and Canada. Yet still there remains a dearth of quality classroom-based research into Media Education. Teachers are welcome to use or adapt our research tools to gather evidence about Media teaching in their own particular circumstances.[1]

For English teachers teaching Media who are not inclined to become researchers themselves, it is hoped that the evidence-based material in this book will provide detailed quality data on which they can make reasoned and reasonable policy and pedagogic decisions.

1 The University of Southampton's Media Education Centre offers a new Master's-level Distance Learning course for teachers designed to introduce them to research-ing their own and others' work in a systematic way. See <www.soton.ac.uk/~mec>

2

Researching Media Education

As suggested in Chapter 1, there has been much rhetoric but little research on Media teaching. That is, there is a dearth of basic research, if research is seen as a process of investigation that is public, systematic, controlled and critical of its own methodological weaknesses (Cohen and Manion, 1994, pp. 4-5; p. 40). Most accounts to date have been concerned with arguing a case (often polemically) for Media Education or providing resources and strategies for Media teachers. As Learmonth and Sayer's survey for the BFI notes, there is a 'marked lack of objective evidence and debate about methods of teaching and learning that most effectively develop students' skills in media education' (Learmonth and Sayer, 1996, p. 9).

The first substantial research on Media teaching took place in the UK in the early 1970s, when the Schools Council funded an investigation into how schools were responding to the burgeoning media culture around television and pop music, and how involvement in this culture was affecting teenagers' commitment to school and educational performance (Murdock and Phelps, 1973). This large-scale survey found that 80 per cent of teachers sampled in (selective) grammar schools and 42 per cent in (non-selective) comprehensive schools felt that the study of the mass media had little or no legitimate claim to classroom attention. The findings were widely used and debated both in the UK and elsewhere, but in the quarter of a century since then, there have been no further detailed large-scale studies.

Empirical Research on Secondary Media Education in the UK

FOCUS	METHOD	AUTHOR	PLACE	DATE
Range and frequency surveys	Questionnaire }	Murdock and Phelps	England	1973
		Butts	Scotland	1986
		Twitchin and Bazalgette	England	1988
		Dickson	England	1994
		Brown and Visocchi	Scotland	1991
	Questionnaire and Interview	Media Education Wales	Wales	1996
	Questionnaire and Focus Groups	Barratt	England	1998
	Questionnaire, Focus Groups and Interview	Livingstone and Bovill	England	1999
Teacher Perspectives	Interview and Questionnaire}	Murdock and Phelps	England	1973
		Butts	Scotland	1986
	Observation and Interview	Hart	England	1993, 1999
	Questionnaire	Davies	England	1996
	Questionnaire and Observation	Goodwyn and Findlay	England	1997
	Focus Groups	Barratt	England	1998
	Self-reflection	Buckingham	England	1995
Classroom Teaching	Observation }	Butts	Scotland	1986
		Brown (DEFT)	England	1990
		Learmonth and Sayer	England	1996
	Observation	Hart	England	1993, 1999
	Observation and Interview }	Buckingham	England	1998
	Self-reflection			

Empirical Research on Secondary Media Education in the UK (continued)

FOCUS	METHOD	AUTHOR	PLACE	DATE
Classroom Learning	Observation }	Buckingham	England	1990, 1993
		Hart	England	1993, 1999
	Self-reflection and Interview	Buckingham	England	1994, 1995, 1998
Curriculum Contexts	Documentary }	Butts	Scotland	1986
		Hart	England	1993, 1999

The rise of qualitative methods in Media and Cultural Studies research has, however, provided much more detailed and nuanced accounts of children's and teenagers' media experiences and their relation to changing patterns of social division, family structures, everyday life, and personal identity. Within education, there has been a vigorous debate about the use of media in schools and about the value of Media Education. More recently, these arguments have been given added impetus by the rise of increasingly interactive media. Yet we currently lack an adequate evidential context for such debates, because no recent study has returned to the full range of questions raised by the 1973 study and explored them systematically across an appropriate range of contrasted educational settings.

Questions about the models of English within which the Media curriculum functions have been explored by Davies (1996) and Goodwyn and Findlay (1997).[2] Responses to Davies's questionnaire suggested that, in the mid-1980's, the 'personal growth' model of English held a great attraction for teachers. That is, teachers favoured an approach to teaching English whereby the development of the individual was regarded as perhaps more important than an understanding of texts. Davies did, however, detect the emergence of a positive attitude towards a 'cultural analysis' model.

Goodwyn and Findlay found that the 'personal growth' model had become almost a matter of faith for English teachers, a rallying cry in order to defeat the 'threat' of a 'cultural heritage' model being imposed. In this context, there was no clear place for 'cultural analysis', the obvious niche for Media Education in English. Yet, in 1997, 87 per cent of respondents to Goodwyn and Findlay's survey accepted the significance of Media Education in the curriculum for English. Goodwyn and Findlay account for these apparent contradictions by the significant rise in teacher support for the 'adult needs' model of English teaching. It seems likely, they argue, that the increasingly strong position of Media Education can be partly accounted for by teachers regarding Media Education as an important aspect of preparation for adult life. Goodwyn and Findlay's

2 See Chapter 3 for an account of the different models disseminated by the 1989 Cox Report.

research, though similar in approach to Davies's, benefited from being conducted in eight LEAs rather than just one and included lesson observation.

There have been several broad surveys of classroom practice Media teaching within the UK, notably from the British Film Institute (Twitchin and Bazalgette, 1988; 1994) and the recent small-scale report by two former Schools Inspectors, referred to earlier (Learmonth and Sayer, 1996). As its title implies, the latter is a study of 'good practice' which relies on reporting the work of the strongest teachers in schools specially selected for the quality of their work in this field. The report, based on eight secondary schools in the UK, is helpful in drawing attention to some of the commonly found strengths and weaknesses of Media teaching, but its primary focus is on appropriate inspection criteria for the evaluation of teaching and learning. It is not explicitly concerned with the relationship between teacher perspectives and classroom practice. It reports on a very small number of Key Stage 4 (age 14-16) lessons, providing detailed information about only one of these (Learmonth and Sayer, 1996, p. 36). However, the observation criteria are generalised rather than Media-specific, i.e. those criteria typically employed by OFSTED in evaluating the quality of teaching and learning in any classroom. In addition, the research explores only one lesson in significant detail and is rather shy in its disclosure of the approaches used and the research methods. It cannot claim to be research in the standard Cohen and Manion sense, since it neither declares its research approaches nor critically discusses its methods.

Barratt's recent questionnaire-based survey of over 700 secondary schools in 129 LEAs, supplemented by focus-group discussions with 39 teachers (Barratt, 1998, pp. 10-12), confirms most of the findings of the Southampton study of Media teaching at Key Stage 4 under the post-Cox National Curriculum for English (DES, 1989, 1993; Hart and Benson, 1993). He found similar disquiet amongst teachers about the coherence and rationale of National Curriculum requirements for Media within English (p. 17). Many teachers were still lacking in confidence (pp. 36-37), especially in assessing Media work and felt restricted by time constraints (p. 27). The majority also felt in need of further training and appropriate resources. Written tasks continued to be the most common form of classroom activity and assessment (pp. 25-26) and film or television adaptations were more frequently studied than original material.

According to Barratt's survey, however, there have undoubtedly been significant changes of attitude and practice since the Southampton study (Hart and Benson, 1993). He discovered much more wide-spread and positive attitudes to Media teaching. Under the post-Dearing curriculum, the majority of respondents (91 per cent) believed Media study had a place in English because of its significance in pupils' lives (p. 19); and a similar number (94 per cent) agreed that Media-related work in English should help to make pupils more discriminating in their use of media (p. 28).

The post-Dearing curriculum and the new GCSE syllabuses for English have meant that many English teachers at Key Stage 4 (43 per cent) are spending as much as a quarter of their time on Media-related work than under the post-Cox curriculum (Hart and Benson, 1993; Dickson, 1994; Barratt, 1998, p. 27. At the same time, Barratt found (p. 22) that 90 per cent of respondents claimed that their departments included Media work within an overall policy document, compared with Dickson's earlier finding of 55 per cent (Dickson, 1994).

Barratt's study is very useful in establishing that there is a growing enthusiasm for Media work and is methodologically explicit. But it suffers from the difficulty which most questionnaire-based surveys experience, a lack of detail on actual practice, as Barratt himself freely admits (p. 38). The use of a few focus groups of teachers to gather opinions rather than to elicit subjective responses in an inter-active way (Wilson, 1997, p. 211) or to explore more deeply issues raised in the questionnaire is also problematic. There is a danger of encouraging normative or consensual responses when focus groups are created from a single profession. In addition, since one of the main potential benefits of using focus groups is the light which may be shed on the gaps between 'what people say and what they do' (Lankshear, 1993, p. 1987) focus group findings need to be supplemented by classroom observation and more in-depth interviews with individuals than focus groups can provide.

In Scotland, where Media Education has been established more firmly than in England, two detailed surveys within five years showed strong developments, supported by the Scottish Film Council (SFC) and by local and national education authorities, in both primary and secondary schools (Butts, 1986; Brown and Visocchi, 1991). A smaller scale postal survey in Wales which addressed itself to heads and heads of department was published in 1996 by Media Education Wales. One finding merits particular comment in comparison with the situation in England. When Media was taught in Welsh lessons, there was found to be greater use of the moving image than in English lessons. The authors of the report do not attempt to account for this, but it is at least conceivable that in bilingual schools (particularly with Media Studies in place) the moving image was used as a source of spoken Welsh, particularly with the prominence of the Welsh language in the media industry in Wales and its consequent availability on Welsh television.

In England, the BFI, in conjunction with the National Foundation for Educational Research (NFER), undertook a survey of schools in late 1993 (Dickson, 1994). The sample was small (482 schools and colleges) and the response rate moderate, providing only 189 replies. There was no opportunity to cross-check these responses with the actual practices in the institutions themselves. Despite these reservations, the survey showed that most institutions claimed that they were teaching some Media Education within English and in 67 per cent of these it was also taught somewhere else in the curriculum; almost three quarters of respondents considered that they devoted between 10 per cent and 25 per cent of curriculum time to Media Education; 69 per cent of respondents thought Media Education was 'very important'. The survey showed that nearly 90 per cent of English teachers in the schools and colleges surveyed used television for showing 'film-of-the-book' adaptations of literary texts. It also showed that the focus of learning in such contexts is often what is learnt *through* using media texts in support of conventional English teaching. But some work is also concerned with learning about the media. It is important to distinguish between them, not because one approach is any more effective or worthwhile than others, but because they are actually different and therefore lead in different directions.

Some researchers have focused more on learning theory and processes than on teaching strategies. The work of Buckingham and colleagues in England offers a series of rich and detailed explorations of student–teacher and student–student interactions in Media classrooms which has been very productive of new questions about learning processes. Buckingham's work has also played a useful role in relating media learning to language-learning theories. His earlier studies on Media Education concentrate on problematising many of the claims made for Media teaching in secondary schools and provide a revisionist account of Media learning in the context of children's social development (Buckingham, 1990a; 1993a). He looks critically at the claims made for group work in developing social skills, learning to work under pressure, understanding team structures, providing opportunities for self-reflection and exploring the idea that reading texts is a process of negotiation. He endorses the view that if pupils share their pleasure in texts with their peers, their understanding is developed. Similarly, some of his more recent research is concerned with the growth of children's evolving understanding of television modes and processes, particularly in terms of how this operates in informal social settings. But this work does not focus on teaching strategies or processes, nor reveal and reflect on its own methodological procedures. (Buckingham, 1993b; Buckingham and Sefton-Green, 1994)

A series of six case studies in London schools (Buckingham, Grahame and Sefton-Green, 1995) also offers useful insights into practical production processes and helpful descriptions of the various methods of enquiry used by the researchers. Grahame's chapter, in which she examines notions of imitation and parody, is particularly challenging. Her work on practical production is especially helpful in exploring some of the complexities of students' understandings of the modality of media texts and the processes of 'imitation'. This line of development is taken further in a new collection edited by Buckingham that explores new approaches to Media teaching in formal education at all levels (Buckingham, 1998).

The emergent trend of small-scale practitioner-based reflexive research, of which Buckingham's, Grahame's and Richards' work is a part, offers detailed insights into classroom interactions between teachers and students and between students. Such work also promises to make useful connections with students' out-of-school media experiences and the perspectives they bring with them to the classroom. But, for all its detail and its ecological soundness in terms of classroom activity, it is rather one-dimensional.

We are lacking detailed and theorised accounts of teachers' work by other teachers. We also need more sophisticated investigations of teacher biographies and the socio-cultural perspectives. Recent research at the London School of Economics (Livingstone and Bovill, 1999) has begun to map young people's media interactions outside the classroom. Using a combination of focus groups, individual home-based depth interviews with children and (separately) parents, questionnaires, diaries of media usage by young people, and interviews with IT teachers and cybercafé Internet users, the LSE project explores in great detail young people's interaction with media in their own homes and at school. It reveals the relative usage by young people of a range of media that together occupy around five hours of their time daily. On average, half of this time is devoted to television, with 99 per cent of young people watching in their leisure time. Music is the next most used medium, with 86 per cent listening for about an hour daily (often as a secondary activity). A similar number of young people (81 per cent) watch videos for a further daily average of an hour. Computer games (64 per cent), non-school books (57 per cent) and other personal computer uses, including the Internet (55 per cent, most often in school) provide the other most frequent media interactions (Livingstone and Bovill, 1999, p. 5).

Beneath these figures lies behaviour that is clearly differentiated by social class, gender and location. For example, twice as many young people have access to IT at school where inequalities of home access are not reproduced and where IT is used for different purposes. The researchers note the vital role of the school in redressing inequalities of access to IT in the home. Yet teachers and schools are overstretched, undertrained and ill-equipped for this task, despite widespread enthusiasm for the potential of IT. (Livingstone and Bovill, 1999, p. 45). The report concludes that a wide-reaching programme of media and computer education is essential so that young people can operate media technology effectively in their work and leisure, process and manage information efficiently, critically evaluate information sources and develop a practical understanding of screen-based forms (Livingstone and Bovill, 1999, p. 53). Given this rich and diverse picture of old and new media usage by young people, we now have a much broader and clearer context for observing, analysing and evaluating what actually happens in classrooms.

3

The Teaching Media in English Project

The project's aim was to fill the research gap described in Chapter 2 and investigate the forms and purposes of Media teaching at Key Stage 4 in English in secondary schools. This research was conducted in schools in the South and South West of England. It attempted to update the findings of the *Models of Media Education Project* (1992-1995) in the light of the post-1995 provisions for National Curriculum English and the GCSE Examination syllabuses arising from them. It also aimed to provide an account of the forms and purposes of Information and Communication Technology (ICT) in English teaching through the lens of appropriate research perspectives. It did not address the teaching of Media through any of the GCSE Media Studies syllabuses available.

The primary research question to be addressed was:

What are teachers of English doing when they say they are doing Media at Key Stage 4 in UK secondary schools?

This question was then broken down into the following underlying components:

- who teachers of English are (experiences, background and training)
- how they see themselves in relation to schools and curricula
- what they say (and think) about Media as a discipline
- how they define their own approach to Media
- what they actually do when they teach Media.

The school environment in the early 1990s

The Cox Report (DES, 1989) provided a clear basis for Media teaching within each of the five approaches to the teaching of English which it had identified. The 'cultural analysis' model seemed to offer the greatest encouragement to teach about the media, but the other models also accommodated Media teaching, albeit in a somewhat different form. For example, the 'cultural heritage' model allowed scope for teaching about 'great' films, placing emphasis on the director as author (*auteur*) and learning to appreciate the craft and art of cinema. The 'personal growth' model, in placing the child at the centre, allowed the child's choice of culture into the classroom and simultaneously endorsed the opportunities for creativity that making media can offer.

The other two models, 'cross-curricular' and 'adult needs' both support a functional view of Media teaching. That is, they allowed for Media teaching as a means to equip pupils with the technologically based information and communication skills that children would need to function in school and, later, in adult society. Here, the emphasis is, for example, on learning how to use computers and the Internet as ways of communicating and accessing information; in these models, the technologies themselves are rarely the focus of study:

Approaches to English in the Cox Report (1989)

A 'personal growth' view focuses on the child: it emphasises the relationship between language and learning in the individual child, and the role of literature in developing children's imaginative and aesthetic lives.

A 'cross-curricular' view focuses on the school: it emphasises that all teachers (of English and of other subjects) have a responsibility to help children with the language demands of different subjects on the school curriculum: otherwise areas of the curriculum may be closed to them. In England, English is different from other school subjects, in that it is both a subject and a medium of instruction for other subjects.

An 'adult needs' view focuses on communication outside the school: it emphasises the responsibility of English teachers to prepare children for the language demands of adult life, including the workplace, in a fast-changing world. Children need to learn to deal with the day-to-day demands of spoken language and of print; they also need to be able to write clearly, appropriately and effectively.

A 'cultural heritage' view emphasises the responsibility of schools to lead children to an appreciation of those works of literature that have been widely regarded as amongst the finest in the language.

A 'cultural analysis' view emphasises the role of English in helping children towards a critical understanding of the world and cultural environment in which they live. Children should know about the processes by which meanings are conveyed, and about the ways in which print and other media carry values.

The original Southampton *Models of Media Education* project in 1992–1993 explored major questions about aims and methods for Media teaching amongst teachers of English (Hart and Benson, 1993). It uncovered several areas of uncertainty amongst teachers and identified a range of models which English teachers consciously draw on in the classroom at Key Stage 4 (age 14-16). The project produced detailed descriptions and analyses of a wide range of classroom strategies for teaching about the media. A range of teaching models was identified that showed how, in the early 1990s, classroom strategies and practices were incorporating new technological developments and ideological debates. By providing two distinct but related sets of data on Media teachers' rationales for their work (from in-depth interviews) and Media teachers' classroom methods (from systematic observation), the study:

- documented different understandings, purposes and practices of Media teachers in a range of locations

- enabled comparative analysis of different approaches to Media teaching in different locations

- encouraged discussion of appropriate models for different locations and purposes

- facilitated discussion of appropriate methodologies for classroom research in Media

- provided a basis for the continuing development of Media as a discipline and for further research in Media

The 1992–1993 project also showed how Media teachers had been supported in the development of their work in the classroom through curriculum guidance and training provided by university education departments and by national advisory bodies like the British Film Institute (BFI) and Film Education. Teachers also had had the benefit of support from professional bodies like the National Association for the Teaching of English, the (now defunct) Society for Education in Film and Television and the Association for Media Education (AME). Also important was the role which central government played in the formulation of National Curriculum policies, especially for English (through the Department for Education and Employment, Her Majesty's Inspectorate, and the Schools Curriculum Assessment Authority (now QCA; formerly, the National Curriculum Council, which was responsible for the Cox Report).

In 1992-1993, at departmental level, there was often a clear expectation that Media work would occur, as mandated by the National Curriculum for English, and there was often discussion and collaboration in the design of units of work that incorporated Media for students at Key Stage 4. So, in spite of the fears and uncertainties of some teachers of English about how others (parents, head teachers, school governors) would see their Media work, it was incorporated into the routine work of English departments. At that time it was rare, however, for Media to be written explicitly into school policies.

In most cases, the lessons observed in 1992–1993 lacked:

- interaction and dialogue (teacher–pupil or pupil–pupil) about media

- space for young people's own media experience and knowledge

- opportunities for active involvement in the social production of texts

- teaching in context through engagement with media processes and technologies

- engagement with political issues

- focus on media institutions

Since that research, new National Curriculum Orders based on the Dearing Review published in 1995 (DFE) have repositioned Media within English. In the 1995 version, the importance of Media was made clearer, though the actual number of Media references was smaller. At Key Stages 3 and 4 the most significant reference to Media came in the *Reading* Programme of Study and required that 'pupils should be introduced to a wide range of media, *e.g., magazines, newspapers, radio, television, film*. They should be given opportunities to analyse and evaluate such material, which should be of high quality and represent a range of forms, purposes, and different structural and presentational devices.' (1f) Many other references within *Reading* would, to the committed Media teacher, have encouraged opportunities for Media. Such encouragement is evident from the examples quoted below:

Post-Dearing National Curriculum English Order (1995)

Pupils should be taught to:

- extract meaning beyond the literal (2a)

- analyse and discuss alternative interpretations (2a)

- consider how texts are changed when adapted to different media. (2b)

- evaluate how information is presented (2c)

- recognise, analyse and evaluate the characteristics of different types of text in print and other media...consider the effects of organisation and structure, and how authors' purposes and intentions are portrayed, and how attitudes, values and meanings are communicated. (3a)

In addition, there were within the *Speaking and Listening* and *Writing* Programmes of Study, ample opportunities for the inventive teacher of Media to bring in quite naturally the study of media texts. For example, the range of forms in which pupils were expected to write included 'playscripts and screenplays' (1c)

However, as we suggested in the Introduction, despite these developments and the strong growth of specialist GCSE, GNVQ and A level courses, Media in English seems to have remained a minor concern for many teachers of English. Learning about the media was re-established by the post-Dearing curriculum, but not in a particularly strong form, that is, not requiring specific commitments to Media work from English teachers. Continuing battles over the purposes of English have created uncertainties and tensions that have sometimes sidelined Media teaching in English.

Yet the environment in schools has now changed in terms of both curricular constraints and the spread of multimedia resources. Some recent studies also indicate a growing interest in IT as an object of study rather than simply as an instrument for teaching and learning. (Goodwyn and Findlay, 1997). So our new research addresses the issues of both curriculum context and the new media environment.

Theoretical framework: paradigms and pedagogy

Three paradigms have dominated the major phases in the development of Media teaching in England in the last 50 years and they continue to provide a useful means of differentiating between different teacher perspectives and classroom practices. Yet all three paradigms remain operational in most educational contexts. The 'inoculatory' paradigm, which seeks to develop discrimination *against* certain kinds of media, corresponds closely to the 'cultural heritage' approach referred to in the Cox Report, to 'transmission' education and to 'protectionist' or 'defensive' strategies. The 'popular arts' paradigm seeks to encourage discrimination between media and corresponds to the 'personal growth' model in the Cox Report. The 'representational' paradigm, which seeks to address issues of ideology, power and the politics of representation, corresponds to Cox's 'cultural analysis' approach and to 'progressive', 'empowerment' and 'oppositional' strategies. 'Progressive' strategies, drawing theoretically on new approaches to audience study, emphasise the activeness and sophistication of audiences and recognise the existing knowledge and skills of students. But such strategies have often done a disservice to students. In an attempt to abolish the cultural and social authority of the teacher and to emphasise spontaneity and informal group work, they have sometimes neglected structured activity, planned learning experiences and teacher direction. Our new study assesses the viability of these three paradigms as a potential theoretical framework for understanding teacher perspectives and classroom practices, especially in the light of the increasing presence of multimedia activities in schools.

Three Media Education Paradigms

	Title	Major Exponents	Cox Report Equivalents (1989)
1	INOCULATORY/ PROTECTIONIST	Leavis and Thompson (1933)	Cultural heritage
2	DISCRIMINATORY/ POPULAR ARTS	Hall and Whannel (1964)	Personal growth
3	CRITICAL/ REPRESENTATIONAL/ SEMIOLOGICAL	Masterman (1985)	Cultural analysis

Although there is a generational element which determines the way teachers conceptualise and realise their Media work, this is not just a matter of the age of teachers, but the product of continuing tensions and debates about the appropriateness of different paradigms in English. There are also contradictions among the various discourses which a single teacher routinely draws on and between these discourses and actual classroom practice. In fact, all three paradigms may be traced in almost every Media teacher. It is also the case that a teacher may voice allegiance to one particular set of beliefs about the purposes of Media teaching but actually contradict them in the classroom.

The continuing power of all three of these paradigms deserves further exploration, because they may provide a key to the confusions, tensions and contradictions between liberal–progressive notions of 'empowerment' and 'critical autonomy' in the classroom and traditional whole-class didactic pedagogies.

Key concepts

The BFI's widely publicised matrix of 'Signpost Questions' (Bazalgette, 1989) is used in this research as a framework for coding, analysing and discussing the main focuses of teachers' aims and classroom activities. It should be stressed, however, that teacher awareness or knowledge of the Signpost Questions is not being used as a touchstone for judging the competence of the teacher. Clearly a teacher can be unaware of these questions and still be an excellent teacher; conversely, knowledge of the questions is no guarantee of the teacher's ability to teach about the concepts to which they relate.

Although the Signpost Questions provide key concepts that are clear and flexible, the framework does not explicitly include study of institutions and therefore risks downgrading the importance of power relationships in the production, distribution and consumption of media texts. This is hardly surprising, since the Signpost Questions are very much a compromise produced from a long process of consultation and discussion with teachers. They are an attempt to provide a consensual framework with which most teachers would be comfortable. Although their blandness is a potential weakness, they remain a helpful tool in conceptualising teachers' aims and classroom activities. In this report we have referred to the more inclusive concept of *Institutions* as well as to *Agencies*.

Signpost Questions	
WHO is communicating with whom?	AGENCIES
WHAT type of text is it?	CATEGORIES
HOW is it produced?	TECHNOLOGIES
HOW do we know what it means?	LANGUAGES
WHO receives it and what sense do they make of it?	AUDIENCES
HOW does it present its subject?	REPRESENTATIONS

The main purpose of this research was to explore relationships between teacher perspectives about and classroom practice in Media Education, to consider how what teachers say is reflected in what they do. As indicated earlier, this exploration of eleven Media teachers and eleven Media lessons mirrors the methods used in the 1992–1993 Southampton research. In this way it is possible to make direct comparisons between the two research projects and speculate on the impact of significant curriculum changes between 1992–1993 and 1998–1999.

Context: curriculum developments and reform, 1993-1999

The 1992-93 project rationale described the development of Media Education from the 1960s to the 1990s. It identified the growth of the VCR, significant publications such as the BFI's curriculum statements (especially the secondary version, Bowker (ed.) 1991) and the BBC's six-part radio series, *Understanding the Media* (Cooper and Hart, 1991) as influential factors. The rationale also considered the emergence in Media Education of significant key concepts (discussed above) since 1989. Another important feature identified in Media teaching at the time was the absence of any formal training for teachers, leading to wide variations in classroom practice. Within the curriculum of the early 1990s, the rationale for the 1992–1993 research highlighted the emerging influence of the National Curriculum but anticipated that children were being offered a fairly narrow, repetitive classroom diet, served up by successive teachers unaware of their pupils' prior curriculum experience.

Between 1993 and 1999 each of these elements has seen significant developments. The VCR remains the dominant classroom technology, but many schools now have satellite connections to a wide range of European television stations and virtually every secondary school is connected to the Internet. While the VCR freed teachers from the tyranny of television programme schedules, the new digital technologies are starting to offer teachers a freedom of choice that could prove overwhelming. (The implications of this are considered in the final chapter.)

For all teachers, including teachers of Media, the time between 1993 and 1999 saw three significant developments. One was the introduction of OFSTED inspections. A second was the introduction of two new GCSE regimes (with another imminent) and a third the introduction of national tests at Key Stage 3. The inspections have had an impact on the teaching of Media in two distinct ways. Implicit in the inspections was a requirement that every English department have a formally written scheme of work for Key Stages 3 and 4, thereby ensuring that Media Education was written into the curriculum and reducing the likelihood of limited and repetitive Media experience for the pupils. But the inspections drove schools towards collective development plans, marginalising training courses without a whole-school focus: quite simply, Media courses were not, during these six years, a high priority for schools.

The first GCSE reform arose from a Conservative government suspicion of 'all-coursework' English examinations. The second reform (1998) was necessary in order to make the new GCSEs meet the criteria of the amended (post-Dearing) National Curriculum (1995). Different Examination Boards responded in very different ways to these challenges (see Chapter 4) but a broad effect was to formalise the position of Media Education in the National Curriculum for English whilst narrowing the range of Media experiences.

The Research
Research Focus
The focus of the 1998-1999 research was slightly different from that in the 1993 study. In 1993, distinctions between what constituted a 'Media' lesson compared to an English lesson were much less clear than they have since become. The GCSE English syllabuses in 1993 offered enormous flexibility and freedom of choice for the teacher – choice to ignore Media entirely, or to offer a very personal interpretation of it. Also, in 1993, the National Curriculum was not yet statutory at Key Stage 4. As a consequence, though all lessons observed in 1992–1993 were taught by teachers of English, certain lessons would have fitted equally well into a Media Studies syllabus or an English syllabus. However, GCSE and National Curriculum changes since then have meant that in 1998–1999 one could predict

that a very clearly defined form of Media Education would be part of every English syllabus in every school. Thus, in 1998-99, all lessons observed were within the English curriculum as defined by the GCSE courses; no Media Studies lessons were observed.

Choice of schools and teachers

A suitable mix of participants from the 1992–1993 Southampton research project and new participants was sought. It was important that a significant number of schools should be taken from the 1992–1993 sample so that some exploration could be made of changes to the Media curriculum within specific institutions. In order to allow such comparison, five schools were chosen because of their previous involvement in the 1993 research and in four of these, the original participants took part again in 1998–1999. A sixth school was invited because one of the teachers in the 1992–1993 project had moved to a new school and taken on a Media responsibility there. The remaining five were chosen from schools who had professional development or initial training connections with Southampton University.

This purposive sample of teachers, though not necessarily typical of teachers of English and Media in the population at large, does, by any set of criteria, represent strength in English teaching in general and in Media teaching within English in particular. The teachers in these eleven case studies had 125 years teaching experience – 3 years for the least experienced and 25 for the most. Amongst them were four heads of English (one promoted to senior teacher), two teachers with responsibility for GCSE Media Studies, one with a responsibility for Media within English and one with a responsibility for the Key Stage 3 curriculum.

The age profile of this 1998–1999 study was slightly different from that in the original 1992–1993 Southampton sample. Then, eight of the teachers had taught for more than ten years; in 1998-99 five had ten or more years experience.

Of the eleven schools, three also offered Media Studies as part of the school curriculum, always within the school GCSE option system (a very similar proportion to the 27 per cent of schools in the 1998 BFI research sample, reported in Barratt, 1998). One other was actively considering taking up GCSE Media Studies and one had, until recent years, offered Media as an 'extra' GCSE within the English curriculum, but had given that up with the removal of 100 per cent coursework in English.

Six of the schools had chosen the NEAB English syllabus; that is, six schools taught Media within English through coursework. Three schools had chosen Southern Examining Group (SEG), one Midland Examining Group (MEG) and one EDEXCEL (London). This pattern is similar to that of the BFI research (Barratt, 1998) in that NEAB dominated (more than half) with SEG being the second most popular. The selection of schools was made before the BFI publication. However, it is interesting to note that these eleven schools represent what might be a plausible cross-section of the BFI sample of more than 700 schools.

Nine of the schools were in Hampshire and two in Dorset. Selection of schools was influenced by an intention to ensure a mixture of types of institution including urban, rural, semi-rural, coastal, mixed gender and single gender: of the eleven schools, eight were mixed-gender comprehensives, two were urban girls' schools and one an urban boys' school.

All schools were contacted by letter and telephone. Of the eight 'new' schools invited, seven accepted. Contact was always through the Head of English who then, in discussion with colleagues, decided who the most appropriate teachers might be. Unsurprisingly, in all cases, strong, confident teachers were chosen, usually with a particular interest or expertise in Media Education. For a more detailed profile of individuals teachers participating, see Chapter 5, 'Media teachers talking'.

Research methods and instruments
Instruments used in 1998–1999
As shown in the diagram below, there were three main elements to the research. Firstly there was the teacher interview, lasting typically for one hour, for the most part conducted in advance of the lesson observed. Secondly there was the five-point questionnaire; this, as

Research Design

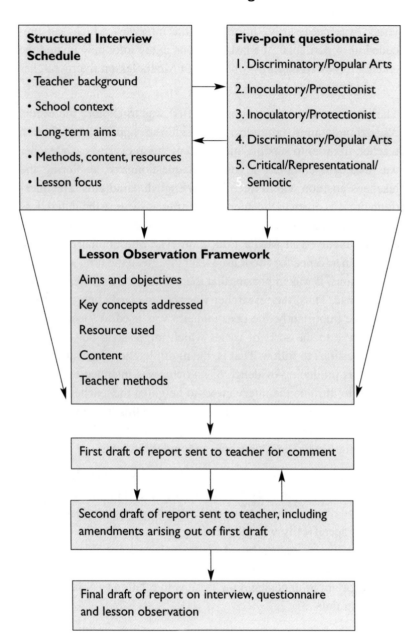

Structured Interview Schedule

• Teacher background

• School context

• Long-term aims

• Methods, content, resources

• Lesson focus

Five-point questionnaire

1. Discriminatory/Popular Arts

2. Inoculatory/Protectionist

3. Inoculatory/Protectionist

4. Discriminatory/Popular Arts

5. Critical/Representational/ Semiotic

Lesson Observation Framework

Aims and objectives

Key concepts addressed

Resource used

Content

Teacher methods

First draft of report sent to teacher for comment

Second draft of report sent to teacher, including amendments arising out of first draft

Final draft of report on interview, questionnaire and lesson observation described below, was used to inform and support the teacher interview. Thirdly there was the lesson observation; interpretation of the lesson was necessarily 'framed' by the interview which had preceded it: in particular, the last questions in the interview invited the teacher to describe briefly what sort of Media lesson the researcher was about to see.

The interviews had three aims. The first was to explore the Media background, aims, attitudes and preferred approaches of each teacher. In order to support this aspect of the interview, each teacher was asked to complete a five-point questionnaire, exploring the teacher's position within three Media/English paradigms. The questionnaire was given to the interviewee after answering the initial, less challenging questions about background and how that teacher had become involved in Media Education. The questionnaire was not sent out in advance for two reasons. Firstly, given the limited number of questions, it was important that there was good and clear quality of response. Thus, the researcher was able to clarify any questions. But more importantly, the questionnaire was used to 'open up' the interviewee to the sorts of issues which might arise out of all the other questions to follow. That is, the multiple-choice questionnaire, as well as producing evidence of its own, was intended to act as a prompt, to intrigue the interviewee, to heighten the teacher's awareness and to set the context for the interview. In this way it was hoped that teachers would not come 'cold' to potentially challenging questions about Media aims, concepts and understandings.

A second aim of the interview was to learn more about the context in which the lesson was taught: it was felt important that the researcher observe the lesson, understanding its prior history and knowing specifically what the teacher was hoping to achieve. The third aim was to gather broad contextual evidence related to the institutional contexts in which the teachers were working. That is, it was important to understand the lessons in relation to opportunities and constraints.

In most cases, observation of the lesson took place immediately after the interview. Where timetable constraints made this impossible, some elements of the interview (those to do with institutional context) took place after the lesson. In every case, however, teachers were interviewed about the lesson aims and the lesson background before the observation took place. The effect of this was to eliminate the possibility of the *post hoc* rationalisation that may occur when teachers provide retrospective accounts of their lessons

Using the lesson observation form as an analytical framework (see below), observational notes were taken on each lesson. In general, the notes took a narrative, chronological form, following the progress of the lesson, but the observational framework provided a checklist to ensure that there was as much consistency as possible amongst all the observations. So, in all lessons, note was taken of lesson objectives, key concepts addressed, resources used, the particular learning focus, the teacher's method and pupils' involvement. This observational framework was further used to interpret the notes during the writing of the report after the lesson. Lessons were audiotaped. In general, the taperecorder was left close to the teacher's position, usually on the teacher's desk. When pupils worked in pairs or groups, the taperecorder was moved, with the consent of the pupils concerned, to monitor some of the pupils' conversations about their media task.

From the interviews and observations, teacher profiles and lesson descriptions were written and copies sent to teachers for comment, clarification and amendment; after first responses from teachers, the reports were edited and returned to teachers for any further comments. In practice, very few amendments were required to reports either of interviews or of the lessons: teachers generally agreed that the reports constituted accurate records of what was said and what was seen.

Significant features of the research instruments and revisions to the 1992–1993 instruments

The original research instruments are to be found in the 1993 document (Hart and Benson, 1993, pp. 16-19). The following paragraphs describe the most significant of the changes made to these instruments in the 1998–1999 research project, and outline the reasons for any change of emphasis. Also in these paragraphs is the rationale for the prompts used.

Lesson Observation Form

The most significant change in this lesson observation schedule is that each broad area of observation (e.g. key concepts) has been supported by a series of detailed prompts.

Aims/objectives: the main focus was to note the degree to which aims were rooted in other experiences. In particular this prompt sought to uncover the relationship of the aims to the past and future learning of a of the students.

Key concepts: these concepts are taken from the commonly used set of 'Signpost Questions' produced by the BFI. (Bazalgette, 1989) What this prompt aimed to discover, apart from the particular concept addressed, was the degree to which these concepts were familiar, made explicit, understood and used

Resources: other than the general issues about quality and sufficiency, the prompts drew the researcher's attention to the availability and use of technological resources (appropriately, the first prompt). Given the increased availability of media technology and Information Technology in schools since 1993, the degree to which Media Education is rooted in understanding and use of such technology is fundamental

Content: these prompts describe content in ways that are familiar to all English teachers and in terms that allow for overlap between Media Education and English. That is, they focus mainly on texts chosen, and the focus of learning within those texts.

Method: these prompts place an emphasis on the role of the teacher and the degree to which she/he manages or intervenes in the learning.

Tasks: these prompts place an emphasis on the role of the pupils and the degree to which they work independently of the teacher and in collaboration with each other.

Research Instruments: Lesson Observation Form

School   **Date**
Teacher   **Year**
Duration of lesson   **Nos.**   **Girls**   **Boys**

Aims/objectives
- To what extent they were Media-based or English based
- To what extent they were made explicit for the pupils by the teacher at the beginning
- To what extent they were reinforced or repeated at the end
- To what extent they related to previous learning
- To what extent they were to be consolidated or developed in future lessons

Key concepts
- Which key concepts were specifically the focus of the lesson
- Which key concepts were supplementary to or implicit in the lesson
- Whether the key concept was new to or familiar to the pupils
- What terminology was used to express the concept
- To what degree the pupils specifically made reference to the concepts

Resources
- Technological; commercial; school-produced
- To what extent the resources were used by the teacher or the pupils
- To what extent teachers/ pupils were familiar with or comfortable with technological resources
- Sufficiency and quality of resources in relation to the number of pupils
- Logistical issues in gaining access to or putting away resources

Content
- Media addressed
- Texts and genres addressed
- Purpose and audience of texts
- Particular focus

Method
- The role of the teacher in terms of learning management, organisation of pupils
- The significance of question and answer
- The significance of teacher explanation
- The significance of teacher modelling of activities or task

Tasks
- The length of time spent working independently, in pairs, in larger groups
- Freedom to choose roles – or allocated roles
- Freedom to choose task or to adapt task – or allocated task
- Effectiveness of collaborative or independent learning
- Number and pace of activities

Research Instruments: Questions for Structured Interviews

Background

- What is your main teaching subject?
- In what areas of English teaching are you most interested?
- For how long have you been a teacher?
- For how long have you been teaching Media?
- Can you describe the process by which you became interested in or involved in Media Education?
- How would you define your approach to Media Education?
- Can you describe your most successful lesson ever?

School context and available support

- What percentage of your current teaching time is given to Media work at Key Stage 4?
- Does this include any Media work outside English?
- What proportion of KS4 pupils have recent experience of Media Education? (i.e.. within this current school year/ or last school year if early in September)?
- Are you able to draw on the expertise of other staff or outside agencies?
- What other Media work is done in the school but outside the English curriculum?
- What form of Media INSET have you been involved in? How recent was the INSET?
- To what extent does English department [and/or school] planning support or prescribe Media work?
- Which GCSE syllabus did you choose?
- To what extent did the Board's treatment of Media Education influence the department's choice?
- What has been the impact of the new syllabus on Media teaching? How do you distinguish between your Media teaching and your teaching about non-fiction texts?
- Did your OFSTED inspection refer to Media teaching? If so, what observations were made?

Long-term Aims

- What are your [long-term Media] aims for your pupils?
- How do you think pupils respond to Media work and to your approaches to it?
- Is your teaching influenced by your own views about the media or society?
- What would you say are the most important 'key concepts' in Media Education
- Are there any concepts with which you personally find difficult?
- How do you see Media Education developing over the next ten years?

Research Instruments: Questions for Structured Interviews (continued)

Methods, curriculum content and resources

- Can you describe in general terms your approach to Media work in the classroom?
- With which areas of Media work do you feel most comfortable, do you feel you teach well?
- Are there any topics or concepts you tend to avoid?
- To what extent do you feel that media technologies are an important element in Media Education?
- To what extent do you use these technologies and feel comfortable using them?
- Do you find any difference in the response of girls and boys to different aspects of Media Education, particularly to the use of technology?
- Which [commercially-produced] resources do you find most useful?
- How far do you find it necessary to produce your own resource materials?
- Has your work in Media Education influenced how you approach other aspects of English teaching?

Lesson focus

- Can you describe the lesson I am going to observe?
- How does it connect with previous or anticipated lessons?
- How does it fit in with the remainder of the English curriculum?
- What are your learning objectives for this lesson, or this series of lessons? What do you wish the pupils to be able to do or understand better by the end of the lesson, and/or by the end of this series of lessons?
- Why do you consider these objectives important?

Questions for structured interview

Background: As part of the background questions, a five-point questionnaire was introduced. This took the form of a brief, five-point questionnaire inviting teacher response to a series of statements. The questionnaire sought to establish the Media paradigm within which the teacher might be working – identified earlier in this Chapter as:

Inoculatory/Protectionist	*(Media paradigm)*	*Cultural Heritage*	(English equivalent)
Discriminatory/Popular Arts	*(Media paradigm)*	*Personal Growth*	(English equivalent)
Critical/Representational/ Semiotic	*(Media paradigm)*	*Cultural Analysis*	(English equivalent)

	Please tick as appropriate: ++ **strongly agree** — **strongly disagree** ? **no clear response**	+ +	+	?	-	- -
1	Media Education should help pupils to judge what represents quality in the media.					
2	Children don't need Media Education as a form of defence against the media: children aren't easily fooled.					
3	Studying film treatment of literary texts is one of the most effective forms of Media Education.					
4	In practical work, understanding of the process is far more important than the quality of the work.					
5	The teacher of Media within English should pay more attention to language and text, and less attention to media institutions.					

Statements 2 and 3 relate to the Inoculatory/Protectionist paradigm. Statements 1 and 4 relate to the Discriminatory/Popular Arts paradigm.
Statement 5 relates to the Critical/Representational/Semiotic paradigm. (see Figure, page 35, Research Design)

Teachers were able to position themselves within a given paradigm by a positive or a negative response to any statement. For example, agreement with statement 1 would suggest a teacher who is comfortable within the Discriminatory paradigm; disagreement would suggest a teacher who rejects the Discriminatory paradigm as a description of their Media teaching. The teacher was also specifically asked, 'How would you define your approach to Media Education?' This allowed the teacher to define such a position in broad terms, though the experience of the questionnaire also helped to focus that definition. Other significant changes to the 1992-1993 interview schedule are described below.

School context and available support: most of the additional questions appear in this section. This is because the educational context for Media Education has changed significantly since 1993. In particular, changes to the National Curriculum have led to a revision of the position of Media Education within it. In this context, questions have been included to consider the impact of the new General Certificate for Secondary Education syllabuses. The constraints of these new syllabuses seem to be encouraging teachers to address Media within very prescribed blocks of time and units of work. It is possible, for example, that Media Education has become more prominent in the English curriculum but less frequently occurring.

Whilst Examination Boards differ in the way in which they manage the compulsory Media element, they also differ in the way in which they assess pupil understanding of non-fiction texts. From the syllabuses, it seems that different Boards interpret this element in different ways and that some Boards do not make a clear distinction between study of media texts and study of non-fiction texts. One of the additional questions explored the teacher's interpretation of the Board's understanding of this issue.

It as anticipated that another significant contextual influence was likely to be the advent of the school inspections carried out by the Office for Standards in Education. Since 1993, all secondary schools have had at least one OFSTED inspection: despite the existence of very specific inspection criteria, it seems likely that the degree to which Media Education is an issue for inspection will differ according to the interests and background of the Inspector and to the preoccupations and priorities of the school. Consequently, two other additional questions appear under 'School Context and Available Support'. One asks whether or not Media Education is encouraged or prescribed by departmental documentation: since OFSTED, every English department has a set of policy and curriculum documents which outline in more or less detail the degree to which particular curriculum elements are taught. Another OFSTED influence has been to encourage schools to have clear development plans, included in which are details about the relationship between curriculum priorities and professional development. Therefore, anticipating the possibility of constraints on courses which are unrelated to school development plans, one question asks teachers about their involvement in Media In-Service Education for Teachers (INSET).

Long-term aims: the phrase 'Long-term' has been added in order to distinguish between these aims and the particular learning objectives of the lesson to be observed (described under Focus).

Methods, curriculum content and resources: Additional questions in this section all relate to the use of new (and old) technologies which have clearly developed in availability. and possibly in use, since 1993. In particular, the teacher was asked about the attitude of male and female students to Media Education in general and to the use of technology in particular.

Lesson focus: the term learning objectives is clearer than the previously used aims. The question was expanded so that teachers could comment on short and long-term objectives arising directly out of this lesson.

Reflections on the process

Inevitably, the research process was never quite as smooth as might be implied by the descriptions of instruments, methods and process in this chapter. For example, the lesson observation framework was originally designed as a lens through which the lesson could, in real time, be interpreted. In practice, the narrative of the lesson demanded the researcher's attention, and, the observation framework immediately took on a different role. It ensured that the researcher's observation of the lesson narrative was informed by a consistent set of criteria (a checklist). In addition, it proved an invaluable tool for retrospectively interpreting observation notes and tapes.

Secondly, the interview sometimes invited teachers to recall matters of fact related to the teaching of Media in their schools, for example, what resources the department owned, or what teaching approaches were commonly used. In such cases teachers would necessarily respond from memory or offer an estimate: schemes of work and resource lists were not scrutinised during the interview. This may have led to some teachers omitting to mention resources or approaches that other teachers in the department may have found significant. In practice, however, the teachers interviewed usually had an official or a nominal responsibility for Media teaching and appeared to have a very clear grasp of the departmental situation.

Thirdly, teachers starved of INSET were eager to talk about their Media teaching, to reflect with another professional on their own practices. On occasions, this led to individual teachers interpreting open questions as suggestions or hints. On such occasions, the researcher needed to 'step back' and to rephrase the question so that teachers did not provide the answers that they thought the interviewer wanted to hear.

Lastly, as described later on in this report, there was a sense in which some of the lessons may have appeared to be a little conservative in approach. It would be understandable if some of the teachers (all veterans of OFSTED inspections) 'played safe' when being observed by an outsider. One consequence of this sort of conservatism might be a disinclination to use technology in a practical, production sense. However, teachers strongly gave the impression that any perceived constraints were curriculum-driven and that the lessons seen were typical of lessons normally taught.

4
Curriculum Contexts: Media Education in the GCSE syllabuses for English

Before exploring the findings of the *Teaching Media in English* research in detail, it is important to consider in some detail those contexts that offer opportunities to or constrain teachers in their Media teaching. In particular, we need to look at how the GCSE syllabuses and examination papers in English might influence teachers in their approach to Media.

Media in the National Curriculum
In the 1980s Media Education in secondary schools was a fast growing area. During that time the National Association for the Teaching of English had its own working party on Media Education, but actual provision was patchy. In 1988 a National Curriculum was proposed for England and Wales, and Media Education was included in the Cox Report, the report on which the Statutory Orders (DES, 1989; 1990) were based. These Cox-based Orders recognised explicitly the value of non-literary and media texts and demanded that they be given some attention, but they also envisaged a wider role for Media approaches within English in recognising that 'the kinds of question that are routinely applied in Media Education can fruitfully be applied to literature' (7.23). However, this attention was strangely confined to the *Reading* Attainment Target.

Although many teachers remained lukewarm about Media Education, many secondary English departments welcomed it wholeheartedly. However, the period 1990-1995 was characterised by enormous changes in Education, with a particular emphasis being placed on a skills-based curriculum. This change of curricular emphasis helped to sideline the cultural analysis approach to English that had allowed Media a space within its curriculum. In addition, teachers spent much of their energy fighting against the universally disparaged Key Stage 3 tests. By contrast during this time, Media Studies as a curriculum option at GCSE level continued to flourish.

In the mid-1990s, the National Curriculum was revised and the new Orders (based on the Dearing Review) were published in 1995 (DFE). As suggested in Chapter 3 it repositioned Media within English: Media was now much clearer and reinforced, though the actual number of Media references in it were fewer.

However, if the number of references to Media was not great, the force of the new statutory curriculum for English and the place of Media within it was enhanced by SCAA's (now QCA) GCSE regulations and criteria (SCAA, 1995) which instructed Examination Boards that 'The range *of reading assessed must also include non-fiction, media* and texts from other cultures and traditions' (p. 37). Thus, many teachers who had feared the demise of Media Education within English, found that it had, in fact, been given the status that, arguably, only comes from a secure position within the assessment system. The possible consequences of that position are discussed below.

(It should be made clear that the following discussion relates to the teaching and examining of Media within the statutory curriculum for English. There are, of course, optional GCSE Media Studies courses available that are much broader in range and place more emphasis on practical work. Discussion of such Media Studies courses is not part of this research. Also, following reorganisation there are now four examining bodies at GCSE level.)

A general effect of the GCSE syllabuses in English that emerged from the 1995 National Curriculum has been to ensure that pupils' understanding of media texts is not only demonstrated but also specifically assessed. Four out of the five Examination Boards, acting on the GCSE Regulations and Criteria described above, chose to position the assessment of Media within English in the terminal examination; only the Northern Examinations and Assessment Board (NEAB) assesses Media understanding within coursework. However, the NEAB's 'non-fiction' paper in English contained elements of Media analysis, and articles from that paper in each tier will be discussed within this context. If the main effect of the new syllabuses on Media Education has been to ensure its continuation within the statutory English curriculum at Key Stage 4, then a second effect has, arguably, been to narrow the range of media texts and media issues to be studied as part of that curriculum. One obvious constraint inevitably arising from the assessment of Media understanding within a terminal examination is the dependence on print-based rather than moving-image texts.

The texts
The classification of texts used in English examinations (as media or non-fiction) is sometimes problematic since not all Boards make clear whether the text offered to the candidate is intended as a media text or a non-fiction text, an important distinction arising from the current National Curriculum for English.

The National Curriculum Document (1995) exemplifies non-fiction as *autobiographies, biographies, journals, diaries, letters, travel writing, leaflets* and media as *magazines, newspapers, radio, tele-vision and film.* That is, 'non-fiction' is defined in terms of specific, print-based, text types or forms; a 'media' text, however, is defined in relation to the source of its production, the medium in which and for which the text was produced. This raises the question as to how Examination Boards classify, for example, a diary or a letter printed in a newspaper. Overlaps inevitably occur. NEAB, for example, used a newspaper article in its non-fiction paper. The Midland Examining Group included in one *non-fiction and media* examination paper an *Independent* third-person article about the yachtsman, Tony Bullimore, and a *Reader's Digest* first-person article describing Terry Waite's life as a hostage in Beirut. In the examination paper MEG did not indicate how it categorises each of these texts; indeed, the implication is that MEG has taken *non-fiction and media texts* as an inclusive category.

(N.B. In the following list the Welsh Joint Education Committee is written as WJEC; the Midland Examining Group as MEG; the Southern Examining Group as SEG; the Northern Examination and Assessment Board as NEAB and the EDEXCEL Foundation, London, as EDEXCEL).

The Media texts selected for examination at foundation and higher tiers in 1998 were:

- *advertisement* – Sinclair's motorised ZETA bicycle (no source of publication or distribution acknowledged) (EDEXCEL)

- *advertisement* – Camelot, for the National Lottery (no source of publication or distribution acknowledged) (WJEC)

- *advertisement* – 'a booklet advertising holidays' for holiday resort of Llandudno (WJEC)

- *leaflets* – RSPB and WDCS, appealing for donations to animal/ bird charities (EDEXCEL)

- *leaflet/pamphlet* (the specific format is not indicated) – the National Dairy Council (MEG)

- *leaflet extract* – produced by the Salvation army, about home-lessness (NEAB)

- *article* – adapted extract about yachtsman Tony Bullimore (*Independent*) (MEG)

- *article* – adapted by Terry Waite (*Reader's Digest*) (MEG)

- *article* – *Over Here – The GI's Wartime Britain* by Juliet Gardner (MEG)

- *article* – *Inside the News* section of the *Guardian*, about home-lessness – (NEAB)

- *article* – about homelessness (newspaper source and section not acknowledged) (NEAB)

- *article* – mainly in diary form, from the in-flight magazine of *Aeroflot* (SEG)

- *article* – the outdoor activity magazine, *Trail* (SEG)

- *article* – the *Sunday Times* environment correspondent on polar trekkers (SEG)

- *article* – from the *Guardian* about a female 'yachtsman' (SEG)

Where relevant (as, for example, in the *ZETA* and *Llandudno* advertisements, and the RSPB and WDCS leaflets) original, very good quality materials were used, allowing candidates to discuss, for example, the connotations of colour. However, several texts were presented as adaptations, typically a black and white copy accommodated on an A4 examination paper page.

Arguably, any discussion of media texts should be framed by some understanding of the context in which the text was produced and distributed. In the 1998 examinations, in the majority of cases, the source of the text was acknowledged, although there were some exceptions. For example, the ZETA advertisement appeared to be an insert, but it would be difficult to speculate on what sort of publication it appeared in. Similarly the WJEC did not appear to indicate where the Camelot advertisement was published. More significantly, the WJEC, having used a 'real', colour advertisement of Llandudno in the Higher tier paper, included in its Foundation tier paper, a (non-fiction) letter from a 'Reverend D. Williams' printed in *The Daily Recorder*, described as 'a daily newspaper'. If the newspaper is unfamiliar or fictitious then opportunities for understanding context are reduced. Board attitudes to context can vary with tiers. For example, NEAB Higher tier candidates were told that their text is from the *Guardian*, but Foundation tier candidates learned that theirs was 'an extract from a newspaper article'. (N.B. Each Board offers examination papers at two levels, Foundation and Higher. The former is aimed at those likely to achieve grades G to C and the latter at those likely to achieve grades D to A*).

However, clarification about textual source is only part of the issue. SEG, in both its pre-release and its unseen material was very clear about sources. For example, it described 'A Lone Wanderer' as an account of a South Pole expedition, written by Fedor Konyukhov and taken from 'the in-flight magazine of Aeroflot, the Russian airline which helped to sponsor him'. Yet this most interesting of sources was not referred to in the questions which followed the text. Indeed, amongst all Boards it was difficult to find any Media questions which took significant account of the context in which the text was produced or published. That is, the pupils were never invited to engage in issues of agencies, institutions or ideology.

The reading questions: writing about the media and about media texts

N.B. In the following discussion, no particular distinction is made between questions assessed according to reading criteria and questions assessed according to writing criteria. There clearly are overlaps. For example, in order to *analyse, review and comment*, candidates must have some issue or some text to provide a focus. Consequently, the section below includes those questions which invited candidates to *write about* media issues in general, or media texts in particular. There is no attempt here to say whether these questions are good or bad examination questions; the issue is simply the sort of media response that they invite.

LONDON, in Foundation and Higher tiers, required its candidates to evaluate the success of the advertisement/leaflets, after consideration of:

- 'the ways in which the subject matter is organised
- the use of language
- the design and layout of the leaflets'

It seems likely from guidance given to teachers by the Board that the order of bullet points was significant; that is, that more importance was placed on candidate analysis of verbal language than of visual connotations. The 'follow-up' writing question in the Foundation tier (*analyse, review, comment*) required candidates to engage imaginatively with the advertisement via a letter to a newspaper defending the reputation of the ZETA bicycle. By contrast, the equivalent Higher tier question very specifically required candidates to evaluate various methods of advertising, including 'the national press, local press, direct mailshots, posters, press releases, leaflets, and billboards'. This question appears to come as near as any media question set in 1998 to 'Media Studies'. However, it seems it is not Media knowledge about agencies and audiences that the Board was seeking in the answers, but a more general, common-sense response. Thus, this generic Media question set by EDEXCEL was essentially a thematic link into the writing rather than a test of media understanding.

For both Foundation and Higher tiers, MEG first required a non-evaluative response. That is, candidates were required to 'summarise' or 'write a summary... trace... and explain.' Foundation candidates were then helped in the analytical element of their response by bullet points, encouraging them to compare the two (survival) passages they were given, and comment on 'the layout; the subject matter; the style of writing and language used by the writers'. The *Independent* article in the Foundation tier paper had the usual newspaper range of headlines, sub-headings and by-line, as well as one graphic (a drawing of the yachtsman in the upturned boat). But the article was 'adapted' and, as with newspaper extracts from all Boards, there was no indication of its position within the rest of a newspaper page. The other article was presented as continuous prose. Higher tier candidates were not asked to comment on layout or any visual features of the two texts offered.

NEAB candidates satisfied the Media requirements of GCSE English within their coursework and this allowed for discussion of moving image as well as printed text. However, NEAB's *non-fiction* paper had arguably more Media elements within it than MEG's Higher tier *non-fiction and media* paper. Both Foundation and Higher tier candidates were expected by NEAB to respond to newspaper articles in comparison with other types of writing, and to comment on how they present information.

SEG required its Foundation candidates to consider two articles (from *Trail* and the *Aeroflot* in-flight magazine), both previously studied with teachers in a pre-release booklet. Candidates, as well as summarising main issues, were required to comment on 'the different ways in which words, pictures and headings are used'. However, given the very particular source of each of these articles, there was (as suggested above) surprisingly little encouragement for candidates to discuss the context in which the articles were published. The Higher tier question invited candidates to compare two broadsheet newspaper articles. The question focused on 'how language and presentation are used *by the two writers*': the emphasis was on individual authorship rather than broadsheet ideology or journalistic practice.

In the media element of its *non-fiction and media* papers, WJEC required its Foundation tier candidates to comment on the advertisement (from Camelot) in terms of 'headline, layout, the use of facts and figures, and the choice of words'. Higher tier candidates were also invited to 'think about the text and pictures' (of their Llandudno advertisement) but, interestingly, were also expected to consider 'what different groups of people ... this advertisement [is] trying to attract to Llandudno' and to say how the appeal to each group was made. Both Higher and Foundation tier candidates were expected to compare two texts (one non-fiction, one media) and discuss their effectiveness in terms of the way in which they presented ideas or sought to influence the reader's views. Of all the Boards, the WJEC most specifically invited the candidates to move outside the particular text to give some consideration to notions of target audience.

Nowhere did any Boards actually discourage consideration of context. Indeed, they might argue that good teaching would encourage candidates to explore authorship in a very broad sense. And, no doubt, some candidates in all Boards took the opportunity to go beyond the scope of the questions, but the constraints of some texts and of most questions arguably invited candidates to remain focused on writers and words, with some limited acknowledgement of layout features.

To illustrate this last point, it is worth considering the assessment objectives covered by the Media examination papers. SEG, for example, lists the objectives covered by its Media paper:

- read with insight and engagement, making appropriate references to texts and developing and sustaining interpretation of them

- distinguish between fact and opinion and evaluate how information is presented

- select material appropriate to their [sic] purpose; collate material from different sources and make cross references

- understand and evaluate how writers use linguistic, structural and presentational devices to achieve their effects and comment on ways [sic] language varies and changes.

The writing questions: producing media texts

It is clear that Media understanding was mainly examined via the assessment of reading. Production of media texts in the examinations was limited, though one must, of course, acknowledge the difficulty of producing any media text in an examination context where resources are confined to pen and paper. However, in various elements of the examination papers for English, candidates were expected to write for audiences other than the examiner. Below is a list of those writing tasks which bear some relation to the production of media texts (N.B. some questions are summarised):

- *A newspaper prints a story criticising the ZETA. Imagine you have used the ZETA.* **Write a letter to the newspaper** *giving your views...* (EDEXCEL Media)

- *There have been many letters in the press recently about how we should celebrate the year 2000 ...* **write a letter to the editor of a national or local newspaper...** (WJEC Media and Non-fiction)

- **Imagine you are a television or radio reporter** *covering an event in a war... Write the report which you intend to broadcast...* (EDEXCEL Poetry and Non-fiction)

- *A* **local radio station** *is running a phone-in to hear people's views about the National Lottery... you prepare yourself by writing down what you want to say. Write your contribution ...* (WJEC Media and Non-fiction)

- *There are many groups of people who struggle to survive in their daily lives.* **You have been invited onto local radio to talk** *about* *the problems faced by one such group... Write what you would say. (MEG Non-fiction and Media)*

- *As a senior student,* **write an advice sheet for pupils** *joining your school. Give them helpful advice on how to survive.* (MEG Non-fiction and Media)

- *As part of the way your school/college tries to help new students settle in... write a lively and entertaining* **'Welcome to...' leaflet** *...'You may wish to show where illustrations would be included in your leaflet...* (WJEC Media and Non-fiction)

- *Many places seek to attract visitors* **by producing publicity material.** *A publisher is producing 'An Alternative Guide to Britain... write an entry for the book.'* (WJEC Media and Non-fiction)

- **Write an article** *for a school newspaper in which you suggest changes that could be made to the meals offered to the children in your school...* (MEG Non-fiction and Media)

- **Write an article for a teenage magazine** *in which you argue the case for more help to be given to the homeless.* (NEAB Non-fiction)

- **Write an article for your school newspaper** *in which you argue either for or against...* (SEG Media and Non-fiction)

- *'Some people are satisfied with having routine jobs while others strive to become high-fliers' –* **Write a short article for your school magazine** *which examines the advantages and disadvantages of each alternative. ....* (SEG Other cultures and traditions)

- *A magazine is running a series of articles in which readers describe their favourite room.* **Write your article** *about My Favourite Room...* (WJEC Fiction, post 1900)

Implications for candidates' writing

The above range includes two advice leaflets (for the writer's peers), two letters to newspapers, three contributions to radio, one entry for *An Alternative Guide to Britain*, and five other articles. Of these five, three were for a school magazine or newspaper, one for a teenage magazine, and one for an indeterminate 'magazine'.

A number of issues emerge. The first is related to the degree to which a given *medium* lends itself to writing in an examination context. For example, radio is used in three questions. One wonders about the difficulties of writing in an examination context for 'talk' programmes, rehearsed or spontaneous. To what degree are teachers preparing pupils for this sort of experience? Though some teachers make a great success of it, radio is not a common feature of many classrooms in the English curriculum.

The second is the degree to which the *technologies of media production* translate to the examination room. For example, writing a leaflet or advice sheet is an entirely justifiable and worthwhile activity in the classroom, where computer technology is available. In the examination, the task must surely offer some frustration to the writer. And it is not clear to what extent pupils in examinations benefit from or are penalised by activities that encourage a range of presentational features rather than extended prose.

The third relates to the *audience* for which pupils are invited to write. From a Media Education perspective, the school magazine as the publishing vehicle for the writer, would appear to offer little encouragement to consider target audiences or mass audiences. Neither would the peer audience appear to encourage pupils to demonstrate their control over the more formal elements of written English, those which are most likely to meet published examination criteria.

Conclusion

Media in the 1998 examinations provided little evidence of writers working within a multimedia society. Also, if one takes the BFI 'Signpost' categories as a summary of those conceptual elements which might make up Media Education, then one can easily see the limits of Media learning as exemplified in the 1998 English GCSE examinations:

LANGUAGES	much evidence of this, with a strong emphasis on the verbal rather than visual
CATEGORIES	implicit in many of the questions, but there are few direct references to genres
AUDIENCES	addressed by WJEC, largely ignored by other Boards
INSTITUTIONS/AGENCIES	no identifiable reference, other than acknowledgement of source
REPRESENTATION	no identifiable reference
TECHNOLOGIES	no identifiable reference

Essentially, despite the prominence that the assessment system gives to Media, within the English curriculum it remains as textual rather than contextual study, with an emphasis on words and writers. For many within English teaching, this might be unproblematic; for those concerned that pupils develop their understanding of media texts, it is not encouraging. From the point of view of our research it is likely to be a constraining factor on the range of classroom work we were likely to observe. The next chapter demonstrates how such constraints might operate in practice as it describes the interviews with the eleven teachers and the observations of their lessons.

5

Media teachers talking

Teachers' backgrounds

Those teachers with least experience (between three and eight years) had little difficulty in answering the question, 'How did you become interested in Media Education?' With one exception, Media was part of their PGCE work and their transition into schools coincided with the introduction of the National Curriculum and its Media element. For them, Media in English is as natural, if not as prominent, as Literature in English. The one exception in this group developed a Media interest through membership of a university film society.

Even the experienced group (between 14 and 25 years experience) talk mainly of the last seven to ten years as being most influential, again citing the National Curriculum as the main motivation. However, one also quotes a remembered need to address the 'fear' of Media as an early motivation and another was alerted to Media by pupils' obvious enjoyment of it. A third remembered when it was regarded as a 'soft option'. The 1992–1993 Southampton research tried to explore those chance elements which drew one teacher or another to Media work. This enabled the research to get a view of what attracts teachers to this particular area, what makes some more interested and/or expert than others. Those distinctions are today much less clear; in a context when all teachers of English must address Media Education it is arguably more difficult to establish what makes the 'Media/English teacher' different from the 'Literature/English teacher'. Indeed, the Literature enthusiast and the Media enthusiast are often one and the same person. Three of the teachers declared their first love to be teaching literature.

Nine of the eleven teachers are women; this is higher than the 67 per cent sample in the recent BFI survey of over 700 teachers (Barratt 1998), but clearly not entirely untypical of the way in which women are represented within English teaching.

These teachers also have strong (though not necessarily recent) connections with 'academic' interpretations of the Media curriculum: seven of them had explored Media teaching at the University of Southampton, either as PGCE students of the last eight years, or as members of Southampton's Media Education Group. For two other teachers Media was a significant part of the PGCE training at other universities.

What these teachers have to say about teaching Media within English comes with all of the authority implied above.

Theoretical paradigms
One research tool attempted to establish the main Media paradigm within which the teacher might be working. (The possible paradigms are identified elsewhere in this report as Inoculatory/Protectionist (Cultural Heritage); Discriminatory/Popular Arts (Personal Growth); and Critical/Representational/Semiological (Cultural Analysis)). This 'question' took the form of a five-part questionnaire, completed by the teacher in the course of the interview. The questionnaire is presented opposite, with the number of responses in each category included.

Although one should be wary of drawing any conclusions from a questionnaire to only eleven teachers, the patterns of response might help point towards a clearer interpretation and understanding of the comments of these eleven teachers.

The very positive responses to statement 1 and statement 4 point towards the position of these teachers in relation to the Discriminatory/Popular Arts paradigm. That is (as with the BFI evidence; Barratt; 1998, p.29), they strongly supported the notion of Media Education as a means by which to encourage discrimination within the media. They were equally strong in their opinion that the creative process, the personal growth of the child, matters more than the quality of the final product. There may be other criteria influencing

	Please tick as appropriate: ++ strongly agree ? no clear position - - strongly disagree	+ +	+	?	-	- -
I	Media Education should help pupils to judge what represents quality in the media.	3	5	2		I
2	Children don't need Media Education as a form of defence against the media: children aren't easily fooled.	I	4	I	3	2
3	Studying film treatment of literary texts is one of the most effective forms of Media Education.	I	4	2	4	
4	In practical work, understanding of the process is far more important than the quality.	5	5		I	
5	The teacher of Media within English should pay more attention to the language and text and less attention to media institutions.	2	5	4		

Statements 2 and 3 relate to the Inoculatory/Protectionist paradigm.
Statements I and 4 relate to the Discriminatory/Popular Arts paradigm.
Statement 5 relates to the Critical/Representational/Semiological paradigm.

this latter opinion: the general discomfort of a few of these teachers with Media technology makes it unlikely that they would give high priority to an area of practice with which they themselves are uncomfortable.

The more mixed or balanced responses to questions 2 and 3 suggest that these teachers are less inclined than they perhaps once were to see Media Education as inoculation against media influences, but the Protectionist model is, perhaps, not yet dead (see *Aims,* below).

The fairly strong support for statement 5 reflects what most of these teachers said in their interviews: for a variety of reasons, teaching about media texts within their institutional context is not a priority for them. However, none of the teachers spoke actively against this notion. Rather they felt that logistical constraints (the syllabus and time) combined with practical constraints (availability of materials and teacher knowledge) made *Institutions* a less significant concept. Indeed, the four ticks in the middle column (no clear response) does reflect the ambivalence of some who felt, philosophically that *Institutions* was something that perhaps they should pay more attention to.

Key concepts: BFI Signpost Questions

From the interview that followed the above questionnaire, it was clear that at least five of the teachers were clearly very familiar with the BFI 'Signpost Questions' (Bazalgette, 1989): i.e. they knew them and could still refer to them in some detail, and four of these still used them in a significant way within the curriculum. The fifth teacher argued that media concepts as defined in the new GCSE syllabus had taken precedence in influencing the curriculum. But one of the five teachers had a scheme of work clearly based on the Signpost Questions. She argued that her department's confidence in using media concepts meant that they could avoid being unduly 'influenced' by equivalent examination syllabus definitions.

It was not that the other teachers rejected the importance of having and knowing such (Signpost) concepts, but, rather, that over the years, concepts in English and Media had merged to make a different set of organising frameworks more significant, a sort of English/Media hybrid. These concepts varied from school to school, but included: *audience, purpose, presentation, style, selection, language, layout, rhetoric, tone, bias, form, structure, and producer.* Of the four schools currently 'using' the Signpost Questions, two had Media Studies departments. If this set of key questions is to remain significant, they may need reintroducing to English teachers.

Of the various concepts specifically referred to in the interviews, *Media Language*, not surprisingly, was most prominent, although this, on occasions, meant verbal language rather than visual and/or verbal language. *Representation*, though often highly significant in the lessons seen, was not much mentioned, other than by two teachers, one of whom saw it as an issue in every part of English, for example in Literature where pupils would study how a character was 'represented'.

The concept of who produces what and for whom (*Institutions* or *Agencies*) was not significant for any of the teachers. That is, they acknowledged its importance but were unlikely to plan for it within English lessons. During the interviews, a number said they were happy to address *Institutions* as and when it arose, but the general feeling was that curriculum pressures and curriculum assessment systems dictated that this concept should have a low priority in the English curriculum. Both the teachers interviewed who ran media studies courses said that *Institutions* for them was a significant issue in media studies, but unlikely to be addressed by them in any meaningful way within English.

If *Institutions* is a neglected concept within English teaching, then *Technologies* as the focus of study seems even more so. Other than in relation to television and video, it was not possible to gather any evidence of teachers focusing explicitly on the contribution to meaning that technologies make. In most schools the Internet had (often recently) arrived and was used by individual pupils for research, but no teacher was yet in a position to address the impact of the Internet on how information or ideas are communicated or received. Given the current media and public interest in the Internet, it is perhaps surprising that it is not faster becoming an issue in the English/Media curriculum. CD-ROM was mentioned as one form of information medium, though one teacher felt that it was already beginning to become obsolete given the rise of the Internet. As with the Internet, teachers said they tended to encourage opportunistic use of word processing or desktop publishing, but were unlikely to focus on the way in which the chosen technology would influence what was written. English teachers were often aware of Information Technology skills taught elsewhere in the curriculum. In 1999 teachers were still citing overbooked computer suites, overworked computer networks and general difficulty of access as obstacles to education through (or about) computers.

If technologies were used or discussed, it tended to be in the context of television or video. Some teachers were enthusiastic about the use of the video camera, though there was no evidence of teachers and/ or pupils editing videos, other than in the video camera – only in one school were appropriate facilities clearly available. One teacher, also in charge of Media Studies, made reference to using cameras for still images and to scanning images into desktop publishers. Interestingly, many examples of the use of video cameras (or computers) came not from the Media aspect of English teaching but from other areas, including retrieval of information about Shakespeare, videoing drama or aspects of performance in Literature, videoing 'speaking and listening' activities or using video in General National and Vocational Qualification (GNVQ).

In relation to new technologies such as e-mail and the Internet, it is worth repeating that many of the schools were currently gaining or had just gained access to the Internet. With many teachers yet to become familiar with these technologies, it is clearly too early to evaluate their position within the English curriculum. At this stage, the overall picture would seem to be of individual teachers and pupils using the Internet as a resource, but, as yet, of no collective attempt being made to consider the new technologies as the focus of any Media study.

Teachers' attitudes to Media Education

By far the most common defining notion to emerge from the interviews in this area was that Media is, or should be *analytical*. More than half of the teachers clearly expressed this, and others, in their discussion (and in their practice) implied this. That is, they were more likely to involve pupils in the analysis of Media texts than in their creation, though more than one teacher was keen to insist that with analysis came room for personal response. Individual teachers had their own variations on this theme. Interestingly, both 'film buffs' were also keen to assert their love for teaching literature – at least as important to both as Media, implying an interest in narrative *per se*. One teacher was keen to define what, for her, Media Education was **not** about: she avoided what she saw as the cliché of advertisement analysis and the standard comparison of two newspaper articles. Another offered an almost crusading perspective, emphasising the 'controversial', and offering an approach to Media texts that would 'provoke and embarrass'.

In general, the teachers felt that pupils responded well to Media Education within English, though three expressed reservations about pupils' response to analysis: there was a feeling from a minority of teachers that pupils were discomfited by the notion that there was not necessarily a right answer to be found. Also, whilst some teachers felt pupils enjoyed practical work, at least one teacher felt that the difficulties pupils encountered in making media proved a discouragement for them. One teacher felt that the pupils preferred Media to the study of literature; another saw no difference between response to English and response to Media work. There was no obvious consensus about perceived responses of boys compared to girls. There was some sense that boys were confident about media, both because of their inclination to use technology, and because the process of media work (analysis followed by 'imitation') suited them. But, equally, teachers who expressed an opinion felt that girls coped well with both the technology and the analysis.

In contrast with the situation reported in the 1992–1993 research, with one strong exception, teachers were generally optimistic or very optimistic about the future of Media Education. Two of the most optimistic said that they perceived teaching colleagues as much more competent and confident in Media than they had been in the past. Two felt that there had been a time of crisis a number of years ago, but that the crisis had passed. One felt that Media had a future though not necessarily within English and one felt that the case for Media Education was unarguable, because failure to address media issues in the current technological age would leave a 'credibility gap' between pupils and education. The one pessimistic teacher had been disconcerted by recent negative press about Media Education; for her, its only chance of survival lay in its retention within the GCSE syllabuses.

Aims

The analytical perspective of these teachers is backed up by their definition of their long-term aims for their pupils. They were essentially concerned with the empowerment of children as *consumers*, helping them to be *informed*, to see how the media are *constructed, to understand technique*, to *critically evaluate*, to be *alert and understanding*, to have *awareness*, to consider *layers of interpretation*. In one sense, this would support Barratt's assertion (1998, p.29) that 'By far the most popular aim of media related work in English is to help pupils become more discriminating users of the media'. Barratt, citing Goodwyn and Findlay (1997) offers this as further support for the notion that 'few teachers now agree that 'English teachers should teach their pupils to resist the influence of the media.' But, as suggested in the questionnaire, it is arguable whether abandonment of the inoculatory paradigm is quite as clear cut as that: two teachers talked about media *influences* and another about media *effects*; other teachers referred variously to *scepticism and cynicism*, to not being *fooled*, to media *social control*, and to *manipulation*.

There is more than the Discriminatory paradigm operating here if one assumes that the analytical perspective given to pupils is in order to counteract manipulative or influential forces. However, teachers are clearly capable of holding these views and still seeing Media Education as a positive force. One teacher stressed the importance of fun; another wanted pupils to appreciate something of the 'craft' of the media. Yet another highlighted the vocational, the artistic in relation to Media aims. A teacher concerned about 'effects on an audience' also insisted she did not teach 'kids to watch out for lying adverts'. And from more than one there was a sense of moving from 'deconstruction to construction'. Only one teacher, however, adopted a position that endorsed cultural relativity: 'All media and all culture is [are] equally relevant.'

Classroom approaches

The emphasis on analysis described above typifies the broad textual approach to teaching about media as well as characterising teachers' attitudes. In general, the lessons seen (see Chapters 6 and 7) were typical of the classroom approaches customarily used by these teachers. However, most teachers provided a gloss in relation to particular emphases not evident in the lessons observed. For example, one teacher is more likely to allow independent, practical Media work to be undertaken by higher achieving pupils, with lower achievers being helped more to understand basic concepts. This same teacher suggested that Key Stage 3 offered more opportunities than Key Stage 4 for experimentation. Another teacher emphasised starting with basic Media concepts and concentrating on the moving image. Both 'film buffs' were likely to link Media and Literature in their teaching.

There was arguably some contrast between teachers' general philosophy as stated (and backed up by their practice) and the examples they offered of their most successful or enjoyable lessons. Unlike many of the lessons seen, these favourite lessons were characterised by practical activities, usually in groups or pairs, often using technology (e.g. advertisements for chocolate, six images of childhood, a video marketing a product, a pop music project). Where teachers exemplified memorable practice through analysis, the analysis was always of the moving image (e.g. two versions of *Twelfth Night*; advertisements; two treatments of Frankenstein; poetry compared to *Blackadder*); by contrast, six of the lessons seen were print based. This may say something about the GCSE syllabus and Key Stage 4 curriculum pressures teachers are now under; it may, however, reflect a statistical reality, that Media lessons are more often print based and analytical (Hart 1998, p. 183).

The English syllabus

All schools in this research project had made a choice whether or not to remain with their current GCSE Board. The eleven teachers were asked to what extent had that choice been influenced by any given Board's treatment of Media Studies.

In fact, in only one school was the treatment of Media very significant. Two other schools said that the treatment of Media was one factor in a range of factors influencing choice. Six schools chose NEAB; three chose SEG, one EDEXCEL and one MEG. (In 1998, two schools actually sat MEG papers, but one has since changed from MEG to SEG). Three schools had recently moved to NEAB, two because of the free anthology which was the core of the English and the Literature syllabuses. Interestingly, one school had contemplated moving to NEAB, but finally declined: the teachers were suspicious of what they saw as the constraints of the anthology. Literature, in some form or another, appeared to be the most prominent factor influencing choice of syllabus. Five schools specifically cited Literature as being especially influential, either because of the particular literary texts prescribed by the Board or because of the Board's treatment of Literature from other cultures.

Teachers were asked to evaluate the impact of their choice of GCSE syllabus on Media Education within the English curriculum. Without exception they felt that the position of Media had been strengthened and most felt that its status had been raised. But there were variations in response, depending on the Board chosen. Those who selected NEAB (where Media is situated within the coursework, allowing the possibility of studying moving images) were much more positive. They felt that colleagues were now more aware of Media, that teachers needed to think more carefully about issues like audience that that the new syllabus had taken Media from the descriptive to the analytical, and the syllabus was more flexible. The most positive response came from one teacher who said that the syllabus 'complemented and enhanced our methods' and, in general, 'teachers find it exciting'. There were, however, seen to be effects on the curriculum. The syllabus that one teacher saw as 'flexible', another saw as 'tight'. There was general agreement that the Key Stage 4 schemes of work needed careful designing, for example by ensuring, in one school, that the Media element was tackled at a fairly late stage when pupils were mature enough to produce good quality coursework.

The SEG teachers (Media assessed in the examination in response to a written text) all agreed that the position of Media had been strengthened. But there were qualifications. One teacher felt that Media was now stronger but narrower. A second seemed to agree, arguing that 'its explicit demands are minimal, and poor in terms of range'. A third felt that teachers in the school had underestimated the demands of the Media curriculum and now needed to rethink.

Teachers of the MEG and EDEXCEL syllabuses agreed that Media was stronger now; one noted a (positive) backwash effect on Key Stage 3, and the other an anxiety within teachers that possibly they were not handling the Media element as well as they might. However, there was no clear consensus on this. Several teachers identified growing confidence in their colleagues' handling of Media Education.

Some teachers were surprised to be asked to distinguish between study of non-fiction and study of media texts. That they were a little hazy about the distinction is not surprising, given the vagueness in some syllabuses, and the failure to distinguish them at all in the MEG syllabus. Most, however, when pressed, were thoughtful about the distinction. A number felt that the study of media texts was characterised by an emphasis on audience, involving notions of 'mass' or 'public domain'. Media study, they felt, was more likely to involve analysis, more likely to include film, television, news and advertising (largely an NEAB response). One teacher felt that it was more likely to involve moving from the text to the context. Non-fiction tended to be defined almost exclusively by the sort of texts which exemplified it – a circular construction: non-fiction includes travel writing, autobiography, and diaries; diaries, travel and autobiography are non-fiction texts. Again, the lack of clarity can be traced back to the wording in the GCSE syllabuses, and, before that, to the vagueness of the National Curriculum description. There was some cynicism in talking about non-fiction: one likened its study to old-fashioned 'comprehension' and another suggested that it can be identified by its preoccupation with 'cosmetic dentistry and garden walls'.

The school

None of the eleven schools reported the existence of any formal cross-curricular or whole-school approach to Media Education, a main thrust of the BFI's *Secondary Curriculum Statement* (Bowker, 1991). The BFI position has been criticised by Hart (1992, p. 43): 'It seems to accept the premises of the National Curriculum as a basis for cross-curricular media education without realising the ideological implications of this position and without recognising the practical difficulties of implementation.'

Two teachers did suggest that Media ideas were informing the school's cross-curricular, literacy policy, but because of the general lack of formal structure it was generally difficult for teachers to be precise about the sort of Media Education that might exist elsewhere in the curriculum. They tended to report examples of Media Education that they had come across – via displays of pupils' work or informal staffroom conversations. No-one reported any formal cross-curricular project centring on Media Education. Also, when teachers mentioned other subjects which appeared to have an involvement with Media work, no clear pattern emerged. Subjects mentioned included History, RE, Technology, Business Studies, Drama, Art, PSS (censorship and representation), GNVQ (Health, Tourism, Leisure, Manufacturing) and careers. Media work outside the mainstream academic curriculum (GNVQ, Careers, PSE) tended to look at representation and deal with practical aspects of Media. In relation to History and RE, teachers sometimes mentioned advertising and newspapers as the most likely forms in which media work would appear.

Teachers were asked how much time they spent on media work within English. It is not possible in any way to offer a clear overview of their responses because of the difficulty of defining what was meant by Media. In particular, though Media was clearly inscribed into the curriculum for English in each school, there was often a difference in whether teachers saw analysis of non-fiction texts as part of or separate from the Media element of that curriculum. Secondly, the way in which the English curriculum is organised also affected the answers. For example, one department works in fairly tight half-term 'units of work'; another has only recently inscribed Media formally into their English scheme of work; where, when and how it is done is left to the discretion of the teacher. In this particular school, the teacher was pessimistic about the amount of time spent on Media – regarded as 'very little... just a few lessons, exam-driven'. In another school, more confident in Media and supported by a thriving Media Studies department, the estimate was nearer 'one quarter of Key Stage 4 curriculum time'. One teacher saw Media as 'integral' to the way the department looked at texts, and therefore could not begin to estimate the amount of curriculum time it occupied.

Between these two extremes a pattern did emerge. The Media 'unit of work' (typically one half-term) was a very clear organising factor in more than half of the schools. In all the departments, Media was formally written into the scheme of work. The way in which Media was written into the scheme of work varied considerably. One department described it as a 'strand'; another had a very clear conceptual framework as the basis of its particular unit; another described the Media element of the curriculum largely in terms of its contribution to written and spoken assessment outcomes (e.g. 'using language to persuade'). In only one school was the Media unit very specifically taught by all members of the department during the same half-term. One school, currently teaching in units, expressed doubts abut the efficacy of organising the curriculum in this way and was seeking to redistribute the Media teaching back into more general elements of the English curriculum.

Nearly all departments had allocated resources (school-prepared and/or commercial) to the particular Media unit or strand, shared by teachers in the department. That unit or strand tended to be described in terms of minimum entitlement or core curriculum. However, the clear pattern emerged of teacher choice predominating over prescribed curriculum. That is, however Media was written into the English curriculum, whether it was taught in units or not, teachers were encouraged to make their own choices: of when to teach the Media element, where to place the emphasis, and which materials to use or which media texts to focus on. Interestingly, though Media was written into every English scheme of work (not the case in 1992–1993, and no doubt since then influenced by the pressure of OFSTED inspections), it seems likely that, within and between the eleven schools concerned, there was still a substantial range of experiences offered in the name of Media Education.

This is not to suggest that any individual pupil would have had a sense of range or variety but that the experience of any individual pupil would still depend very strongly on the choices made by the individual teacher within a given English department. For example, those pupils who did in-depth analysis of John Ford's film *The Searchers*, would have had that experience because one particular teacher's enthusiasm led her to film analysis. Within the same school, even within the context of a clear scheme of work, another pupil's Media experience could have been represented by in-depth analysis of a number of television advertisements. The question to be answered by this school (and every other school) would be, 'What would give coherence to the course's constituent units... Is there an essential body of knowledge and information? If so, what is it?' (Masterman, 1980, p.3). As Masterman goes on to suggest, without coherence a Media Education course could be 'orientated towards content rather than process, asking different questions of different media and developing no consistent line of enquiry'.

This is not to criticise the quality of lessons observed. Indeed the vast majority of pupils observed clearly had very good Media learning experiences. The point is that regardless of the constraints of terminal examinations or the openness of coursework and despite the inscription of Media into every English curriculum, choices made by individual teachers of English were still crucial. Where one teacher would allow the limits of a print-based, examination-based syllabus to describe the limits of their teaching, another would see film analysis as an invaluable means by which pupils could be encouraged to produce writing designed to *analyse, review and comment*. It is worth reflecting that, whatever model of English or Media teaching guides the curriculum, it is the underlying perception that English teachers have of their own role that is just as important. There was clear reluctance on the part of virtually all the heads of English concerned to impose a curriculum on their teachers, believing rather that personal choice for the teacher was crucial.

Given that all schemes of work contained descriptions of Media entitlement, and given that such entitlement has largely been enforced by the OFSTED process, it is perhaps surprising, not to say a little disconcerting, that no teacher in the most recent OFSTED report on English was able to testify to the department's treatment of Media as being significant. It may be that in eleven Media-confident schools, inspectors saw only Media-competent teaching and saw no reason to make a specific observation. Or it may be that for the OFSTED inspectors concerned, Media was not a high curriculum priority or was even 'invisible'.

Context: resources

Whilst some teachers made their own resources and collected authentic media texts from their daily life (pamphlets, leaflets, advertisements etc.), it was more common for teachers to adapt commercially produced texts. There is little doubt, even in this small sample, that the English and Media Centre's *Advertising Pack* (1993) has become ubiquitous. Eight out of the eleven schools had this resource and clearly did use it; some teachers felt it particularly useful for those colleagues who were less confident about Media Education. Interestingly, they most often referred to one specific unit within the pack, a study of a series of television commercials for Levi Jeans, of which the video in the pack contains a number of popular examples. It is interesting to speculate for a moment on the degree to which Media Education within English is being taught via this particular section of this particular resource. The English and Media Centre was cited as an important distributor of Media resources for English teachers. Two other publications by the Centre mentioned by teachers were the *News Pack* (Grahame, 1995), and *Klondyke Kate* (Bleiman *et al.*, 1995) Other resources to get two or more mentions were the free materials distributed by Film Education and BBC schools broadcasts. In addition, teachers tended to use appropriate sections from GCSE 'course books' such as those produced by Longmans or Oxford. BFI materials were referred to obliquely, never by title, by only a small minority.

In-service training for teachers

By the very fact of their involvement in this project, most of the eleven schools had arguably demonstrated significant confidence in their Media knowledge. This was a group of teachers who know about Media Education.

Most teachers stressed the importance of the informal sharing of ideas, and the significance of this should not be underestimated. The general picture, however, is of a lack of Media INSET in the past five years. Although several of the teachers have had contact with the Southampton Media Education Group, such contact with local teacher networks was never recent. In fact, the Southampton Media Education Group became the Media Education Centre in 1996 with a greater focus on academic research rather than on teacher support and INSET. Eight of the eleven teachers indicated that they could recall no external formally organised Media-specific INSET in recent years. But INSET did occur. There was some evidence of limited provision by the GCSE Examination Boards to support their new 1998 English syllabuses. Where this occurred, it would typically involve one day's training, of which the Media element of the syllabus represented one part. The scope and quality of these days depended significantly on the scope and quality of the particular Board's syllabus, and, as Chapter 4 argues, in some cases the view of Media offered is rather narrow.

In three of the four schools where Media Studies was taught, the teacher responsible for Media Studies had a formal or semi-formal role in providing INSET for teachers of Media within English. (In the fourth, Media Studies was the responsibility of the Creative Arts faculty.) Links between Media and English departments were very strong, and the consequent positive impact on teachers' knowledge about and confidence in Media in English was evident. Typically, the Media specialist was a frequent attender of courses in Media Education, and so the internally generated training was supported by external expertise.

Of those teachers who could recall recent and relevant Media INSET, the most likely sources were the BFI (courses at the South Bank, and the Waterfront), the English and Media Centre and the University of Southampton. On one occasion, these INSET providers had combined to offer a local authority 'area training day' on Media at Southampton University. However, this was the sole example offered of a teacher attending local-authority INSET in Media. There was no evidence of systematic certificated professional development.

There were two models of INSET which appeared to be successful. The first was the model described above, with training emanating from internal Media Studies expertise, supported by regular external support. The second was a school without a Media Studies GCSE course (though considering it) which made a point of encouraging a range of teachers to make frequent and regular use of the variety of courses offered by the English and Media Centre, several of which, each year, tend to focus specifically on Media. This approach was characterised by a desire to acquaint as many teachers as possible with as broad an experience as possible. However, this school had also allowed the teacher with the most Media expertise one day 'off timetable' to develop curriculum materials for a Media unit of work.

Of the five teachers who had received (or were about to receive) recent Media training, three were the newest to the profession. Indeed one head of English commented on how teachers new from PGCE courses were important in contributing to new ideas about teaching Media. It may well be that the greatest INSET needs are those of long-serving teachers, who either received no specific Media training, or training that dates back a number of years.

In some cases, teachers felt they were fighting against other institutional pressures for INSET time. For example, two of the schools faced imminent OFSTED inspections and one of these commented on how preparation for OFSTED tended to drive perceptions of training needs. Two others referred respectively to Special Educational Needs and Boys' Achievement as two agreed school training priorities which were effectively tying up training resources. Though the evidence from this small sample is not strong, it may be that the tendency in recent years for formally adopted School Development Plans (partly driven by OFSTED) has made it less likely than in previous years that English departments establish their own training priorities.

In these eleven schools, a general picture emerges of a Media curriculum centred on analysis and heavily determined by the GCSE syllabus, especially if is assessed in a terminal examination. A general effect of the constraints and of teachers' own preferences is a tendency to underplay context (e.g. institutions and agencies) and to put text (often print-based) at the centre of study. The teaching of this sometimes conservative curriculum is in the hands of committed and optimistic teachers who recognise the new status that Media has in the English curriculum. Their approach is generally 'low-tech', but there is a tension between their favoured approach (involving media production in group-centred activities) and the approach which many feel that the examination system requires them to adopt. They maintain their enthusiasm by supporting each other and relying, where possible on the guidance of an 'expert' in the department. It is just as well that such teachers are so committed and resourceful because school priorities serve to limit severely teachers' opportunities for professional development within the field of Media.

6

Media teachers teaching

Background to the lessons

When reflecting on the lessons an important context to consider is that ten out of eleven were in the first year of Key Stage 4. Six of those year 10 classes were observed in the Autumn term when department schemes of work tended to includ some notion of induction. Thus, several lessons served to introduce Media Education to the pupils in some way. Of course, all pupils had, theoretically, a Key Stage 3 Media experience on which to build.

A second context was that several teachers, in their keenness to co-operate in the research project, taught a lesson 'out of sync' with their normal teaching programme. That is, although the lesson taught was typical, it was not necessarily the lesson that would have been taught at that time by that teacher. The combination of induction factor and rearranged teaching programme gives some of the lessons a sense of detachment from the rest of the planned curriculum.

Aims

It is generally true to say that most teachers expressed their intentions for the lesson in terms of broad aims rather than specific objectives, more related to types of understanding they wanted to develop than to specific Media concepts they wanted to be understood. On some occasions, the aims were described more specifically in relation to enhanced understanding of a given media text. None of this is to say that the lessons lacked focus. Indeed, the majority were related to developing the understanding of a very specific, narrow segment of media text: they were sharply focused in a textual sense.

Lessons with the broadest aims included one which introduced pupils to advertising (as part of a communications model of Media Education), and another which encouraged a group of boys to explore self-image in relation to other images of masculinity found in newspaper headlines. The lesson with the clearest objective required struggling learners to use Media concepts and terminology appropriately within a given sentence – an objective measurable by the end of the lesson. Another lesson with a narrow objective (albeit within a broader set of aims) required pupils to come to accept a very specific understanding: that John Wayne's character, Ethan, in *The Searchers*, represents 'a hero who does not fit'.

Three of the lessons in some way aimed to develop pupils' understanding of how different elements of media combine to produce new meaning. These included the exploration of sound and image (the opening to David Lean's film, *Great Expectations*); the exploration of printed text and image (newspaper coverage of Britons on holiday); and the intertextuality to be found within the Levi Jeans advertisements.

In two of the lessons the aim was for pupils to come to an understanding of a very specific piece of written text: an article from the *Big Issue*, and two contrasting articles about women in work. Both these lessons were very strongly connected to coursework or examination outcomes, with the emphasis on pupils arriving at a common understanding of how these texts operate.

The remaining two lessons, in very different ways, aimed to use media approaches in order to enhance pupils' understanding of literary texts. One involved the use of storyboarding to explore and re-present poetic imagery and narrative. The other lesson explored the marketing of film (through posters and trailers) as a way of enhancing pupils' understanding of the literary texts on which the trailers and posters were based.

Texts and contexts

Barratt's observation (1998, p. 40) that original TV drama features rarely in media work in schools is borne out in the conversations with teachers and in the eleven lessons seen. Indeed, though television sets and VCRs were used in four of the eleven lessons, no lesson in any way tackled the vast output of television drama, news, documentary or popular entertainment. The VCR was used in three cases to show film (of Shakespeare, Dickens and John Ford's *The Searchers*). Where the moving image was taken from television (the Levi Jeans advertisements) it came as part of a pre-packaged study of advertising. Clearly, all four studies of the moving image were, in themselves, entirely valid media explorations. The noteworthy point is the apparent absence in the eleven lessons of study of material taken directly from television broadcasts. If this pattern were replicated in large numbers of schools it would suggest that film and advertising dominate the study of the moving image.

Seven of the lessons focused on the printed text. These texts included an imaginary poster advertising English lessons, an article from the *Big Issue*, a collection of newspaper headlines, a newspaper story with accompanying photographs, news reports in contrasting newspapers, a Calvin Klein advertisement and a poem. With the exception of the poem, all printed texts took the form of black-and-white photocopies. This, of course, is inevitable where the teacher wishes between 15 and 30 pupils to discuss the same media text. It does however raise the question about context. Clearly, the meaning of any printed text is affected by the print and images which surround it in the publication in which it appears. In the eleven lessons seen, the emphasis was on text rather than (immediate) context. However, broader contextual issues (e.g. whether an article was published, say, in the *Sun*, the *Big Issue*, or the *Mail*) were raised.

Media concepts

Not surprisingly, the Media concept, which featured most strongly, indeed in virtually every lesson, was that of *media language*. In addition, given that seven of the lessons were print based, it is not surprising that *media language*, in practice, often meant the connotations of words and the use of rhetoric. This particularly applied to the investigation of the *Big Issue* and the articles from the *Sun*, the *Mail* and the local newspaper, and to the study of representations of males in newspaper headlines. In the lesson which explored the marketing of Shakespeare, the connotations of graphic and presentational features of printed texts (in posters) were also considered. In two lessons in particular (focusing on *Great Expectations* and on representations of holiday makers abroad) there was strong emphasis on the notion of anchorage: teachers deliberately created disjunctions between word/sound and image in order that pupils could consider how the former can be used to 'fix' the meaning of the latter.

When the focus was on visual, non-verbal signs, the discussion often centred on the significance of cultural codes rather than, for example, codes of camera shot, focus, colour or light, though these conventions were, of course, addressed. This particularly applied to the analysis of the Calvin Klein advertisement and the study of John Ford's film, *The Searchers*. The former dealt with, for example, the significance of facial features and clothes; the latter paid particular attention to (American) Western artefacts or 'props', costume and the body language and relationships of the prominent actors. The *Searchers* scheme of work suggested that codes related to 'framing' and 'Technicolor' were covered in other lessons. The lessons which most strongly focused on medium-related codes included the exploration of *Great Expectations* (connotations of music, the human voice, graphics, and point of view); and the analysis of the marketing of Shakespeare (moving-image codes contrasted with print-based codes).

The second most prominent concept to emerge was that of *representation*. In interviews with teachers the term was sometimes used by them to describe the way in which literary and other texts *portray* characters or themes (For example, a teacher might say that storyboarding was used to *represent* poetic imagery in visual form.) But the term was also explicitly used to mean the selective portrayal of social, economic or gendered groups in society. In the eleven lessons, such representation was considered in relation to masculinity, women in work, Britons abroad, the native North American, the unemployed, (American and British) youths, and cinema 'stars'.

Given the traditional emphasis within English teaching on purpose and audience in writing, the media concept of *Audiences* did not feature as strongly as one might expect. *Audience*, however, was inevitably an issue in those lessons which dealt with advertising (Calvin Klein, Levi Jeans), and in English lessons. Also, in discussion of the various texts, references were made to likely or intended readership (e.g. of the *Big Issue*, of the Shakespearean posters and film trailers, of the *Sun* article), but, other than in the work on Shakespeare, audience was not often the most significant feature of any discussion.

Categories (or genres) inevitably featured strongly in that nearly every lesson involved the selection by the teacher of one specific text type. So, *Categories* (as described in the section above on texts) included the film trailer, film opening credits, and complete film text. It also included television advertisements, magazine advertisements, newspaper and magazine reports and articles. But *Categories per se* was rarely the focus of the study. For example, though *The Searchers* represents the Western genre, and it was discussed in that context, knowledge of other Westerns and other genres was implicit, rather than explicitly discussed. Similarly, all printed texts were considered as single texts or pairs of texts, but the way in which different elements of newspapers or different newspapers themselves can be categorised, was not significant in these lessons.

Since *Agencies/Institutions* was regarded by virtually all of the eleven teachers as interesting, but not necessarily a feature of the English curriculum, it was unlikely to be prominent in the lessons. But there were examples where this concept did become significant. When Agencies did arise, it tended to be in the narrower sense of the word 'agency' with the emphasis on a single agent or narrow group of agents. For example, discussion of *The Searchers* focused strongly on the role of the director and the significance of the star (areas also considered in the lesson on Shakespeare). Comparison of the *Sun* with a local newspaper raised issues about the responsibility of editors to constrain what their journalists might write. And one lesson on advertising emphasised the role of the advertiser (i.e. copywriter) in exploiting the weakness in the consumer. Agencies, however, in the sense of large institutions with networks of ownership and control, did not feature in these lessons.

Technologies featured as a media concept only in the discussion of film and television advertising where reference was inevitably made to the conventions of camera shot and sound effects. But there was little discussion of the degree to which any textual message is influenced by the technology of the medium in which is produced. Given the relatively 'low-tech' level of the lessons and the common problems of access to computers, this is not surprising. Four lessons involved use of television, one an OHP and one an audio player. Though teachers reported class and individual use of computers for the purposes of gathering information and processing writing, use of information technologies did not feature in the lessons seen. A note of caution is needed here. Most of the schools interviewed had quite recent or very recent access to the Internet. Most teachers were interested but few were very experienced in its use. Prior to the Internet, information accessing was done mainly via CD-ROM, a medium over which teachers had been able to exercise significant control. The Internet raises very different questions about access to and confidence in information databases. How schools address the Internet with pupils (and it is unlikely to be an issue solely for the English department) is, perhaps, a subject to which researchers should return within the next two to three years.

Teaching approaches

The eleven teachers were clearly very skilled; issues of discipline or indiscipline amongst pupils simply did not arise. Also, teacher interviews revealed that they used a variety of pedagogic approaches. This chapter, therefore, only outlines the predominant approaches seen in the eleven lessons; it does not, of course, attempt to describe how these teachers typically operate.

With one exception, the teacher, usually at the front, was strongly in control of the progress of each lesson. The most common approach was teacher-led question and answer, interspersed with pair, small-group, or individual activity. This was most obvious in all the lessons based on printed texts – the teacher would, typically, take the whole class through an analysis, allowing and encouraging all responses, but clearly defining the limits of what a given text might or might not mean. Such lessons were nearly always balanced by the teacher handing back the learning to the pupils, inviting them to work in short bursts, on small segments of text. In no lessons did teachers insist that pupils worked as individuals, in isolation from their peers; the general pattern was of informal collaboration in groups of two, three or four.

Three out of the four lessons which used VCR and television involved strong control by the teacher over the progress of the learning. To a degree, this was related to access to the technology: in all four lessons, only teachers had access to VCR controls – what pupils saw and heard, and when they heard and saw it, was controlled by the teacher. Within these constraints, teachers were obviously keen to involve as many pupils as possible in the discussion of film and television images. In one lesson (analysis of Levi Jeans), however, the teacher's role was very low key; she devised a clear strategy of group activity supported by analysis 'frames'; in addition she allocated to pupils specific responsibilities within the group for the analysis of one particular feature of the 'text'. This teacher remained in control of the technology, but handed most of the responsibility for learning back to the pupils.

Practical activities

As indicated elsewhere in this report, several of these lessons were introductory and others were adapted to accommodate a visiting researcher. Thus the lessons seen were never likely to feature very much practical activity, assuming, that is, that practice would usually be preceded by exploration of theory. In only one (on Shakespeare) was there an intention to produce a videotape as an end product to the project. In one other, storyboarding was used, but as a means of interpretation rather than as a step on the road to production. Any practical activity during these lessons, or planned as a consequence of them, was likely to involve writing, some of it analytical, some 'persuasive', replicating the technique of the text studied.

It is interesting to speculate how skilled teachers such as these would teach about the Internet. Its interactive nature would necessitate the balance of responsibility for learning shifting towards the pupil. Its capacity to offer large chunks of (sometimes unverified) data would provide the teacher with at least two further challenges. The first would be to find ways to encourage pupils to validate the data; the second would be to encourage pupils to adapt and re-present information in new, creative and productive ways. Certainly, the model of teacher-led analysis of a text, however well managed, would seem inappropriate for learning about some of the new technologies.

7
Changes in Media teaching: 1993–1999

On a very practical level, it is first worth comparing the lessons taught by the five teachers who were common to both research projects. Interestingly, four out of five used the same medium on each occasion (two print and two television) and the fifth 'switched' from television to print.

Secondly, it is worth comparing the range of lessons in the two studies. Although the 1993 report noted few opportunities in lessons for space to be given to pupils' own media experiences, compared to 1998–1999 there was a strong element of popular culture in the lessons: in 1992–1993 three dealt with the making or marketing of popular music and another with the analysis of comics. In the 1999 report there are no obvious examples of popular culture being addressed, other than in the study of the Levi Jeans advertisements. Arguably, the curriculum freedom offered in 1992–1993 allowed for a more open interpretation of media experiences, but this freedom had its disadvantages. Between the eleven teachers there was less of a common purpose, more of a sense of individual preoccupations being explored. Indeed, three of the lessons in 1992–1993 had no specific Media aims at all.

In 1998–1999, although there appeared to be a narrowing down of the Media curriculum, from all teachers there was a clear purpose; each teacher had a sense of the place of Media within the English curriculum, and each lesson was clearly designed to fulfil an identifiable Media requirement of the appropriate GCSE syllabus. It is possible to interpret the changes that took place between the two studies as a development of coherence and focus in Media, but, perhaps at the expense of inclusiveness and creativity.

Significantly, the study of film featured in this report included interpretations of literary greats (Dickens and Shakespeare) and one film genre (the Western) – the most famous of film genres, but arguably not one that attracts young people to the cinema now.

Status, coherence, and progression

There are areas in which significant advances were made. For example, the 1992–1993 researcher noted the doubtful status of Media Education within the English department. In 1998–1999 that status had been significantly enhanced, and there was a strong sense that most teachers in most English departments were gaining confidence in their Media expertise, or, at the very least, recognising the need to gain more expertise if they were to do justice to their pupils. The motivation for this, of course, was the new GCSE requirement that Media is assessed in all syllabuses. This may, however, not be altogether good news. Where the GCSE Board elected to test Media within a terminal examination, there was a strong emphasis on analysing printed texts, considered without the benefit of their original context. Where the Board elected to test Media understanding within coursework, there was much more likelihood of study of context and of moving image.

If the status of Media within English had been enhanced, then so had its coherence within the English curriculum. OFSTED inspections have ensured that every school now has clear curriculum statements outlining curriculum content and opportunities for progression and continuity. (Ironically, inspectors were extraordinarily consistent in their failure to make the teaching of Media in English a significant issue.) There were clear examples in 1998–1999 of such curriculum statements having a significant impact on the Media curriculum, and being strongly based on some conceptual model of Media teaching. It seemed that there was now much less likelihood of pupils, for example, endlessly repeating advertising projects as they progress through the school with each teacher unaware of their pupils' prior curriculum experience. Collaboratively produced units of work, supported by relevant and centrally held resources (particularly from the English and Media Centre) were the norm.

But a word of caution is needed here. In most cases, in 1998-1999 the final choice for curriculum content at lesson level still resided with the individual teacher. Teachers can use such freedom to 'play safe' to rely on tried and tested lessons taken from a collectively produced scheme of work. Or they can use the freedom to assert their individuality within a coherent curriculum framework. Thus continuity and progression for the learner can be guaranteed, but not necessarily at the expense of a narrow or limited Media diet. For teachers to make informed choices they need the benefit of research such as this. They need to see the advantages of common purpose, but, at the same time, to recognise the dangers of the curriculum straitjacket. A very careful balance between collectivity and individualism needs to be struck. A purposeful and 'progressive' Media curriculum is now more likely, but not guaranteed.

Teacher consensus and support

In 1992–1993 the National Curriculum framework was still 'bedding in'. By 1998 the National Curriculum had been largely accepted or at least tolerated. Teachers themselves were likely in 1992–1993 to have entered Media Education down a variety of avenues; in 1998–1999, regardless of length of teaching, memories of first encounters with Media Education tended to be forgotten, with teachers now linked by the National Curriculum connection. With this new uniformity, there is arguably a common base on which teachers can agree and move forward, though some may regret the loss of diversity.

Yet if teachers teaching Media can now look with more confidence to the English curriculum and to their English-teaching colleagues for authority and support, they are likely to find the whole-school context more of an obstacle. In 1991 the BFI were, perhaps misguidedly, advocating that the main Media thrust should be cross-curricular (Bowker, 1991). Certainly, there has been no obvious development of cross-curricular Media initiatives since then, and

OFSTED-driven whole-school imperatives have made it harder for the English teacher to justify leaving her class to attend Media-related courses. Media INSET in 1992–1993 was noted as being sporadic and inconsistent. In 1998–1999, with the collapse of much local-authority-based INSET, Media training seemed something of a rarity.

Technological change

Five years of technological development have meant that teachers are beyond the stage of struggling to get on computer training courses, or talking about the importance of 'keyboard skills'. From the various teachers in 1998-99 there were references to the use of scanners, digital cameras and, of course, the internet. In practice, however, in relation to technology, the pattern of lessons in both research projects seems very similar. That is, Information Technology was not used in any lessons seen, though folders of work and lesson plans suggested that the use of word processing was common enough outside these lessons. The Internet in 1998-99 was beginning to be used as an information source to support study of film and literature. But still, such technologies were tools of occasional use rather than the focus of study.

A significant and surprising feature in relation to choice of technology remains the absence of television broadcasts as the 'texts' to be the focus of Media study. If television broadcasts have yet to gain a major foothold in the English curriculum then what chance interactive game play or Internet usage?

Contexts

Whatever texts were studied, a common thread in the 22 lessons featured in both studies was the significant absence of context. Printed texts were commonly seen as isolated fragments, and though broad institutional contexts were raised, the emphasis was nearly always on engaging with the text itself. Five years have made little difference to teachers' attitudes towards teaching about Agencies, Institutions or Ideology. The 1998–1999 teachers were never opposed to the notion that the context of production was important, but considered the issue too slippery for pupils to grasp, or too low a priority in a crowded curriculum that offered no encouragement to go beyond the text itself. Indeed, the Media Studies specialists, those most likely to know about Institutions and Ideology, were no more likely than any other teacher to bring these issues into the English classroom: they were strong in their assertion that such matters were best tackled in a discrete Media Studies context.

Media pedagogy

Despite the curriculum and technological changes of the past five years, teachers' aims and approaches seemed to have changed little. They still sought to empower their pupils with the ability to 'analyse', 'understand' and 'deconstruct', with a hint of inoculation in the empowerment. Their approaches within the classroom also remained broadly similar. Analysis was still likely to involve teacher-led discussion, with learning handed back to pupils once the parameters of textual understanding had been defined. This seemed especially strong where television technology was used, with teachers finding it difficult to separate control of technology from control of learning. And the outcome of textual analysis in a production sense was still more likely to be the essay than the video, not surprisingly, given the ever-pressing need to produce assessment evidence. The gap between teachers' descriptions of their most successful or favourite Media lessons and the lessons observed reveals a tension between what teachers do teach and what they wish to teach. They would often cite as successful those lessons which were group based or technology dependent which some teachers find difficult to accommodate within the current English curriculum.

8

Conclusion: moving image media and the digital future

Our research investigated Media Education in the curriculum for English in secondary schools during 1998–1999. The lessons to be learned from it need to be considered in the light of curriculum changes since then. In other words, we need to learn the lessons of the past and apply them to the present and the future.

The moving image

The most obvious change is the clarification and expansion of the role of Media Education in the latest Curriculum for English (QCA, 1999). As outlined in the Introduction, there are new emphases on purpose, form and audience. More significantly, for the first time, the moving image has become the responsibility of the English teacher; a position long advocated by the BFI.

The campaign for more attention to the moving image is best reflected in the influential report Making Movies Matter (BFI, 1999). At the heart of this document is an ambitious, well-structured model of progression, describing five stages of learning in relation to 'FVT' (film, video and television). The model outlines what children and students should know about and be able to do in relation to texts (Film Language), contexts (Producers and Audiences) and meaning (Messages and Values). In the past, Media Education has rightly been criticised for failing to describe clearly what subject progression looks like. On this basis alone, the model should be welcomed, and, indeed, it has a number of clear strengths. Its basic structure

(Language, Producers and Audiences, Messages and Values) allows for easy integration with the BFI's 'Key Concepts' (Bazalgette, 1989). This should reassure any teacher who fears an extra or competing conceptual framework. The progression model is inclusive in the sense that television and video are part of its notion of 'cineliteracy'. And it does not duck the thorny issue of terminology, recommending the particular vocabulary that students at each stage of progression should be introduced to (e.g. stage 4 includes reference to *montage, surrealist, cinéma verité* and *ideology*).

However, as Buckingham and Jones have argued, this 'apparent narrowing of the field at a time of media convergence is, to say the least, paradoxical' (Buckingham and Jones, 2000, p.13). The report's title is taken from the last sentence of its introduction, 'We want to remind you that movies matter' (p.7). Although the report takes account of video and television, the introduction and the title perhaps point to the real concern of the BFI: when it talks of the moving image, in reality this means film. Given that the BFI's own recent study, (Barratt, 1998) draws attention to the general neglect of television, and the absence of television drama from the Media curriculum within English, one needs to be careful that, for the new curriculum, television and video do not simply become the means by which film finds its way into the classroom. At the same time, there is here a strong emphasis on 'cultural heritage' approaches to the study of moving image media, a concern with appreciation and enjoyment at the expense of critical engagement. This would be retrogressive. And at a pragmatic level, there is a further danger that focusing so strongly on the moving image might mean that radio will continue to be neglected, and that Media analysis of print texts might come to mean little more than simple retrieval of information and a cursory check for bias.

We do not agree with Bazalgette's assertion that 'Media Education is not a subject. It's incoherent, it's unmanageable, it's a theoretical hybrid, it's trying to do too much. It can never form the basis of a coherent model of learning...' (Bazalgette, 1999, p. 4). Over fifteen years ago, Masterman (1985), in calling for an holistic approach to studying the media, argued that Media Education had very little to say about the 'distinctive nature of TV, radio, or the press' (p. xiii). He called for 'critical approaches which students can apply to any media text' (p. xiv). The logic of this argument seems even stronger today. In the twenty-first century, if one's starting point for Media Education were the uniqueness of each medium, then teacher and student could easily be overwhelmed by the extraordinary range of digital media developing almost daily. Even with 'old' media, distinguishing between the moving and still image can sometimes lead to fruitless and misleading debates. A holistic approach is firmly embedded in the conceptions and structures of the new Media Studies A/S level courses.

Developments in the last decade mean that it no longer makes sense to study individual media in isolation from each other. The social and cultural issues raised by the media pervade them all. Increasingly, as in the case of Rupert Murdoch's News Corporation, media operations have become diversified across different media in order to operate effectively on a global scale. Murdoch's News Corporation is one of the world's largest media companies with total assets as of March 31, 2001 of nearly US$39 billion and total annual revenues of about US$14 billion. Its operations in the United States, Canada, continental Europe, the United Kingdom, Australia, Latin America and the Pacific Basin include the production and distribution of cinematic films and television programming; television, satellite and cable broadcasting; the publication of newspapers, magazines and books; the production and distribution of promotional and advertising products and services; the development of digital broadcasting; the development of conditional access and subscriber management systems; and the creation and distribution of popular on-line programming.

In addition to cross-media ownership, there is also an increasing convergence between media, with the Internet acting as a meta-medium for carrying digital radio and television signals, and the integration of digital communication capacity into domestic media like television sets. At the same time, there is a constant cross-referencing between media like radio, television and newspapers and cross-media promotion of programming and other material (e.g. the tabloids' promotion of soaps through features, soft news items and scheduling information). It follows from these developments that Media Education needs to develop new literacies that are genuinely cross-media.

Nearly all accounts of Media Education describe its aims in terms of the ability of students to critique the media. It is essential that such an ability is founded on general principles and concepts that allow the student to engage with any medium that she or he encounters, including those media barely imagined, let alone developed and marketed. To study the media in terms of the *moving image* only would seem to be potentially disempowering. In the classroom, fragmentation of Media Education seems likely to lead to greater reliance by teachers on individual, favourite resources, lessons or exercises. Our own research points to the (understandable and reasonable) tendency of teachers to use and re-use well-known materials, for example, the Levi Advertisements' package from the English and Media Centre's *Advertising Pack* (Grahame, 1993). But teachers need a Media Education framework inclusive enough to deal with the unfamiliar, the unimagined and the 'unattractive'. And that framework needs to be flexible enough to allow consideration of a range of media and media forms within the context of a single lesson or series of lessons. As Tweddle argues, we 'require a language for talking about texts which derives from a theory about texts, about what they are, how they are constructed ...and how they are used', a language which should 'apply both to texts that already exist and to possible new texts or types of texts that may emerge in the future' (Tweddle *et al.*, 1997, p. 49).

Holistic approaches to Media Education

The lessons we observed suggested that in some teachers at least, there already exists a capacity for teachers of English to deal with familiar film narrative. We saw detailed study of John Ford's *The Searchers*, David Lean's *Great Expectations* and adaptations of Shakespeare, but there was no television drama, no study of quiz, chat or game shows or comedy, and no attention to the distinctive nature of press institutions (rather than attention to newspaper articles). We saw four lesson on news in print, but none on television news. We found no evidence, in observations or conversations, of attention to radio.

Perhaps what was more significant was that we found little evidence of comparative analysis and few attempts to treat the moving image as something applicable equally to factual to and fictional narrative. But this sort of holistic approach is needed. It is not only that Media Education needs the capacity to deal with several different media at once, it also needs the capacity to deal with those text forms that, in themselves, borrow from a range of other forms, genres, traditions and technologies. Graddol (1994, p. 142) draws attention to some important media tensions or overlaps. He argues that television news is a hybrid, 'drawing on both literary realism and realist cinema', and that this 'reflects a constant tension between verbal and visual com-munication'. News, he argues is both a knowledge system (factuality rather than fiction) and a genre, (not documentary, docu-drama or chat show), and needs to work hard to establish the security of the former and the distinctiveness of the latter. As Graddol suggests, the message carried by the news audio channel (to do with causes) may well differ from the message carried by the visual channel (to do with effects). To know about its visual messages implicitly involves knowing in what ways television news differs from still photography on the one hand and cinema narrative on the other. And any study of television news might beneficially involve consideration of news in other media: in print, on the radio and on the Internet.

In practical terms then, what teachers need is an analytical frame-work that applies to television and cinema, print and the moving image, factuality and fiction. The framework below (drawing on Graddol and adapted from Southampton University's Distance Learning Course, *Examining Media**) offers a broad analytical, inclusive framework designed to be a starting point for talking about a media text. (A more detailed framework, taking particular account of digital media, is discussed later in this chapter.)

---

*   *Examining Media* (2001) a Master's-level Certificate in Advanced Educational Studies (by Distance Learning) Southampton: Media Education Centre <www.soton.ac.uk/~mec>

When responding to a media text one might consider:

1. Written and spoken language, including the use of modal verbs, use of the passive

2. Camera codes and conventions of perspective and gaze, including viewpoint, distance, angle, light, colour

3. Cultural codes, including facial expressions, dress, body language, and situational contexts

4. Editing, narrative or genre codes, including notions of author, character, closure and chronology

5. The relationship between verbal and visual codes, including the ways in which one can give meaning to or 'anchor' the other

Talking about a media text

How might this operate in relation to film and to television news? As suggested above, the narrative of television news (point 4 in the framework), arising as it does from pictures taken after the event, often shows effects rather than causes, the causes being handled in the accompanying verbal text. Also, news narrative can move backwards and forwards in time without adopting the special conventions that realist film narrative needs to use (e.g. switch to black and white) when it disrupts chronology. Cultural codes (point 3 in the framework) in film narrative are usually described in terms of *mise-en-scène*, the notion of selecting costume and contextual background to suit a particular narrative. Although television news would seem to allow the more 'natural' cultural codes brought to its narratives by the people who appear in it, it is not unusual for television news to 'set up' interviews, for example, by representing an academic in front of her/his bookshelves.

Media understandings:
implications for the new curriculum

Implicit in the discussion above is the notion that teachers are familiar with the commonly accepted Media 'Key Concepts' as articulated by the BFI (Bazalgette, 1989). By and large, the teachers we saw and spoke to were. But it was also clear that between 1989 and 1999 the original meanings of these concepts had, understandably, slipped or become hybridised, with some loss of clarity in teaching and learning. Now would seem an appropriate time for teachers to reconsider the central Media Education concepts and their relationship to the English curriculum.

Representations seems to pose the fewest problems. The teachers in our research were familiar with this notion whether it related to how writers might represent characters in novels, or how different social, ethnic and gendered groups are represented in news and advertising media. Surprisingly then, in those lessons where representations were most strongly dealt with (of masculinity, indigenous North Americans, women in work, and cinema stars) it was only in the first of those, in Mary's lesson on masculinity, that *Representation* was declared to be a prime learning objective of the lesson. In an English curriculum with Media at its centre, it seems reasonable that the notion of *Representation* should sometimes be the main learning objective of the lesson, rather than the 'by-product' of a study of language or literature.

There was a similar issue related to how the teachers in our study thought of or taught about *Audiences*. All felt comfortable with the notion because it was, and always has been, a 'natural' and inevitable part of studying texts. Where advertising was the object of study (Levi Jeans and Calvin Klein) *Audience* was an explicit focus. Other than in those lessons, however, *Audience* did not feature as strongly as one might have expected, given the long association of the concept with the teaching of literature. The newest statutory curriculum requirement is to teach pupils 'how audiences and readers *choose* and *respond* to media'. The danger is that teachers, like those in our study, will see it as unproblematic and tick it off as one thing they already address. But there is a world of difference between acknowledging a potential readership of a given text (literature or non-fiction) and making readers and audiences the focus of study.

More to the point, the implications for audience/readership study might shift significantly depending, for example, on whether the texts in question are novels, poems, plays, newspaper articles, television news broadcasts, films or advertisements. Indeed, notions of 'choosing' and 'responding' themselves become problematic. For example, one cannot really study advertising without considering how advertisers try to 'create' audiences for products or 'reposition' products so that they appeal to different (social, age, ethnic or gendered) groups. In this context, the notion of audiences 'choosing' media is, at best, ambiguous. It is not always clear who is making and selling what to whom. Many television programmes, in fact, 'make' audiences, which they then sell to manufacturers of other products via the advertising agencies employed by them.

In any case, teaching about textual response involves rather more than considering the 'effects' of moving image media on mass audiences or the individual's engagement with printed texts. Writers like Buckingham (1998) and Tobin (2000) would argue strongly that mass audiences are made up of individuals, who are not easily led into the choices that the producers of texts would have them make and who, in fact, *use* the mass media, to help establish their own social identities.

It is easy to see why many teachers at this point might sigh with frustration. After all, what they are likely to want from a text like this one is enlightenment rather than problematising. But there is an essential truth that has to be faced here. Audience and readership studies is a fascinating but complex area and not one easily dealt with in one point in one paragraph in an already demanding curriculum. Teachers must first acknowledge the complexity of Media in English. They should then quite reasonably expect the QCA, their Examination Board, and various in-service providers to support them in this area of study.

Similarly, it would be reasonable to expect a little more support and direction for teachers in relation to the study of *technologies*. As has been mentioned frequently in this book, the newest National Curriculum for English in the UK has a paragraph on Media Education, where the focus is on understanding the language codes used in media texts. It also has a paragraph on ICT-based information texts:

Media and moving image texts
Pupils should be taught:

- how meaning is conveyed in texts that include print, images and sometimes sounds

- how choice of form, layout and presentation contribute to effect...

- how the nature and purpose of media products influence content and meaning...

- how audiences and readers choose and respond to media.

Printed and ICT-based information texts
- To develop their reading of print and ICT-based information texts, pupils should be taught to: select, compare and synthesise information from different texts

- evaluate how information is presented

- sift the relevant from the irrelevant and distinguish between fact and opinion, bias and objectivity

- identify the characteristic features at word, sentence and text level of different types of text.

Nothing in one paragraph contradicts the other. That is, the Curriculum certainly allows for the integration of Media and ICT within English. The problem is that, historically, within English ICT has usually been about skills and production, and Media has been about concepts and understanding. To a degree, although both paragraphs appear in the 'Reading' section of the National Curriculum, this 'tradition' is reinforced in the wording: for ICT, students 'should be taught *to*', but for Media 'they should be taught *how*'.

In the twenty-first century, one might hope to see teachers supporting students in their interrogation of a very wide range of texts found on the Internet. To do so, they would, of course, need to consider relationships between words and images, to consider the nature and purpose of the texts, and to evaluate the quality of the information. In other words they would need to *integrate* ICT and Media skills and concepts. Given the speed of technological development in this area it is hardly surprising to find that the teachers in our research were not yet in a position to involve themselves in this type of 'cutting edge' analysis. It would be expecting a great deal of them if one assumed that, without very specific guidance and support, they were able to develop within a print-centred curriculum a pedagogy for multimedia texts.

The basis of such a pedagogy does exist. Tweddle *et al.* (1997) developed a framework for textual analysis capable of dealing with traditional texts and digital texts. To the familiar *form, purpose* and *audience*, Tweddle's 'continuity continuum' adds *originator, representational medium, mode of transmission* and *gatekeeper.* This analytical framework has the potential to go beyond the current set of Media Key Concepts, but it needs to be taken up and developed. As suggested earlier in this chapter, the current Media Education front runner is the *moving image.* Indeed, Bazalgette has argued that we should 'refocus the media education project on the moving image media alone' (Bazalgette, 1999, p.5). There is a danger that this heavily promoted approach might inhibit the development of a more integrated approach to Media.

For very different reasons, from the evidence of our research, *Agencies* did not feature strongly in planning Media lessons in the English curriculum either. *Agencies* and general institutional issues were seen by virtually all the teachers in our study to be an area, in principle, worth addressing, but, at the same time, rather complex and not a priority. The latest version of the UK's National Curriculum for English refers to the 'nature and purpose of media products' as a focus for study. This might include but does not necessarily require a study of *agencies* or *institutions.* If institutional issues are not addressed, there is a possibility that study of Media in English will simply mean a study of a wider range of texts and communication codes. Clearly, this issue needs further debate if teachers are to be persuaded that a study of agency and institution will lead to a better understanding of how a text functions. Teachers can hardly be blamed if there are insufficient case studies of good practice in this respect.

Our evidence suggests that of the main Media concepts, *Technologies* poses the greatest challenge to teachers. By contrast, the concept with which our teachers were most familiar and most confident, not surprisingly, was *Languages*. All teachers were skilled in considering conventions and codes of print-based texts, and there were some good examples of the study of communicative codes as applied to music, the human voice, and the moving image. The only caveat here arises from the evidence that some teachers said they felt more comfortable in dealing with *Language* in relation to print. That is, some of our teachers chose not to deal with moving image codes because they felt less assured working with them. The natural tendency for teachers to teach what they know best will need to be addressed by every head of English department if the new requirements related to the moving image are to be dealt with adequately. Our research suggests that, if these teachers were typical of other teachers nationally, there would be significant freedom of choice within an agreed departmental curriculum. Teachers uncomfortable with Media Language as applied to the moving image would be able to avoid it. Clearly, in the new curriculum, that will no longer be appropriate. Perhaps the first task for heads of English is to ensure that teachers within their departments build on the *linguistic* expertise they already have and from there develop confidence in teaching about *moving image* language codes.

But even more than *Languages*, the Media concept likely to present fewest problems in adapting to the new Curriculum demands is that of *Categories*, or, as English teachers are more likely to say, genre. Understanding of genre was implicit in virtually all lessons observed. That it was not often the focus of study is almost certainly to do with the curricular tensions between English and Media rather than with teacher subject knowledge. Though many departments may have schemes of work which are genre-based (typically science fiction) it is probably more common for literature teaching to be related to the work of individual writers. In any case, most students will have gained their knowledge of genre from films rather than books. (Students will usually know most of the conventions of the Western, but are unlikely to have read a single Western book.) It might well be that teachers' greatest need in this area is access to appropriate resources rather than any conceptual development. Anthologies of short stories, whatever the genre, are easily accessible. Collections of moving image texts on which to base inter-textual studies are harder to come by. However, Film Education is already an excellent, often free, resource base for genre study in film, and, indeed, many of the resources produced by them in the 1990s are worth revisiting in the context of the new Media demands of the National Curriculum for English (e.g. *Media for English* and *Film Language*).

Planning for Media – units, concepts, progression and assessment

Both conversations with and observations of teachers raised a range of planning issues in relation to Media in English. As suggested above, the liberalism of most heads of English departments tended to make them reluctant to **impose** a curriculum on any of their teachers. The challenge remains, of course, to ensure that, given freedom of curricular choice, all teachers of English do cover those Media areas that they might find unfamiliar.

A second issue concerns the way in which the Media elements are made part of the English curriculum. To best ensure syllabus coverage of Media, most teachers in our study had opted for discrete modules of work; the 'Media Unit' was typical. Some, however, having gone through such a process, felt that there was a mechanistic element in dividing the curriculum up into manageable 'chunks' and opted to reintegrate Media into the curriculum. The new, post-2000 curriculum demands will, no doubt, leave many departments in this dilemma: the holistic approach or the unit-led curriculum? Our experiences suggests that though it may be slightly artificial or contrived, there is some merit in the Media Unit, at least until teachers feel that they can teach about the moving image with the same confidence that they bring to print-based texts.

However, what matters most is that the Media element of the English curriculum is led by Media Education concepts and learning objectives. As outlined in the Introduction, the curriculum requirement is to teach *about* the media in English, not teach English *through* a study of the media. This presents teachers with two substantial problems. The first is that assessment objectives in the new curriculum are, understandably, so broad as to be largely unhelpful where Media Education is concerned. For example, the reading assessment criteria at level 7 require pupils to 'show understanding of the ways in which meaning and information are conveyed in a range of texts'. The second problem is that there is, as yet, no model of what progression in moving image interpretation looks like when it applies to the Reading element of the curriculum for English. There are sources that the English teacher can turn to, but they are not wholly satisfactory. Schools that run discrete GCSE Media Studies courses will be able to refer to that syllabus for some sense of progression in Media. Indeed, the evidence of our research suggests that the specialist knowledge provided by Media Studies teachers had a significant impact on the Media-related professional development of teachers in the English department. However, the Media Studies assessment criteria of GCSE Media Studies syllabuses are too specialised for the English curriculum, and, in any case, only cover pupils in years 10 and 11. As indicated at the start of this chapter, there is the BFI's own model of progression (1999), but it is a model that excludes print texts and is, therefore, limiting for the English teacher.

Given the absences described above, let us consider the practical implications of planning for Media within English: how to turn *English through Media* into *Media in English*. On page 106 is a unit of Media work. The commentary that follows draws attention to those characteristics of the unit that are particularly significant for Media Education.

Commentary

Beginning with concepts is important. (Column B). Not only does it focus the learning for this particular unit, but it ensures appropriate coverage of a Media curriculum. As indicated earlier, Media Education is, unlike English, conceptually organised. Planning a Media curriculum needs to take account of this. The texts chosen (Column C) are, in this example, 'moving image', but it is likely that much Media work will integrate print and moving-image texts.

Planning a unit of Media work: Moving image narratives in fiction and non-fiction

	Media Concepts	Media texts	Media learning objectives	Media analytical activities	Written or practical outcomes
Weeks 1/2	Media language	Extract from a television news bulletin reporting war	To understand how meaning is conveyed in non-fiction moving image narrative; to identify relationship between sound and image, especially the role of the news reader	Watch images without sound; anticipate words of news reader; compare actual script with anticipated script	Students write alternative verbal track so as to affect meaning of visual images in two items in a news bulletin
Weeks 3/4	Media language	The opening ten minutes of a film depicting a story from the Second World War	To understand how meaning is conveyed in, fictional moving image narrative; to identify relationship between sound and image, especially the use of music; to distinguish between fiction and non-fiction approaches	Listen to soundtrack without images visible; anticipate images; compare actual images with those anticipated; discussion of use of words and use of music to anchor meaning of visual images	On separate audio tape recorders students prepare alternative music tracks so as to affect meaning of visual narrative
Weeks 5/6	Agencies/ Institution	Television news extracts depicting war	To understand how the nature and purpose of the media text affects its meaning; to identify the criteria that determine what gets into the news (news values)	From an analysis of two national news bulletins broadcast on the same day by different channels devise a set of criteria that would allow the students to predict what is likely to get into the news	Students write a commentary on a third news broadcast, explaining how the news items meet or fail to meet the news inclusion criteria devised by the students
A	B	C	D	E	F

Each of the three rows of learning objectives (Column D) is intended to echo the English assessment criteria ('understand how meaning is conveyed'), and offer reassurance that this work is directly relevant to the English curriculum. However, in reality, there are three very specific Media learning objectives contained within them. The first is to identify relationships between sound and image; the second is to compare sound and image relationships in fiction and non-fiction; the third is to identify the criteria (news values) that determine what gets into the news and how that news is ordered. What makes this a Media-focused project is not the fact that it contains use of the moving image, but that the project is conceptually-based and has clear Media Education objectives. Yet it remains firmly within the English curriculum; news and narrative have always been important elements of English teaching and learning.

In essence the activities themselves (Column E) are not Media-specific. It is common practice in English teaching to disrupt texts in some way (as in cloze or sequencing tasks) to help students engage with sub-text. The text disruption here is simply 'tweaked' so that it applies specifically to the moving image. If one wishes to consider the relationship between sound and image then it makes sense to divorce sound and image temporarily to see more clearly how one affects the other. The final column (F), which outlines the student portfolio evidence arising from the activities, is important. Teachers of English (as in our research) sometimes feel that Media work forces a choice between attractive but complex, technology-based practical activities with no written outcomes, and written outcomes dependent on sometimes arid textual analysis. The examples offered here are designed to meet both concerns. The writing of the newsreader's script is a brief, practical activity, though not dependent on technology. The preparation of the music track is low-tech, without the necessity for editing equipment. The commentary on the third broadcast is supported by the visual evidence of the news bulletin and arises naturally out of the work preceding it.

The argument for an holistic approach to Media would suggest that the above unit could be expanded to take account of digital as well as more familiar film, video and television texts. For example, to the planning columns of *Media concepts* and *Media texts* in the table above, one might wish to add notions from Tweddle's framework for textual analysis (see above) of, say, *originator, gatekeeper* and *form.* These notions would encourage teachers in their planning to give consideration to collaborative as well as individual creativity, institutional control and censorship. For example, in the above unit, one might wish to extend the study to consider, say, how war is represented on Internet news websites. In such a case, one might plan to teach about the roles of webmaster (originator), Internet provider (gatekeeper) as well as hypertext (form). And of course, the column headed *Written or practical outcomes* might well include artefacts in the form of *web page* or *electronic mail.*

The sorts of ideas represented in this plan should represent a starting point for Media in English, an advance on English through Media certainly, but still only a beginning. The real potential for Media in English might best be represented by the work of Andrew Burn when he was at Parkside Community College, the first specialist Media school in the UK. His own account of his work there (Burn, 1998) draws our attention to the possibilities, but also to the distance between where we are now and where, ideally, we might be. He writes of £10,000 work-stations, of 'non-linear editing', and of 'a new semiotic order' redrawing the boundaries between writing and the visual arts. To get to where Andrew Burn now is, there are three formidable obstacles. Money of course: the work stations remain a dream for most schools. The second obstacle is the need for teachers of English to understand and have expertise in media 'writing' rather than reading (the production processes; how many teachers will have a clear sense of what is meant by 'non-linear editing' let alone be able to practise it?) But the third and greatest obstacle is conceptual rather than financial or technological. We undoubtedly do need to think in terms of a new semiotic order, but this involves a reconceptualising of the subjects English and Media, and it is not clear from where the impetus for such a development might come.

Examination syllabuses: English and Media Studies
Choosing an English syllabus with Media in mind

The teachers we studied were unlikely to make syllabus treatment of Media a significant criterion when choosing an English syllabus at GCSE level. While that was understandable given the status of Media in English at the time, the increased demands of the Media element of the new curriculum suggest that the criteria for syllabus selection might need to change. At the very least, teachers may well seek a syllabus where the Media element is part of coursework. It is difficult to imagine how the moving image can adequately be addressed in a terminal examination. Indeed, when Boards are required by QCA to amend their syllabuses, it seems likely that Media in coursework will be the norm. Beyond that, teachers will need to be convinced that the Chief Examiner for the chosen syllabus has a clear view of conceptual issues in Media Education, and that the syllabus-specific training adequately deals with the sorts of issue raised in this book.

Links between syllabuses in Media Studies and English

As we have suggested earlier, English teachers who find themselves in a school where GCSE Media Studies is taught are fortunate in that they can draw on the expertise of the teachers who run the course. However, the existence of GCSE Media Studies also implies the need for some element of collaborative planning. Where Media Studies is offered in the school's option system its take-up tends to be relatively high. Therefore, for the sake of the many young people who study Media in English *and* Media Studies, it is important that teachers are aware of the ways in which the two syllabuses coincide. In addition, given that the new GCSE Media Studies syllabuses (from WJEC, OCR and AQA) have, as indicated earlier, undergone recent substantial revision, links between the two subjects need to be reconsidered by English and Media Subject specialists.

In particular, QCA requires the Media Studies syllabus to share the core criteria for the English curriculum, the nearest statutory curriculum to Media Studies. Thus, the new Media Studies syllabuses are required like English, to address cultural diversity, the historical development of their (media) texts, and the use of ICT within the subject. Significantly also, the three new Media Studies syllabuses are organised, much more clearly than before, within a conceptual framework. The concepts vary slightly between Boards, but, essentially, those Key concepts discussed earlier in this chapter can be identified in each syllabus. The most important issue in relation to the English and Media Studies overlap is that conceptual interpretations and use of terminology are consistent within a single school or college and that repetition, particularly in relation to popular areas of Media like advertising, is avoided.

However, teachers of both subjects need to be aware of differences as well as similarities. One of these relates inevitably to the amount of time available in a dedicated subject such as Media Studies compared to Media within English, where Media is one curriculum element amongst many. That is, the extra time in Media Studies means that concepts are studied in more depth, and practical production is a much more significant element. Where practical production is involved, Media Studies syllabuses demand that students are able to reflect on and analyse their own media products. This sort of a self-evaluation as part of the student's assessment evidence is not traditionally part of the curriculum for English. Given the absence of a clear model of progression for Media in English, English teachers need to think very carefully about the way in which they respond to examples of practical Media production in their own subject.

Introducing Media Studies into the school curriculum
Some of those teachers of English not fortunate enough to have Media Studies already up and running in their school might consider that now is the time to introduce it into their school's curriculum. Given the level of Media expertise that the new National Curriculum for English demands of teachers, it might be reasonable to assume that such expertise could fruitfully be developed and applied in a specialist environment. Those making this sort of choice might want to scrutinise the syllabus specifications of the three Boards, all now available on the Internet.

In practice, it seems likely that teachers might opt for the Board they already use for English. However, teachers would be wrong to assume that a given Examination Board that offers both English and GCSE Media Studies has already taken account of possible overlaps between the subjects. Some Boards might function in this way, but it is by no means normal practice and it is quite conceivable that the examiner who writes the GCSE Media Studies specification does not liaise with the examiner who writes the English specification. Before making a choice, it might be worth asking the Board about any appropriate curriculum liaison that has already taken place. But regardless of the Board's own good practice, there are two important issues that an English department should bear in mind when choosing a Media syllabus. The first is the way in which the syllabus deals with conceptual issues. This is potentially a complex area, and it is important that teachers have confidence that the Board is clear and consistent about the way in which it treats Media concepts and builds them into the curriculum. The treatment of Media concepts in a syllabus specification should be capable of clear interpretation by someone not expert in the subject. If the conceptual basis for the Media Studies syllabus is not clear, then it is unlikely that the rest of the syllabus will be consistent and manageable. Secondly, English teachers entering Media Studies for the first time need to consider how the syllabus deals with practical production. Those in-experienced in Media should ask themselves if the syllabus speci-fication's technological demands in terms of resources and skill are reasonable and manageable for a department not used to teaching Media Studies

From GCSE English and Media Studies to A/S level Media Studies
The three Boards (WJEC, OCR and AQA) that offer GCSE Media Studies also offer Media Studies at A/S level. (WJEC also offers Film Studies at A/S-level.) These post-2000 A/S level specifications share one common feature: they are all modular. Titles of modules vary slightly between syllabuses (e.g. Forms, Representations, In-dustries, Texts and Contexts, Issues and Debates, Audiences and Institutions) but essentially, these syllabus specifications are more similar to each other than are those at GCSE. As at GCSE, teachers choosing a Media Studies syllabus at A/S level should expect to see more emphasis than previously on the historical context of media

development, again a shift quite consciously led by QCA. Also required by QCA is some demonstration of how in a single Board, GCSE and A/S level syllabuses relate to each other. For this reason, progression between Media Studies at GCSE and at A/S level should, in theory at least, be comparatively unproblematic. However, one final word of caution is necessary for English departments venturing into Media Studies. All the evidence suggests that if Media Studies at GCSE or A/S level is offered, it will quickly become a very popular subject, with large numbers of students opting for it. If a school starts along the Media Studies road then it should expect the English department to grow, and plan accordingly.

Bridging the gaps

Reading about the experiences of other Media teachers can be up-lifting, inspiring or downright depressing, depending on the quality of those experiences and one's own starting point. For example, the work of Andrew Burn, introducing students to successful use and understanding of digital media (see above), may well inspire the committed Media teacher. But the English teacher who is less secure in Media teaching may become despondent at the size of the gap between where she/he is now, and where she/he could be, or needs to be. This is an especially significant problem, given the existence of another gap our research has revealed, the gap in professional development opportunities for teachers of Media.

For a teacher teaching Media, whether in the English curriculum or in specialist studies outside it, standing still is not an option. As one teacher in our own research noted, failure to use and address technology will produce a credibility gap between the experience of young people and the education they are offered in schools.

The majority of schools may always fall behind the technology used in commerce and by the general public. And, realistically, there will always be a time lag between the technological know-how of teachers and that of their more advanced, more adventurous, 'try it and see' students. However, there is no need for English teachers to be despondent. Their role is not necessarily to get their hands on all the technology, or even to master all the skills. But they do have the opportunity and the obligation to understand the relationships between the new media and its users. Helping young media users make the most of those relationships is surely what Media Education needs to be about. Teachers need to explore and interpret such relationships and reflect them back to their students.

The metaphors used to describe the rapidly-changing media environment are, of necessity, changing with it. Notions of inoculation, discussed elsewhere in this book, will surely become obsolete. Janice Hughes (Hughes, 2000, p.8), a marketing consultant on the technological environment, describes the future consumer's home as a 'walled garden'. In this 'garden' an extraordinary range of broadcasters, communicating through a variety of media, vie to 'control the portals and gateways'. But this 'garden' is no prison. Indeed, with the new PVRs (personal video recorder system – vivo is the brand leader) Hughes sees the consumer creating 'tailor-made channels and unique viewing schedules which could radically alter viewing habits and reduce advertising revenues'. This notion of the viewer with PVR as 'television scheduler' is taken up by John Sutherland in The *Guardian* (28 May 2001). Speaking as an educator in the US as well as a journalist, he sees a very important role for education in helping young consumers understand and make the most of this new power. 'Television watching is not just a fact of childhood life, but the biggest fact. It should be in the national curriculum.' In a way, of course, it is. But that curriculum needs interpretation and elaboration to help teachers help students make sense of it.

It would be encouraging to finish on a note of optimism, to imagine the teacher as sort of guide or companion, supporting the child or student in their new mastery of 'smart TV'. But this scenario assumes a largely benevolent environment with the consumer gaining the upper hand in any struggle that might exist. Not everyone will have access to the garden. Hughes warns of a different sort of credibility gap. She suggests that there could develop two societies, 'the information rich and the information poor' with the poor largely excluded from the 'knowledge economy'. She stresses the importance of education and training to ensure that 'the communications revolution embraces everyone'.

However, whether one imagines the communications revolution as benign or beneficial, threatening or divisive, it seems clear that teachers do have a Media Education role to play. What is more, there should be no need to fear the gap between students and teachers as technology users, or the gap between where teachers of English are now and where they need to be. Teachers will continue to do what they do best: help their students to interpret and interact with the communication environment in which they find themselves, whether that is an environment of print or image, still or moving. They will ensure that studying the gap between the information rich and the information poor will necessarily be at the heart of any future Media curriculum.

Appendix
Interviews and lessons

This is a detailed account of the interviews with and lessons taught by each of the eleven teachers in the research. All interview analyses are written in a similar format: they begin by outlining the route whereby the teacher came to teach Media, and her/his attitude towards it; thereafter, the teacher's aims and approaches are considered, particularly in the context of the 'Key Concepts' in Media Education. Finally, each analysis reviews other significant contexts in which Media is taught, including the school/department, the choice of examination syllabus, teaching resources, and the availability of INSET. Each interview is followed by a detailed account of the lesson observed, informed by the Lesson Observation instrument described in Chapter 3. Each account ends with a summary of the main characteristics of the lesson and an evaluation of the media learning that has taken place.

The lesson observations are organised into three groups. The first group (Group 1) consists of the five teachers who took part in the *Media in the Classroom* research of 1992-93 (Hart and Benson, 1993) and were revisited in 1998-99 (Evelyn was now teaching in a different school). In the next group (Group 2) the emphasis is very strongly on response to verbal, printed text, with some aspect of mass-media communication at the heart of the lesson. Lessons in the third group (Group 3) are linked by a common emphasis on authorship, both literary and cinematic.

Group I

Evelyn:	Community comprehensive
Frances:	Rural comprehensive
Helen:	Semi-rural comprehensive
Jane:	Rural comprehensive
Joan:	Urban girls' school

In 1992-93 Evelyn's focus was on analysis of children's comics and magazines with a focus on target audiences. In 1998-99 she again chose on magazine elements, in this case a single magazine advertisement selling male perfume. *Representation*, *stereotyping* and *Audience* were significant in both lessons.

In 1992-93 Frances used storyboarding to encourage interpretation of poetry, leading to a television presentation of a poem. In 1998-99 she encouraged her pupils to look analytically at a series of television advertisements for Levi Jeans. In both lessons *Representation* was an important element of the Media understanding.

In 1992-93 Helen, alongside her head of department Harry, focused on magazines, particularly newspaper colour supplements, and the relationship between the advertisements they carried and their audience. In 1998-99 Helen again looked at magazines, in this case one 'persuasive or manipulative' article from the *Big Issue*.

In 1992-93 Jane led the class in a shot-by-shot analysis of a pop video, relating the work to work already done on imagery in poetry. In 1998-99 Jane led the class through a shot-by-shot analysis of the opening of David Lean's film, *Great Expectations*, though the emphasis was more strongly on film narrative than literary narrative.

In 1992-93 Joan led her pupils through an analysis of a literary adaptation – the BBC television serialisation of *Jane Eyre*. In 1998-99 she focused on analysis of two newspaper reports in which women at work are represented in contrasting fashion. In 1998, Joan strove to reinforce pupils' understanding of central Media concepts.

EVELYN
School: Community comprehensive

Teacher background

Evelyn began teaching in 1991 after doing a PGCE at Southampton University as a mature student. Media Education was an important element in the course. She enjoyed Media immediately and was quick to see connections between analysis of texts generally studied in the English curriculum and analysis of media texts. She sees Media as 'more theoretical than practical... the pictures, the symbolic side of things was really easy for me to pick up.' Her Media experience was put into practice in her first school which, in an effort to boost the number of GCSE successes, offered Media Studies as an 'extra' for some very bright students within the GCSE English curriculum, 'subverting English time.' At the time Evelyn felt 'Media was seen as a soft option'; but 'it's changed since then'.

She joined the Southampton Media Education Group at Southampton University. Straight after her initial training, Evelyn began studying for an MA (Ed) at Southampton University, where one of the units studied was Media Education. She was interested in establishing links between Media work and curriculum management, being particularly interested in 'Media in the curriculum.' When she came to her current school, two years ago, she was asked to institute Media Studies as a GCSE subject. Though she is a part-time teacher, as well as her commitment to the English curriculum, she also has responsibility for GCSE Media Studies. Thus, she has taught Media Studies as well as Media within the English curriculum in each year of her teaching career to date.

Media Studies takes up approximately one quarter of Evelyn's total teaching time and Media Education about one third of her English curriculum time. Inevitably, her background in Media, both academically and professionally, means that her approach to teaching English is significantly affected by a Media perspective.

Teacher attitude to Media Education

Her attitude to Media Education is language-based. She tries to take pupils from analysis to practice, or, as she describes it, from deconstruction to construction: pupils, she says, move 'from description, through analysis to production'. Indeed, she recalls her best lessons as those in which pupils, 'with basic learning in place (e.g. understanding of *Audience*, so they know what they're producing something for), moved from analysis to independent production'. She is also concerned that pupils learn that one can read pictures in the same way that one can read words.

Evelyn prefers the Media she teaches as part of the GCSE Media syllabus to the Media which she teaches in English lessons and which she finds 'less exciting'. An exciting lesson for Evelyn might involve giving a camera to pupils and inviting them to capture six images of childhood: 'They come up with some terrific ideas.' In GCSE Media she feels they can 'apply Media knowledge more'.

Although Evelyn feels that children aren't easily fooled by the media she does believe that pupils need to be aware of media influences. She implies that it is the teacher who might help children to be aware of such influences, including the influence of media institutions.

Aims, concepts, approach to teaching

Teaching about *Institutions* is, she says, imperative, 'the most difficult of concepts, but [difficult] only because you haven't seen something in practical application'. She feels that pressures on curriculum time prevent her doing what would be important in teaching about institutions, that is, visiting organisations to 'see them in action'. But, at the same time, she regards it as the weakest area in Media work 'unless you are talking about people copying up information... I'm interested, but I don't want to waffle... I want to get some basic concepts in my mind and be comfortable.' When tackling *Institutions* she would like more practical hands on work, discussion and exploration She feels that children need to know how institutions are organised – 'the who and how of production.'

But she does feel that the extent to which she tackles *Institutions* is severely limited by the constraints of the curriculum. Therefore, she feels that teaching Institutions is, in an English curriculum, more likely to be implicit or superficial rather than explicit. She is inclined to address the general ways in which organisations work rather than deal with specific institutions: 'We look at how something is organised, and what influences it might have, and who is influenced – but once you start getting into a global context, and multimedia and all that stuff, it's beyond the children.' Despite this she feels that 'influence and effects and cultural background is really relevant' to the GCSE syllabus. 'You've got to understand a kind of market side from this point of view – how something represents a group and a product.' In addition, Evelyn links issues of *Institutions* to syllabus criteria for achieving A or A* at GCSE; she feels that knowledge of the social contexts in which texts are produced is only really required of pupils aspiring towards the highest grades. In other words, in an English curriculum, the concept of *Institutions* is something which, for the vast majority of students, it is possible to ignore.

Evelyn has a positive attitude towards technology in Media Education, but her own use of it is severely limited by lack of resources. Where possible she uses cameras to capture still images, but has no darkroom, and resources (film etc.) are limited. One recently purchased video camera has just become available for use, but there are no editing facilities and Evelyn feels that her own editing skills have declined through lack of use. She is, however, likely to use a scanner to introduce images into DTP, for example in work on magazines and advertising, possibly producing collages to show pupils that they can select images appropriately. The Internet has only recently become available within the school, so that issues, related to information production and access in this medium do not yet feature in any way in the curriculum. The Technology department, does, however, have a responsibility to introduce computer skills to all pupils throughout the curriculum. Whilst Evelyn is likely to use the scanner and DTP, she suspects that most colleagues in the English department are likely to limit their use of computer technology to word processing in the context of production of written assignments. All students have access to all available technology in their own independent time.

Boys, she feels, are more confident in their use of technology than girls. Indeed, boys are generally more inclined than girls to take risks in Media... to cut corners. Girls, Evelyn feels, are more likely to address the production process systematically and are more likely to achieve good results. They are likely to know whether what they do is right or wrong. But when girls are encouraged they will go on to take risks; they work hard and have more self-control.

Evelyn's approach to teaching about any aspects of the media differs depending on the age and ability of the class with which she is working. Though all her work is, she says, language-based (implying an emphasis on close analysis of text), with higher-ability classes she is more likely to allow opportunities for 'hands-on Media work... more independent learning, more media texts in class, more practical'. Pupils of lower ability spend more time being guided into important understandings of terminology and Media concepts. Equally, there is a difference in Evelyn's approach at Key Stage 3 and at Key Stage 4. At Key Stage 3 pupils are more likely to experience pamphlets, storyboarding, comics and scanning of images into computers; at Key Stage 4, she argues, there is much less time. As a consequence, the approach at Key Stage 4 has to be much more analytical. In addition, she feels that the current GCSE syllabus does not justify much more time being spent on practical work, as 'the curriculum is biased by the 60 per cent examination.'

Her long-term aims for pupils are related to her own beliefs about media and society: she believes that children need to grow up to be 'critical' ('in the true sense of the word'). They need to be aware of the influences of media texts. 'Young people are influenced by such a range of texts.' Alongside this analytical model, Evelyn holds a view about the importance of Media Education in a vocational context. That is, she feels that Media Education, should, in some way, take account of career opportunities in the media and in media-related institutions – in order that pupils learn to cope and work in a media-dominated world. In addition, she believes that with the growth of media in society and Media Studies in the curriculum, pupils might be inclined to continue with Media in the sixth form and 'develop their artistic side'.

Though she feels that pupils react positively to her approach to Media, she is aware that, in the early stages when Media is introduced (assuming no previous experience in primary school, or little experience at Key Stage 3) pupils are, at first, a little perplexed by the way in which they are challenged. That is, they are perplexed by the teacher's emphasis that there are no right or wrong answers, that they are required in media work to think more independently, to initiate their own ideas. She believes that children, because of their experience in writing across the curriculum, expect to 'get it right', whereas in media work, the process is more important than what is produced.

Evelyn, nevertheless, is very optimistic about the way in which Media Education might develop over the next ten years. There was, she feels, a time when Media Education was in crisis. She now sees her teaching colleagues, once lacking in Media expertise, as more aware, more confident and competent.

Context: the school
Evelyn is aware of other media work taking place in History, RE, Technology and Business Studies. This she gathers from discussion with students about where they acquire specific media skills, and from informal discussion with other teachers. There is, however, no formal school document which makes reference to Media Education, although, after the school's very good GCSE Media Studies results, Evelyn has no doubt that

the subject has genuine status in the school and is taken seriously: 'It's acknowledged as being a well-taught subject and a worthwhile subject within the school.'

Media Education is inscribed into the English Department's formal schemes of work, but the specific choice of ideas and materials is left to the individual teacher. 'We have some formalised schemes of work and we do share common schemes of work which include Media; in the upper school the requirement is one formal piece (the Levi piece or anything you wish to use yourself.. most people who are not confident use the Levi).' Evelyn is inclined to adapt any commercially produced resources which she encounters; she is particularly keen to collect and maintain her own range of current media texts, including greetings cards, leaflets, contemporary newspapers and comics. She dislikes using other people's ideas. She has access to a set of Longmans Media Studies course books (she also makes use of *Understanding the Media* (Hart, 1991)). Her colleagues, however, are most likely to rely on the media examples within the department's more general English coursework books. In addition, they might use Media units 'imported' from other schools; these include work on the series of Levi Jeans advertisements in Jenny Grahame's *Advertising Pack* (1993). Interestingly, Evelyn herself has never used this very popular resource, preferring, as suggested above, to make her own resources or adapt others.

In the school's OFSTED inspection, there was no significant reference to Media Education, either positive or negative. Evelyn does, however, recall that inspectors commented favourably on the fact that she had just introduced Media Studies as a separate GCSE subject. Also, they seemed to regard Evelyn's teaching a year 7 class to read pictures as innovative, an activity she felt to be 'normal'.

Context: INSET
There are few outside agencies that Evelyn can call on to support her in her Media work. The Southern Examining Board does offer support in its annual INSET related to its GCSE syllabus, but Media will only be a small part of this single-day activity. SEG also offers support via individual visits from those who request them. Southampton University, where Evelyn trained and did her MA (Ed), was another agency that she used to call on, but she has limited contact with the university now. Since Evelyn is the Media specialist in the department, it is she who is expected to support others. There has, however, been no recent departmental focus on Media INSET, and Evelyn's expertise is shared informally with like-minded col-

leagues rather than inscribed into the departmental scheme of work. In addition Evelyn produces some units of work, mostly used by her head of department. In recent times, therefore, no-one in the department, including Evelyn, has experienced any formal or organised Media INSET. Evelyn points to the way in which preparation for OFSTED inspection tends to determine INSET priorities and school and department development plans.

Context: the syllabus

With the introduction of the new GCSE syllabuses (1996) the English department moved from MEG to NEAB. The Boards' treatment of Media played no part in this decision; the most influential factor was NEAB's provision of a (free) anthology on which the literature element of the examination is based. The department now partly regrets this decision – it is interesting to reflect on the 'institutional' issues in one Examination Board taking over most of the 'market' via its provision of a free anthology. That is, much of the statutory literature study in the examination depends on a substantial anthology of texts which the Board provides free for each pupil. This is especially interesting given NEAB's link-up with a publisher: the syllabus is free, but the essential support material is sold to schools. Within the NEAB syllabus, Media Education is assessed and, therefore, taught within coursework, allowing teachers the scope to tackle film and television. However, Evelyn points out that the NEAB non-fiction examination also requires Media skills; any Media coursework is, therefore, seen as additional preparation for the non-fiction examination. Evelyn distinguishes between Media and non-fiction in a number of ways. For example, with media texts, *Audience* is likely to relate to any texts which communicate to mass audiences, but *Audience* might mean a single reader when applied to non-fiction. Non-fiction texts, including travel, biography and autobiography, are likely to involve 'pure written texts' rather than visual language. Also, when studying media texts, Evelyn would expect explicit consideration of issues such as *denotation* and *connotation*. *Commerciality* would also apply more to media texts than to non-fiction.

Evelyn is in no doubt that the new syllabus has confirmed and enhanced the position of Media Education in the English curriculum. 'It has accentuated the need to have some more uniform idea about what Media involves and has encouraged quite a lot of discussion, but also some fears of inadequacies on the teacher's part.' But she does see in her colleagues an increased awareness of and confidence in the teaching of Media texts.

Her planning for the lesson observed shows the particular influence of the syllabus: writing, as part of the coursework requirement, is likely to emerge from the reading. As a consequence, any teaching of Media, Evelyn feels, must equip pupils with the ability to manage sophisticated concepts and terminology in such a way as to demonstrate their understanding in their writing.

THE LESSON: STUDYING AN ADVERTISEMENT: *CALVIN KLEIN*
Teacher: Evelyn

The class
The class is a year 10 lower set of 15 boys and girls, 9 of whom were present (the rest were involved in NVQs). The teacher says that, in some ways 'they are quite quick – they've actually picked up on symbolism for example.' The best pupils in it are expected to achieve grade C GCSE, and the lowest, hopefully, no lower than E. This group is recognised as one with behavioural problems. It is supported by a Special Needs Assistant who was present in this lesson. They are at the very earliest stages of their GCSE syllabus.

Lesson aims
Evelyn's expressed aim was to 'introduce Media Language' through a Calvin Klein advertisement. By 'Media Language', she meant a range of Media terms which pupils would need to understand within this unit of work. Within this, there were a number of other aims. One aim was to persuade the pupils that pictures could be read in the same way as verbal texts. Another was to introduce two particular Media concepts, *Audience* and *Representation*. A third was to provide the pupils with appropriate terminology and train them in the use of it. The terminology included media terms like *image, product,* and *manufacturer*, but also English lexical items such as *masculine,* and *handsome*. An important aim was for the (visual) reading experience, allied to appropriate terminology, to supply the pupils with phrases and sentences which would later inform and support their writing. Evelyn's aims for this lesson were wide-ranging and need to be seen in the context of her more general aim that these pupils are helped to achieve their potential within the context of the GCSE English syllabus. In addition, she had a clear set of objectives for this lesson: 'I would hope by the end of this lesson they could use a word like *image* or *product*... I think the concept of *Audience* is something that they'll quite easily pick up but in

a superficial sense.' In the longer term, she wishes them 'to interpret and read a broader range of texts... not just read passively'.

This work had begun in the previous lesson, in which the image provided by the teacher had been considered largely in terms of denotative content – i.e. what pupils could see in the picture, 'the image of the man in detail – face, shirt, hair hands'. Notes had been written on the board and in pupils' notebooks. The intention was to move from content to issues of meaning and purpose: 'What is in the picture, then what it represents... then why is it giving us these ideas and then why was the whole thing put together in the way that it was put together... I'm trying to lead them through to realise that reading a picture is like reading a text.'

This unit of work has three main elements, designed to last up to four weeks. The first element is the analysis of this shared image, 'one advertisement and its effects'. From more able pupils she expects a comparison between two advertisements. The second main element involves independent analysis of a different image, a personally chosen advertisement. The third element is production of an advertisement; as Evelyn describes it, 'they deconstruct and then construct'.

The lesson aims were communicated at the start of the lesson via a recap on previous learning. The aims were constantly reinforced via reference to the hand-out on which all significant terms and lexical items were listed. In addition, homework diaries were used at the end of the lesson to confirm the follow-up work: to take five of the Media terms/lexical items and use them in sentences in order to demonstrate that they had been understood. In this way Evelyn was able to see the extent to which her lesson objectives had been met.

Content and teacher approach

Evelyn made it clear that her approach in this lesson was significantly influenced by the emotional and behavioural problems of the pupils in the group. As a consequence, the lesson was heavily managed by the teacher from the front. (Normally, Evelyn's approach would be much more 'hands on', with more access to a range of texts and more pair or group work.) When independent work was required, the nine pupils would work individually, supported by Evelyn herself and by the Special Needs Assistant. Evelyn made it clear that she likes these pupils, and they respond well to her, but their relationships with each other are such that pair or group work would be ineffective or counter-productive. In addition, she felt that their limitations in terms of intellectual response mean that they would benefit most from teacher management of individual contributions, rather than from 'sharing' ideas in a looser framework. Although this approach has control at its centre, it was clear throughout the lesson that relationships were informal. The lesson itself was very tightly focused with short-term objectives to ensure that all pupils were able to succeed. Evelyn is very concerned to improve the self-confidence and self-esteem of this group; she feels that the best way to prepare them for their examination is not to train them in specific examination techniques but to give them a broad framework of support so that, when faced by unfamiliar texts, they know they have a range of questions which will help them in their interrogation of those texts.

The lesson was characterised by very good pupil–teacher relationships, and good humour.

Despite the working level of the group and its behavioural problems, Evelyn was determined not to underestimate what the group could achieve. Thus, the list of terms used (see below) includes notions such as *connotation* and *anchor*. For example, she felt that the metaphor implicit in anchor would allow it to be understood by all the pupils in the group.

There were two main elements to the resources used. One was a black-and-white photocopy (originally colour) of a *Calvin Klein* advertisement for *Eternity for men*, an *eau de toilette*; each pupil had a copy. It consisted of a single image of an open-shirted young man, gazing directly at the camera; no words other than the name of the product, its form and origin appear on it. The second element was a handwritten support sheet for pupils. (Evelyn has consciously moved away from elaborate, word-processed materials, to what she sees as more immediate and relevant materials that relate to the aims of the lesson in question). This sheet contained a series of words (some media terms, some lexical items), accompanied by brief definitions of each:

- *stereotype*   typical of, a sort of standard

- *image*   the picture you can see

- *product*   the item or thing being sold

- *manufacturer*   the maker of the product

- *audience*   the person or people looking at the advertisement, the potential buyer of the product

- *symbols*   e.g. the ring on the man's finger; symbols stand for or represent something

- *masculine*   like a man e.g. a masculine model = very manly

- *handsome*   good-looking

- *connotations*   ideas associated with people, things or words e.g. the wedding ring gives connotations of a reliable steady married man, a person you could trust

- *anchor*   an anchor is something that holds down an idea or connects and makes more secure the ideas that are being expressed

Stage 1: *(20 minutes)*

This involved teacher/pupil discussion of *Representation* within the *Calvin Klein* advertisement.

The teacher first recapped on what had been established in the previous lesson: 'We thought he was in his late twenties.. not very clean shaven... eyes nice and dark... hair bleached and highlighted... a serious but casual look... his lips are soft but he's not smiling... things you said.'

The teacher began this lesson by exploring the significance of the words, in particular, the name *Eternity*: 'The man is wearing a wedding ring... eternity, for ever.' Following a comment from a pupil, the teacher discussed what one might learn from his hands ('clean, possibly an office worker'). She then introduced the idea of the model representing other men in terms of his wealth, considering whether or not he was 'rich or poor.. or comfortable financially,... or could afford to buy aftershave'. The teacher briefly explored issues of *Institution* via the names of *Calvin Klein* and *Versace*. When one pupil volunteered '*Miss Selfridge*' as another producer of fashion/style, the teacher suggested, 'That's a company', distinguishing between a store more generally known for sales of fashion and two names known for fashion and perfume 'design'.

Moving more directly to the issue of *Representation*, the teacher raised the issue of the man's clothes and, in particular, his open shirt: 'Why do we put it on our neck or chest?'; and, summarising the discussion, 'slightly sexual – this is where the perfume/aftershave/*eau de toilette* is worn... it's an invitation really.' She was concerned to look at 'the ideas that are selling us something'. The teacher, at this stage, was also keen to address directly the specific concept which she was moving towards: 'I'm giving you a new word... If I said to you the man *represents* the sort of person who might want to buy or wear this aftershave or *eau de toilette* would you know what I meant?' (Pupils nodded in response). The teacher then led a discussion on the gender-related connotations of *eau de toilette*, including who the likely purchaser might be.

The issue of *Representation* was reinforced in two ways. Firstly, the teacher explored who the possible purchaser of this product might be: 'Would a woman buy this aftershave... how old?... would it be at 16 to 18 or in your twenties?' Secondly, the issue was explored via its use in a given syntactical context; i.e. the teacher wrote on the board, 'This man *represents* (stands for) the sort of person who would buy or wear this product.' To link this specific media meaning to more general understandings of *represent*, the teacher then explored with the pupils its more common use: 'I want you to learn this word, *represents*...'Who do you *represent* Stephen?... Daniella, you *represent* the school... you wear school uniform?' The teacher questioned individuals to ensure that the word had been grasped. She also reminded the SNA that, of all the words on the hand-out, *represent* was the most important to reinforce in the learning of those pupils she supported. The teacher summed up by suggesting that the model was *representing* the idea that 'if you wear *Eternity* you're this sort of man...sexy'.

Stage 2: *(20 minutes)*

This stage moved from the advertisement to the prepared list (handed out to pupils), and exploration of some of the words on it. Whilst pupils were working independently, the teacher pursued with individuals the meaning of some of the words from the list, including *product, image* and *stereotype.*

Then the teacher drew the class together. To begin with the teacher was concerned to persuade pupils that images could be read in the way that words could: 'We're going to go a little further into exploring the ideas... *did* you think you could read pictures?' (the emphasis on *did*, aiming to boost the pupils' confidence, suggesting what they had already achieved). She added that 'looking at the picture gives you words, doesn't it?... look at all the words we've produced.'

Then 'ideas we get from reading the picture and the words' was written on the board. Turning to the list, the teacher began with the first word, *stereotype*, appropriately linked to notions of *Representation*: 'Would you say I am a *stereotype* of a teacher because I am quite serious.. short hair .. look fairly strict?' She explored with the pupils whether or not she, and the female SNA, were stereotypical: 'We both use our hands and voices to express ourselves.' Then, moving from the general to the specific, the teacher constructed a number of questions and statements including the word *stereotype*: 'If I said to you the man has been *stereotyped...*', and, 'He's a *stereotype*, he's typical of that sort of model...' 'Is he *stereotypical* of the good looking man who has a car... Does he have a mobile phone? What sort of car does he drive?... Do we understand this word *stereotype* that's on our list?' As with the word represent, the teacher was concerned to connect its meaning to areas of experience with which the children might be familiar. This second stage of the lesson culminated in pupils writing a sentence in which they demonstrated that they could comfortably and appropriately use the word *stereotype*. (All examples were copied from the board in order to support the pupils when they would come to write an analysis of the advertisement). The teaching emphasis was more on pupil grasp and use of the term stereotype than on how stereotypes function more generally in advertising.

The third word/concept which dominated the discussion was *Audience*: 'Find the word *audience...* if this man is attractive and he's trying to sell a product to an *audience...* do you understand what I'm saying?...Why do we need an *audience* for an advert?...Why would they buy it?...Who might be the *audience* for this product?.. How old would they be?' To summarise, the teacher wrote on the board, 'The *audience* for this product might be 16 or more... It's the picture and the ideas about the product which are actually attracting people to buy it.'

Drawing the several issues together she asked the class, 'What would you use to represent that perfume... if it was a unisex one': reassuringly the answer came, 'A man and a woman'.

Stage 3: (10 minutes)
This constituted a summing-up. Also homework was set, which was intended to consolidate the learning in the lesson. In keeping with the activities of the lesson, pupils were asked to select five of the words on the list and use them in sentences to demonstrate that they understood their meaning.

Pupil response
The advisability of the tight focus and teacher control was evident in the opening minutes of the lesson when one boy arrived, clearly fresh from

some personal emotional conflict; though he did not positively contribute to the lesson, he co-operated with all activities, and the good humour of those more actively involved was unaffected.

Given the organisation of the lesson, interaction between pupils was not possible, but all pupils in this small group of nine interacted in some way with the teacher or the SNA. During the teacher-led discussion of the image and associated concepts and terminology, two particular pupils were most vocal in their response, accounting for the vast majority of extended ideas or volunteered responses. One was Nathan, a potentially difficult pupil who, on this occasion, was keen to use his wit to good effect whilst trying to extend the limits of what could reasonably be said. He was especially keen to explore the sexual connotations of the advertisement. When the teacher was considering the model in terms of 'sexy areas' where the perfume might be applied, 'neck or chest... the areas you might want to snuggle up to', Nathan suggested, 'Put it on your bum.' When distinguishing between aftershave and *eau de toilette*, Nathan played momentarily on the *perf* of *perfume* making it sound like the *perv* in *pervert*. Before the lesson the teacher had indicated how, with groups like this, the discussion of sexuality was always an issue to be wary of, needing sensitive handing. Nathan also asked 'what happens if you buy a man woman's perfume?' When the teacher established that the man in the image was comfortable financially, Nathan, with some sharpness, added, 'and mentally'. But though Nathan was keen to be divergent in his answers, he certainly did get the point. For example, he visualised alternative representations which would not be as effective: 'If they put a tramp on the picture, who would it attract?' Nathan was also the one most keen to relate the purchase of perfume to his own experience, citing an occasion when he had bought perfume for his mother.

The other most vocal pupil was Daniella, always involved and keen to please. She was the first to confirm the activities of the previous lesson. 'You had to look at it, see what you liked and write it down.' Whereas Nathan's contributions tended to take the discussion off at a tangent, Daniella was most likely to follow the teacher's lead in any answer which she supplied. In response to the teacher seeking confirmation about understanding of *represent*, Daniella replied, 'Yes, he (the model) wants people to notice him', and in response to the question seeking to establish the *audience* for the advertisement and the product, Daniella volunteered, 'people about his age'. She was the pupil who clarified the most common understanding of the word *represent*: 'You *represent* your school, you wear your school uniform.' When Nathan suggested that *Miss Selfridge* might be similar institutionally to *Calvin Klein*, Daniella was unsure about the relationship and suggested, 'That's a shop.'

Though most pupils were much more passive than Daniella and Nathan, their level of concentration and approach to the note-taking and writing tasks suggested that they were able to achieve the limited but clear objectives set for the class. That is, by the end of the lesson, they seemed able to use terms like *represent* and *stereotype* in ways which were at least syntactically plausible, if sometimes less secure semantically:

> *He is a posh stereotype.*

> *He is a stereotype of a masculine role, quite rich.*

> *This man is a typical stereotype model and you can tell him from his clothes and his looks.*

Media concepts and Media learning

It is not clear how far the understanding of terms like *stereotype* or *represent* went beyond the syntactic towards the semantic. After all, this was a wide-ranging introductory Media lesson with a year-10 low-ability group. Two main Media concepts were addressed, *Representation* (with its associated *stereotype*) and *Audience*.

Representation: clearly, this was at the heart of the lesson. moving from the general use of the word in everyday conversation to its more particular use within Media Education. In particular, the focus was on certain representations of men and associated stereotypes.

Agencies/Institutions: this was touched on in the brief discussion of the relationship between *Calvin Klein, Versace* and *Miss Selfridge*, and in the very brief references to product and manufacturer.

Audience: pupils specifically considered who might purchase the product and whom the advertisement might be aimed at; they also briefly considered hypothetical, alternative audiences (e.g. a tramp).

Language: this was addressed in a broad sense, in that consideration was given to notions of *image, anchorage* and *connotation* (the last two offered on a circulated list of media terms).

Categories: only the single print-based advertisement was considered.

Technologies: this concept did not feature in the lesson.

In this unit, the media concepts, like the Media element of the syllabus, were embraced by the more general need to learn how to use specific lexical items related to a given subject. That is, as well as understanding media concepts for their own sake, pupils needed to assimilate terminology in order to make their writing plausible. ('For getting a grade C or above they really have got to understand more complex language... by C they're asked to be critical as well as personal... the parameters of writing, i.e. style, form and organisation, are influential in the marking'.)

In the four weeks remaining of this unit of work, teacher and pupils would return to these concepts and reinforce understanding.

Main characteristics of the lesson

Media concepts and terminology were the focus of this lesson. In particular, the teacher wanted the pupils to learn to use specific terminology (Media terms and more general lexical items) in the context of their own writing. That is, she wanted pupils to demonstrate their understanding of the terms by using them in sentences which they constructed.

The teacher's control over pupils' learning was tight throughout. The lesson was characterised by short-term, very specific learning objectives. All discussion was managed from the front by the teacher. When pupils were asked to explore ideas in their own writing, the emphasis was on individual work, supported by the teacher and the classroom assistant. The control that the teacher exerted over the progress of the lesson was partly determined by the behavioural history of the class, and partly by the need to offer clear support structures for students with learning difficulties.

The text studied was a black-and-white photocopy of a *Calvin Klein* advertisement consisting of a single dominant image with minimal verbal text. The particular publication in which this advertisement appears was not a significant feature of the lesson. That is, the text was offered as a means by which pupils could explore their understanding of media concepts and terminology.

Though *Media Language* and *Institutions* or *Agencies* were referred to during the lesson, the emphasis was on *Representation* (*stereotype*) and *Audience*. In exploring these concepts, the teacher concentrated on the connotations of a range of cultural codes, including what is signified by body and facial features, earrings, clothes (and the way in which they are worn) and vehicles. No practical work was involved in this lesson and no information or communication technologies were used.

FRANCES
School: Rural Comprehensive

Teacher background

Frances teaches only English. She has been teaching for 14 years and teaching Media for about half of that time. She is second in the English department with a responsibility for Media Education. Her interest developed via National Association for the Teaching of English (NATE) materials and publications that stressed the importance of Media Education. Also, she attended some conferences and took part in a number of courses at Southampton University. Though enthusiastic about teaching Media now, Frances says that, to some extent, she was drawn to Media teaching by a need to address a fear of it: it was regarded as a difficult area of English, something which needed to be faced.

Teacher attitude to media education

Frances partly defines her attitude to Media Education by describing what, for her, Media Education is not. It is not, 'comparing two newspapers', not 'just news and ads'. Her approach is text-based, but in a broad context. So she will include publication and ownership as two important issues. Also, she is inclined emphasise film and the moving image. She recalls her most successful English lesson as a parody of chocolate advertisements, whereby the pupils were asked to make their own video using 'lard', as the product to be sold. Apart from the understanding of advertisements that pupils gained, what made it successful for her was the pupils' enjoyment and involvement, to the extent that they were willing to make the video at home in their own spare time.

Aims, concepts, approach to teaching

Frances's approach to Media teaching is the one summed up under Context: *the school*. That is, her approach is textually based, starting with media concepts which are very close to those 'Key Concepts' originally published by the BFI. Her own views on society do influence the way in which she sees Media Education. Her main aim is that pupils should be able to make informed judgements about the world around them on the basis of knowledge: ('I want them to see that people lead you down roads'.) For example, she would wish them to understand the implications of being a consumer. She also wishes pupils to understand why they might enjoy one media product more than another (exemplified in the lesson on advertising which follows). She is very positive about Media Education in general.

She lists important concepts as *Audience* (which she feels is, anyway, part of English) and *Agencies* (which she personally finds particularly interesting: she notes that, in some cases, a media institution is 'really only owned by one person'). However, the concept which she feels is particularly significant in that it distinguishes English from Media is *Representation*. But she stresses that you can't really teach one without the other. She finds no particular concept difficult or especially challenging. She feels generally comfortable teaching any of the recognised media concepts.

Frances enjoys and includes practical Media work in her lessons, but believes that other teachers are more confident in the use of technology than she is. However, she is generally optimistic about her developing confidence in the use of technology. She sees technology as an important but not essential element in Media Education. She considers skills in the use of technology to be more relevant, for example, to those who might wish to go on to study Media at A level. She recognises that boys are happier in their use of technology in Media lessons than girls, but feels that there is no gender difference in terms of general response to media work.

Frances is optimistic about the future of Media Education. She feels that there was a time, some years ago, when it was threatened, but thinks that it has now survived that. ('A couple of years ago I would have been more pessimistic than I am now'.)

Frances is clear that teaching about Media has changed her approach to English teaching in general. She is now more likely to take a wider view of any text, to move outside any text (e.g. to look at *Agencies*). For Frances, Media ideas have had the effect of blurring the distinction between Media teaching and English teaching, in that the Media approach to texts seems to encompass other aspects of English teaching.

Context: the school

At Key Stage 3, Frances described the Media content of the English department's scheme of work in any given year as 6/39 of the curriculum; that is, this minimum time allocation constitutes a departmentally agreed Media syllabus. The Media element of the scheme of work, which Frances devised, has a strong conceptual basis (adhering closely to the BFI 'Key Concepts Signpost Questions'). The scheme is supported by a set of teaching ideas from which all teachers may select, though the scheme may be interpreted differently by different teachers. This is a minimum Media requirement and any teacher (especially Frances) is likely to do other Media 'bits and pieces' elsewhere in the curriculum. At Key Stage 4 the amount of time spent on Media Education in a given year is similar (6/39 in each year). However, at Key Stage 4, the conceptual basis is more likely to be directly linked to assessment criteria described by the NEAB syllabus. (It seems the department's prior, explicit use of Media concepts makes it likely that they are less influenced by the NEAB's conceptual framework than might be the case with a less 'secure' department.) At both Key Stages the school scheme of work includes significant elements of film/video and DTP. Frances feels that, compared to six years ago, she can be confident that more Media work is being done by other teachers in the department, who often initiate ideas.

Other expertise has, in the past, been available via the BFI; also, the department makes use of the *Southern Echo* in its newspaper work (a top English group will soon visit its offices).

Frances assumes that elements of Media Education are likely to occur elsewhere in the curriculum (e.g. in Drama and in GNVQ Manufacturing). School planning does not specifically make reference to Media Education, though Media ideas are informing the school's cross-curricular forum on literacy. In the past the department considered opting for Media Studies as a GCSE subject but rejected the idea. However, given the department's improved technological facilities (e.g. editing suite, own camera, availability of IT) it may reconsider its position.

Frances and the department use a range of commercially produced resources, but are most likely to use materials from the English and Media Centre. In particular, Frances speaks of the usefulness of *The Advertising Pack*. (The department does not have the English and Media Centre's equivalent *News Pack*). The department also has lots of books about Media Education. Teachers in the department still produce many of their own worksheets, but Frances is most likely to produce her own resources when, for example, particular [up-to-date] video clips are needed for a lesson.

Frances recalls no significant reference to Media in their OFSTED inspection two years ago.

Context: INSET

Frances's own Media INSET is not recent. Most of it occurred about five years ago (e.g. at Southampton University). In recent years INSET has largely been determined by agreed school policies and priorities. For example, a recent school focus has been on the performance of boys.

Context: the syllabus

The school uses the NEAB English syllabus. It moved to NEAB from SEG when the newest GCSE syllabuses were introduced. NEAB's attitude towards Media Education (placing it within the coursework) and towards literature from other cultures was a significant factor in this choice. Frances is very positive about the syllabus in general. She feels that it allows teachers a great degree of flexibility, although she also acknowledges that the new syllabus is very full. Talking of Media Education, she says that a current problem which didn't exist six years ago is 'fitting it all in'. Despite this, she feels that the syllabus has raised the status of Media Education and made it 'less frightening' for some teachers. One implication of the new syllabus for the department is that they now try to fit all coursework elements in by December in year 11, leaving January to June for examination preparation.

Frances is clear in her distinction between Media (assessed in coursework) and non-fiction (assessed in the examination): for her the difference lies in approach rather than in the texts which are selected for analysis. Non-fiction she equates with 'comprehension' where the main aim is to look at the meaning in a text. In Media Education she anticipates consideration of the Media concepts, moving outside the text. The examination preparation for non-fiction involves no particular acknowledgement of a discrete textual genre or form. Frances feels that the sort of curriculum which the department offers pupils (including Key Stage 3) is adequate preparation for what pupils might face in the examination. ('They are used to a variety of texts'.)

THE LESSON: ANALYSIS OF ADVERTISING :
LEVI JEANS
Teacher: Frances

The class
This is a year 10, low set (four of five, probably GCSE English grade C to E). 12 boys and 4 girls were present.

Lesson aims
There were a number aims for this lesson. In particular, Frances wanted the pupils to explore ideas of intertextuality. She also wanted them to understand the way in which an advertisement is constructed. She stressed that the emphasis here was not on technical construction but on the concepts which make up the advertisement.

The pupils had already finished their 'official' GCSE Media unit (creating a film version of Hamlet, having already studied two versions of it, using BFI materials). The class had looked at how the film versions of *Hamlet* had differed from the text. In that unit, the Media assignment that the pupils handed in took the form of a letter. Also, in that unit, broad issues of intertextuality emerged, and Frances saw that issue as a link with the work on advertising. She saw in the *Levi Jeans* series of advertisements opportunities to explore familiar cultural references, particularly to film and music.

However, Frances was equally keen to move away from the notion of film adaptation and give the pupils something entirely different, i.e. curriculum variety was another motivation for this lesson. This particular lesson was the second within this small project; the previous day the pupils had looked at the Levi Jeans series of twelve different, and very well-recognised advertisements taken from *The Advertising Pack*. (The music accompanying these advertisements is actually available commercially on a CD). Having been introduced to the advertisements, pupils then played the 'caption game' (captioning each advertisement) and also studied some factual information from the pack about *teenage heroes, the history of the Levi advertisements*, and *intertextuality*.

It was not Frances's intention to develop this particular project much beyond the discussion which she has set up. That is, she saw this as essentially a speaking and listening activity and felt it important that not all English work has written outcomes; in any case, the written element of the NEAB syllabus had already been satisfied in the *Hamlet* unit of work.

Content and teacher approach

As indicated above, this lesson focused on a series of advertisements commonly known as the 'Levi advertisements' from *The Advertising Pack.* Other resources used included a television set and VCR. In addition, the two lessons involved three work sheets taken unchanged from the pack, or adapted to suit the particular task. This one-hour lesson had three stages of roughly equal proportions.

Stage 1: (15 minutes)

Frances reminded the class what was expected of them, an activity set up at the end of the lesson the previous day. Pupils were today asked, in groups of five or six (some absences), to view the advertisements again, this time making notes under given headings. Each group was given the same headings (*gender representations, representations of age and youth, cultural references* and *shared images*) and within each group individual pupils were given the responsibility for taking notes under one of these headings. The notes taken were then to be discussed by the group and (in a future lesson) group responses considered in a whole-class context. Frances's role in this first stage of the lesson was low-key, reminding the whole class of what was expected of them, but mainly responding to individuals and to groups, clarifying the task and pointing to the significant elements in the task sheets. For example she elaborated on two of the prompts, *Who wears them most frequently and how are they worn?* and *What sort of people admire them?* (in the latter example drawing pupil attention to a character's gaze in the narrative which the viewer might notice). In one sense this was less the beginning of a lesson than a continuation of a previous one.

Stage 2: (20 minutes)
The second part of the lesson involved observation and note taking by individuals. Pupils twice viewed the twelve advertisements without interruption (sound and vision) taking notes in accordance with their given area for analysis. These notes were recorded roughly in columns under headings which captioned or labelled each of the advertisements, e.g. the pupil responsible for cultural references would make appropriate notes on *cultural references* for each advertisement in succession.

Stage 3: (20 minutes)
The third part of the lesson involved collective discussion (i.e. at group level) of the notes which had been taken. The teacher's role was to circulate amongst the groups, supporting and guiding the discussions. Throughout the lesson the teacher acted to facilitate the pupils' learning rather than guide pupils to any particular response or predetermined understanding. There was no plenary session; whole-class responses were to be gathered in a future lesson.

Pupil response
This group of pupils was clearly used to working in this particular way. That is, they understood both teacher expectations that they should co-operate in groups; and note taking in this guided fashion seemed not unfamiliar to them. During the watching of the advertisements they remained entirely attentive, stopping appropriately, as directed, to take notes. Like any group of pupils in this sort of context their consequent discussion was a mixture of task-specific comments (e.g. 'What style of music does that song fit

into?') and 'off-task' but associated discussion (e.g. recounting with enthusiasm in detail the latest Levi advertisements not actually included in the clip – including one featuring a transsexual and one connected to martial arts). Given the number of advertisements viewed and the timescale for viewing, their notes were necessarily brief, a prompt for focused discussion rather than a detailed analysis.

In relation to the theme of intertextuality, not surprisingly, pupils seemed more likely to draw on *shared images* and more general *cultural references* (e.g. to typical locations like the pool hall, or the bar), than to specific references to, say, other American films or genres. One group did recognise the film *Grease* in several of the advertisements, especially in the one set in the Launderette, but did not elaborate on specific connections. The pupils seemed more assured in identifying the genre of music accompanying each advertisement ('70s or 80s', or 'Eddie Cochrane') and the mood that the music sought to establish. They were clear about the American aspects of the culture and, in particular that the advertisements often implied less affluent, rugged environments ('the American outback' as one pupil described it).

Given that there were twelve advertisements (seen twice) it is not surprising that the discussions were likely to deal with *audience, representation* and *cultural reference* at a fairly general level. Although this lesson did not provide much evidence about the degree of detailed understanding of media concepts (nor was it meant to), pupils did not seem uncomfortable by being faced with a direct set of references to *representation, target audience* or *shared images.*

They were most inclined to use specific media terminology when clarifying their roles in the activity, as in, 'What have you got in your notes about *target audiences*?' (As well as using specific media terminology in the prompt sheets and work sheets, Frances tended to use similar terminology in discussion with the pupils: to one pupil she explained what was meant by 'juxtaposing'; to the whole class she made reference to 'media texts'. She did not try to shield pupils from contact with media terminology, but did not necessarily expect them to use such terminology directly in discussion.)

The responsibility for learning given to the pupils in this lesson appeared to be mirrored in their Media writing. For example, in one assignment where pupils were asked to produce a 'guide' to *The Mayor of Casterbridge*, they were also required to write a self-reflective commentary:

'Evaluate and compare your guide with at least three others from the class.' This sort of activity, while common in Media Studies and Communications syllabuses, is comparatively rare in English syllabuses where assessment criteria tend to focus exclusively on the creative effort.

Media concepts and media learning

Categories: in a broad sense, this was central to the lesson in that the issue of intertextuality (listed on the prompt sheet as *cultural references* and *shared images*) was the main organising principle under which the advertisements were studied.

Representations: the pupils' prompt sheet guided the pupil discussions.

Language: because of the nature of the task, much of the discussion related to cultural codes (e.g. music, clothes, and locations) rather than to codes specific to television.

Audience: several, in their groups, spoke confidently with understanding about *target audiences*.

Agencies/institutions: although these issues were not prominent during this lesson, evidence from pupil Media folders suggested that they are, elsewhere, specifically addressed. For example, in an assignment analysing news and news institutions, one pupil made specific reference to *news conventions, newsworthiness* and to the notion of a media *gatekeeper*.

Technologies: this concept did not feature in this lesson; television and video technologies were used.

Main characteristics of the lesson

The teacher wanted the pupils to understand the way in which an advertisement is constructed. In particular, she wanted that understanding to be framed by explicit reference to particular media concepts. She also wanted pupils to be able to consider advertisements in relation to the ways in which they draw on other texts.

The teacher felt able to hand most of the responsibility for learning and analysis to the pupils; to facilitate this, pupils were given very specific analysis 'frames'. Further support was offered via the allocation of different roles and responsibilities to the pupils in each group. Thus, an individual pupil would take responsibility for a particular media concept and view the advertisements in relation to that concept, taking appropriate notes. Reporting back within the group (rather than to the whole class) then followed.

The texts analysed included twelve Levi advertisements taken from *The Advertising Pack* (Grahame, 1993). No printed text was considered, other than a range of supporting materials and prompts, again taken from *The Advertising Pack*. Context was also important in that the cultural environment in which such advertisements are produced, and from which such advertisements borrow, was a focus of the lesson.

Media concepts were foregrounded – a familiar process in a department which habitually makes concepts and terminology explicit for pupils. *Audience* was briefly considered, but the emphasis was on *Representation* and, in particular, the *cultural references* on which *representations* draw. Institutional issues did not figure significantly in the lesson. The emphasis was on points of reference within advertisements rather than on the professionals who produce them.

No practical activities featured in the lesson. Technologies used were those which supported analysis, namely a television set and VCR.

HELEN:
School: Semi-rural Comprehensive – 13 to 18

Teacher background
Helen was in her first year as head of English, having come to the school as a newly qualified teacher seven years ago. She did her PGCE at Southampton University where Media Studies was an important element in the training. Helen also teaches Drama and General Studies. She has been teaching Media all of her career and it was a significant element in her teacher training at Southampton. Media Education was, therefore, an important part of her early experience of teaching. For the first four years of her time at the school the English department offered Media Studies as an extra GCSE within the English curriculum, linked into English coursework, and Helen taught Media Studies as part of that curriculum. Because of the move from coursework to examinations, and because of pressures on curriculum time, the department was no longer able to offer Media Studies as part of the English curriculum.

Teacher attitude to Media Education

She describes her approach to Media Education as essentially analytical. Typically, Helen's Media work involves deconstruction of selected texts. She believes strongly that, 'Media Education should help pupils to judge what represents quality in the media.'

The department has no editing facilities and her Media teaching does not much depend on technology. However, she recalls her most successful lesson as one where pupils used video cameras as part of a project involving the advertising and marketing of a product. This was successful partly because of the commitment of pupils to the roles they adopted, (as competing advertising agents) but also because, in the advertising and marketing of the product, the pupils were sharp and thoughtful in their analysis: ('really quite an analytical viewpoint', and 'they used each other's skills and ideas...'). She prefaces this account by suggesting that her best lesson was not likely to be 'technical ... because of my lack of training and skills'. Not surprisingly, therefore, for Helen, in practical Media work, understanding of the process is far more important than the quality.

Aims, concepts, approach to teaching

Helen's long-term Media aim is to highlight how media texts work (though not, she stresses, in a technical sense). She wishes pupils to be able to see [as readers/consumers] how things are constructed, how things are being done to them, 'to be able to look around them and see how that was constructed in the way it was.' She feels a combination of scepticism and cynicism towards the media, but beyond this she does not feel that her own views about the media or society particularly impinge on her teaching.

She believes that pupils are very positive in response to their Media work. 'There's a certain immediacy; it is around them.' She says that they particularly enjoy study of advertising and collecting of advertisements. Much of her approach to Media Education now is driven by the requirements of the SEG syllabus and the need to equip pupils to be able to deal with its particular form of examination assessment.

Helen regards the use of technology as essential. Pupils working with Helen are likely to use video cameras (though she now finds more time for this at Key Stage 3) but are unlikely to be involved in any editing of video material. (The school has no appropriate facilities.) Though the department does not specifically teach desktop publishing skills, these are taught elsewhere in the curriculum and the skills are utilised within English. Things are, however, likely to change in the near future. The next academic year would see the English department with an IT suite dedicated to English teaching. Also, Helen points to current, intermittent use of new technologies, including a digital camera and use of the Internet to find background information about Thomas Hardy. However, the new technologies are not at the centre of the English curriculum; for example, there is as yet no focus on how one can validate information gained via a web site.

Helen notes that though boys and girls are equally enthusiastic about Media work in general, boys are particularly enthusiastic in their use of technology.

Media concepts (as in the BFI Key Concepts) are not significant in Helen's teaching – she is not aware of them. She is more likely to employ concepts from a broader notion of language study, particularly emphasising the importance of *rhetoric*. Generally, she is more confident in analysing and teaching about printed material (including presentational and visual representations) than moving image. Within the context of moving image she feels that her experience and training have better equipped her to manage analysis of advertisements than film, an area in which she feels less confident (e.g. she says that she is less able to talk about camera angles). In particular, she recalls a useful element of her PGCE course which involved analysis of advertisements.

She is neither particularly pessimistic nor optimistic about the future of Media Education, ('I'm not sure it's flourishing now') though, as described above, she regrets its narrowing via the GCSE syllabus. In her teaching, she is likely to try to maintain some breadth, regardless of syllabus constraints. But she feels that, at Key Stage 4 opportunities are limited: 'We can't actually do very much Media ... we can't actually call it Media Studies.'

Context: the school
Helen finds it difficult to quantify the amount of curriculum time allocated to Media at Key Stage 4, largely because she sees Media as integral to the department's general approach to analysis of text within English. She sees rhetoric, manipulation and persuasion as key elements of Media Education and these, she believes, apply to the way the department approaches study of texts in general – including the study of literature. 'It is ...rhetoric rather than Media in a broad sense.' That is, the focus is on rhetorical language. Much of her attitude derives from the SEG syllabus which, she says, 'is

quite specific in how language is used by the media, and how language seeks to persuade us.' Helen, therefore, argues that Media Education in this school is spread throughout the curriculum and not, for example, placed at the end of the course in preparation for the Media examination.

As indicated above, the department has experience in teaching Media Studies through coursework, though Media Studies is not currently available within the school curriculum. Media Education is written securely into the department's scheme of work. 'Because it's central to the examination, there is a chunk there.' It is described in terms of a range of experiences that pupils must have. Individual teachers then interpret those experiences in the classroom, though some units of work (like the advertising project which Helen developed) are commonly used. Teachers who are less secure in Media are offered support by other teachers; in addition the department maintains a folder containing other Media ideas. The school has no particular Media policy though Helen wonders whether one might be appropriate. She suspects that Media work occurs in other subjects such as RE and History (pointing to advertisements and newspaper work on display around the school).

Commercial resources are most likely to be purchased from the English and Media Centre. In particular she cites the *News Pack* (Grahame, 1995), which she describes as 'excellent', and *The Advertising Pack* (Grahame, 1993). She also refers to *Klondyke Kate*, (Bleiman *et al.,* 1995) though this resource tends to concentrate more on non-fiction than on media. Helen and the department also make much use of Film Education material, with which she is impressed, particularly since it does offer ways into the analysis of film, 'often very relevant to literature as well ... and it does explain a lot of those camera angles.' She also makes use of Schools television broadcasts on the subject of Media. The department prepares a lot of its own materials via 'cut and paste'.

The department's OFSTED inspection was approximately one year ago, but Helen does not recall Media being mentioned either in the verbal or written feedback. Though Helen herself was conscious that, for logistical reasons, Media did not feature much in lessons during inspection, this was never raised by the OFSTED inspector.

Context: INSET

Though Helen recalls Media-related issues as part of some INSET provided by Sabrina Broadbent of NATE, she has received no specific Media INSET since her PGCE training seven years ago. For new ideas and keeping up with developments, she relies on incoming staff to offer their experiences and draws on the range of up-to-date Media publications that the department purchases (mainly from the English and Media Centre).

Context: the syllabus

The English department has always used the SEG syllabus and saw no reason to change when the newest GCSE syllabuses were introduced. The syllabus treatment of Media Education did not play a significant part in the making of that choice. Helen rejected the NEAB syllabus (the only syllabus to offer Media as coursework) because she disliked the constraints of its Anthology, around which most textual study is based. She feels that the impact of the SEG approach to Media has been to make Media teaching more specific, but much narrower. The recent (first) examination of the new syllabus required, at both Foundation and Higher level, comparison of newspaper/magazine articles published in the Board's pre-release material. The questions in the 1998 Media examination made no mention of *Aeroflot*, whose in-flight magazine provided the source for the text, concentrating instead on the writer's use of language and presentation. (The department had prepared pupils to discuss the social context in which the text was produced.) Helen feels that these examination questions are closer to traditional comprehension questions than Media questions. 'One of the first things you do is look at the audience', says Helen, pointing out that no sense of audience was needed in the examination paper. (Discussion of *Audience* was later to occupy a significant part of Helen's lesson).

Helen's approach to distinctions between non-fiction and Media texts are, to a degree, constrained by the syllabus. Indeed, in the context of the SEG Media examination, there is little encouragement to distinguish between Media and non-fiction. Helen sees very little difference between them: 'The distinction', she says, 'within English is by what they're asked to do with it [i.e.. the text]...' She identifies the most important difference in relation to the purpose of the writer. That is, her teaching of Media texts is, much more than for non-fiction, influenced by notions of *Audience* and *manipulation*. These concepts are not likely to feature significantly in Helen's teaching of non-fiction texts.

THE LESSON: PERSUASION AND RHETORIC IN THE *BIG ISSUE*

Teacher: Helen

The class

This group is of mixed ability: 11 girls and 8 boys in year 10.

Lesson aims

The main aim of the lesson was to make pupils aware of the purpose of the text (an article from the *Big Issue* provided by SEG) and the methods used by the writer to persuade or manipulate the reader. A more pragmatic objective was to prepare pupils for the SEG Media examination; the material which they were to analyse had been provided by SEG for just this purpose. (Pupils would end up with 'a whole list of things' that they might expect to look for in a similar text in the examination.) Helen would also, in normal circumstances, ask pupils to go away and find an article of their own that they could then analyse for themselves.

Though this was a typical Media lesson for Helen (the materials and the approach have been used before) this lesson did not relate directly to previous learning. Indeed, this is not the normal time for this class to tackle Media, and Helen had arranged this lesson at this time in order to contribute to this research project. There is no special media vocabulary which Helen expects the pupils to become familiar with, nor does she feel that the SEG syllabus suggests there should be.

On this occasion, Helen was not expecting any written outcome; in other circumstances she might have expected the pupils to express their thoughts in writing – probably, a formal examination 'answer' to the text. Such writing would involve discussion of rhetorical devices and persuasive techniques. In it, Helen would expect pupils to use appropriate analytical terminology/ vocabulary, though this would not necessarily be recognisable as Media vocabulary. In this lesson, as part of Helen's usual practice, pupils would end up with a detailed annotation of the text, reflecting their own analysis and the ideas emanating from their peers and from the teacher.

The lesson aims were communicated to the pupils, at the start of the lesson, via rehearsal of a set of questions that this class has previously been taught as a way into textual analysis (e.g. Who is it for? How is the message conveyed? What is it about?) This was essentially a linguistic/literary approach. The examination context of this textual study was also made clear. At the end of the lesson, Helen did not specifically return to these aims, but the lesson finished with the analysis half-completed; presumably, the learning would be reinforced at the end of the next lesson.

Throughout the lesson Helen reinforced the aims by highlighting, praising, and recording on the blackboard any pertinent observations from pupils (e.g. references to the use of scientific evidence about the harmful effects of the sun's rays, or examples of puns in the headlines or summary).

Content and teacher approach

Each pupil was given a black and white A3 copy of an article from the *Big Issue*. The article was an ironic attack on users of sun-beds, entitled 'Sun Vampires'. The article included a cartoon of a 'cooked' female suffering from excessive exposure to the sun-bed's rays. Copies of the *Big Issue* itself were not actually used.

Helen's approach was to lead whole-class discussion/questioning, follow up with pair discussion (during which Helen would support individuals), and hold a 'plenary' before returning to paired discussion. Thus there was constant fluid movement between teacher-led analysis and pupils' own responses. Helen was always involved, either leading class discussion or supporting paired discussion. Though there was clearly a given understanding which Helen was leading the pupils towards, she was also careful to acknowledge and highlight interpretations that she had not anticipated.

In drawing pupils' attention to rhetorical techniques, Helen referred to a number of 'flashcards' on the wall which offered reminders of such techniques (e.g. *scientific evidence, ridicule, puns, sarcasm*). Another consistent element of the lesson was a requirement for the pupils to label or annotate the text in preparation for and as a consequence of any discussion.

Helen began the analysis by exploring the possible readership of the *Big Issue* via paired discussion; in this way pupils were able to give a media context to the analysis which followed. Pupils then continued exploration of *Audience*, this time in pairs. Helen then drew the class together and noted on the blackboard examples of potential purchasers of the *Big Issue*. This process of teacher-led discussion, paired discussion and annotation of text, followed by a 'plenary', was, more or less, repeated for consideration of the cartoon, the text's introduction and for the consideration of the text itself. The first 35 minutes of this one-hour lesson were devoted to headline, introduction and graphic image, so that attention to the opening paragraphs (the last 20 minutes of the lesson) was rooted in a secure context.

Summary of stages of the lesson:

1. Teacher and class discussion of possible readership of the *Big Issue*

2. Paired discussion of readership and individual annotation of text

3. Whole-class discussion of readership

4. Teacher and class discussion of cartoon and summary

5. Paired discussion of cartoon and summary and individual annotation of text

6. Whole class discussion of cartoon and summary

7. Consecutive reading of opening paragraphs

8. Teacher and class discussion of opening paragraphs

9. Paired discussion of paragraphs and individual annotation of texts

10. Brief plenary of pair observations of paragraphs

When discussion of the main body of the text began, three pupils were asked to read aloud the first four paragraphs of the text as a preliminary to discussion. Helen clearly offered the pupils opportunities to respond as individuals, concentrating as much on what they noticed as on what the writer was doing. But pupils did not read the whole text before analysis; i.e. after general discussion of the *Big Issue* readership, the pupils were immediately led through a carefully managed analysis of the text itself.

Pupil response

This was a class that, behaviourally, had given some cause for concern in year 9. However, the vast majority were committed to and involved in the analysis; i.e. there was no hostility to the notion of analysis in this form. Indeed, boys and girls seemed equally engaged in the task. The paired and whole-class discussion provided plenty of evidence that these pupils were familiar with notions of *persuasion* and *rhetoric* and were alert to appropriate devices, such as the inclusion of scientific evidence.

At each stage of the discussion, assisted by Helen's prompting, pupils were able to draw out a significant number of issues from a limited amount of material. In relation to the potential readership of the *Big Issue*, teacher and pupil together made reference to age, availability of money, charitable disposition, the sellers themselves, and environmentalists. There was a little confusion amongst some pupils between notions of sellers and buyers ('they all look like Swampy'; 'people that like that hippie sort of thing'), but Helen drew the pupils' attention to the confusion. In relation to the headline, pupils made reference to the incongruity of the sun being connected with *vampires*.

The discussion in relation to the text summary (in bold) and to the cartoon was more developed, including reference to:

- similarity of sun-bed to coffin (referred to in text)
- linking of burnt flesh to cremation
- humour – cartoon form
- nature of the reclining figure – 'female'; 'alien'
- absence of full stop (and bold lettering) making the reader want to read on
- play on words, inventing words – 'tanorexics' used by text to describe sun-bed 'addicts'
- play on words – 'sun-fix': connection with addiction
- paradox of coffin being 'high-tech'

In the main body of the text, pupils made reference to use by the writer of adjectives; 'slang' ('prepared to fork out'); scientific language; repetition and exaggeration; quotation to bring in expert opinion; humour; and rhetorical questions

Media concepts and media learning

It is interesting that although Helen did not use much media-specific terminology, she did not shy away from using other complex terminology/ language in helping pupils to interpret the text. For example, apart from what was contained within the flashcards on the wall, Helen, in the lesson, specifically referred to: *connotations, nomenclature, incongruity*, and *paradox*.

Two Media concepts were central to the lesson. The most important concepts were clearly *Media Language* and *Audience*.

Language: this mainly related to verbal rhetoric with brief reference to presentational and graphic connotations, particularly in relation to thoughts induced in the reader by the cartoon.

Audience: although Helen in her outline of the lesson made no specific reference to audience, this was clearly a significant part of the lesson, going beyond notions of implied readers towards a brief consideration of social characteristics of potential purchasers of the magazine in which the article was printed.

Agencies/Institutions: though this was not a significant feature of the lesson (beyond a brief reference to sales of the *Big Issue*) it was clear that Helen was hoping to develop this later. She suggested that she might move on to a wider consideration of the significance of the context in which the article was written: e.g. who writes for the *Big Issue*? What are their motives?

Representation: although not central to the lesson, *representation* was touched on when one pupil mentioned that the choice of female for the cartoon sun-bed figure might be sexist.

Categories: *genre* did not feature prominently; i.e. the *Big Issue* was not considered in relation to other publications

Technologies: this concept did not feature in the lesson.

Main characteristics of the lesson

The teacher's primary concern was to make pupils aware of some of the ways in which written texts can manipulate or persuade. Her approach was essentially one taken from Literature, with an emphasis placed on the use of linguistic rhetorical devices in a print-based text.

Although concerned to encourage independent learning through annotation of text and paired work, the teacher maintained careful control over the progress of the lesson, so that a common understanding could be reached, and pupils would be in a strong position to respond to any examination-style questioning.

To a degree, study of the text was related to the context in which the text met the public's attention: there was some discussion of potential audience for the *Big Issue*. However, pupils encountered an extract provided by the Examination Board rather than actual copies of the publication. The emphasis was on text rather than context, and analysis rather than personal response.

The predominant media concerns of the lesson were *Media Language* and, to a degree *Audience*. References to *Representation* and *Media Categories* were implicit rather than explicit. Issues of *Institution* and *Ideology* were not significant.

Information and communication technologies were not used within the lesson. The lesson involved no practical media-making.

JANE
School: Rural comprehensive

Teacher background
Jane has been teaching for 15 years. She began teaching Media while a student teacher. Her first department successfully offered Media as an alternative to Literature. She has continued to teach Media since that time, with the exception of a three-year interlude in a school where the management were resistant to Media being taught. Jane teaches only English; within English teaching she favours close reading and analysis of text – she enjoys deconstructing texts, including poetry. She feels that, for a long time, Media teaching in the South of England was less developed than in the Midlands where she formerly taught, but she now feels that that gap has probably closed. Though experienced in teaching Media within English (her first department was used by Len Masterman for development work), Jane, nevertheless, feels that her own Media training is comparatively limited. Despite this, she recognises that there are many teachers who have much less Media experience.

Teacher attitude to Media Education
Jane's approach to Media teaching is analytical rather than creative, with less emphasis on practical Media work. Her most successful sequence of Media lessons was one taught about five years ago involving a project centred on pop music videos; Jane feels that the success of the project arose from the absence of pressure at the time to produce any particular piece of coursework; also the subject caught the pupils' interest and enhanced their motivation.

Aims, concepts, approach to teaching
Jane's main Media aim is that pupils learn to see the choices made in any media text, that they understand the way in which media texts are consciously constructed. She feels that pupils respond well to her (analytical) approach to media; she is conscious that too much analysis could be seen as 'dry' and is, therefore, careful to avoid an excess. Typically, she might invite pupils to analyse game shows. Part of this work requires pupils to devise and perform their own game show, an attempt to 'dilute' the analysis, put learning into practice, and make it fun. Her own dislike of soaps and tendency to watch very little television makes her uneasy about her own familiarity with some aspects of the media.

Jane regards *Media Language* as the most important 'Key Concept' and certainly more important than *Institutions*. However, she feels that *Institutions* is a concept which she neglects, and which it is difficult to keep up with or on top of. She is aware of the BFI Signpost Questions, but says that they are no longer directly significant in shaping or framing her Media teaching: the language and terminology used by the Examination Board is now more significant. Jane is optimistic about the future of Media Education and expects it to flourish over the next ten years.

Jane's approach to Media, as indicated by her attitude towards it, is largely analytical; her lessons are more likely to involve television and VCR than, say, the use of the video camera. Her Media lessons tend to be 'low-tech'. This is partly philosophical in that she feels that media concepts and understandings can be conveyed with the minimum of technology. In addition, she prefers to avoid the logistical problems that go with organising the use of technology in the classroom. In practical work, therefore, Jane feels that understanding of the process is far more important than the quality of the work produced. However, departmental access to video cameras has recently improved and this is likely to have a positive impact on future Media practical work.

Jane does not regard Information Technology as significant in a Media context, and is happy that it remains outside Media work. However, teachers have recently had in-house training in the use of Internet and e-mail. Clearly it is too early to talk in terms of these new technologies being embedded in the English curriculum, but Jane sees this as an area ripe for development.

When she does use technology she finds boys particularly enthusiastic and motivated; girls too are positive, but no more so than in response to other features of the curriculum or of Media. Jane feels that some boys appear to have difficulty in some of the analytical writing which studying the Media demands. For example, she feels they have struggle to write about social codes (like dress and speech) in ways which are not merely descriptive and superficial.

Jane feels that her Media teaching has had an impact on other aspects of her English teaching. In particular, because of it, she feels more comfortable in dealing with image; this is exemplified in her use of Mike Benton's publications linking poems and art, and in her analysis of book covers before reading begins.

Context: the school

For Key Stage 4 pupils, Media work occupies a minimum of one twelfth of Key Stage 4 curriculum time in that the school's interpretation of the GCSE syllabus requires pupils to tackle a 'unit' of Media work (a maximum of one half-term, though units may occupy less time; the head of department is keen for two media pieces to be tackled, one moving image and one printed text). However, Jane will also introduce elements of Media work where appropriate throughout the curriculum. The department works from a common department Media policy which Jane wrote; the policy outlines appropriate Media experiences and offers guidance. It requires attention to be paid both to print and to moving image. It is up to the individual teacher how the policy is interpreted, and where Media is placed. Jane regrets that she has been unable to find a satisfactory way of describing progression within Media Education. Instead, the department is in the process of 'mapping' the English curriculum which is currently taught and describing the Media experience, retrospectively, within it.

As a consequence of the Media policy, all pupils at Key Stage 4 should have a similar Media experience, and 50 per cent have recently done some Media work. Though the Key Stage 4 Media curriculum is largely delivered via the Media 'unit of work' (and 'units' have been commonly used within the department), Jane, and the head of department, are now uneasy about the notion of the 'unit', regarding it is an artificial teaching construct. Indeed, Jane is currently considering ways in which she can redistribute the Media 'unit' more 'naturally' into the curriculum.

Within the rest of the school, Jane thinks that some Media Education probably takes place within Art. Expertise in the use of video camera is available from other members of the teaching staff, including the head of Drama, head of English and head of Art. There is currently no GCSE Media Studies course, though the department is actively considering whether or not to introduce it; in particular, the department is considering whether or not its teaching of Media within English would be enhanced by the greater expertise that might come via teaching Media as a discrete subject.

In relation to commercial resources, Jane is most likely to use the BFI teaching materials or those produced by the English and Media Centre, particularly *The Advertising Pack'*. Typically, Jane will adapt commercially produced resources for her own use.

Jane has no recollection of Media featuring significantly in the OFSTED feedback or written report.

Context: INSET

That the department values Media Education is evident from the attendance of its members at virtually all courses run by the English and Media Centre, two or three of which in a given year tend to be Media based. In addition, Jane was recently allowed one day's INSET in order to develop a unit of work for the department (on *Jurassic Park* and *The X-Files*). It is common for the members of the department to describe to each other what they have done, and this includes descriptions of successful Media activities. Jane had recently attended an 'Area' INSET day on Media (Autumn, 1997); the day was led by contributors from the BFI, the English and Media Centre, and Southampton University; the head of department in the school was involved in its organisation.

Context: the syllabus

The school has chosen the NEAB English syllabus. Its approach to Media Education was one of many factors involved in choosing a syllabus, though not especially influential. The NEAB syllabus was seen as supportive of Media Education in that it placed the assessment of it within coursework rather than in the examination. (The school has a background of commit-ment to coursework.) The implications of Media within coursework, though positive, are complex and need to be reviewed. For example, Media bears the brunt of the coursework writing, so it would benefit pupils if it could be done as late as possible when pupils are more mature. Also, Media analytical skills are particularly relevant to the textual analysis required in the 'non-fiction' examination, and pupils would benefit from Media work as near as possible to the examination. However, the pressures encouraging Media work to be tackled late in the curriculum are matched by similar pressures from other areas of the syllabus; the implications for curriculum organisation are currently being considered. Jane feels that the curriculum is now so tight that teachers cannot afford to 'get it wrong'. One particular problem which Jane and other teachers are reviewing is the lack of reward that coursework (and consequently Media coursework) receives compared to the great effort which it demands. In this context, she feels that teachers need to reconsider the importance of the examination itself which might be underestimated at present.

Jane distinguishes between media (assessed in coursework) and non-fiction (assessed in the examination) largely via a description of the different texts to which they might relate: e.g. travel and autobiography would be non-fiction, leaflets and news would be Media. This description corresponds to the way in which the Board itself defines the distinction. Jane refers to the necessity to comment on 'presentational devices and layout' in media texts, though she acknowledges that, for some non-fiction texts, these issues also become relevant. For example, the non-fiction examination requires awareness of authorial intention and attitude to the reader. She suspects that pupils might differentiate between media and non-fiction in terms of *how* they respond, regarding media as something watched or viewed (moving image) rather than read (print). In general, she feels that the new syllabus has highlighted the importance of Media Education, but that it has increased the pressures involved in teaching it since, as a significant element of the coursework, it is so important to 'get it right', and there is so little time to do so.

THE LESSON: ANALYSIS OF FILM OPENING: *GREAT EXPECTATIONS*
Teacher: Jane

The class
The class was a small group of year 10 pupils of lower ability, mainly boys (11 boys; 14 out of 15 pupils present) Coming from different classes, their prior Media experience in year 9 was mixed, depending to a degree on the enthusiasm of the year 9 teacher.

Lesson aims
The aims were strongly Media-based (rather than English-based). Jane wanted the pupils to understand some of choices made by makers of film, to realise that nothing in a film is there by chance. In particular she wanted them to understand the relationship between sound (including music) and image and to see the way that a film's effect on the viewer is created. She hoped that by the end of the lesson pupils would be in a position to begin to consider specifically the impact of particular camera shots. This was the second lesson in a small unit of work (two to three weeks) leading to a written analysis. It is was Jane's intention that this particular unit could possibly form the Media assignment for this class, though there would be another opportunity to address Media issues in year 11 (possibly in response to print).

In future lessons Jane intended to discuss how the film is presented or marketed via its packaging, the video box in which it is distributed. The first lesson, the previous day, had particularly focused on the idea of camera shot, with pupils, for example, standing on desks to consider the impact of different perspectives. The aims were made clear to the pupils at the beginning of the lesson. At the end of this lesson Jane indicated to the class that future lessons would involve a closer look at 'shots' and 'how the mood of the film is created'.

Content and teacher approach

The resources used were the videotape, VCR and television set; the approach arises out of Jane's previous Media experience and her understanding of the film. In order to develop the lesson aims described above, Jane chose David Lean's 'classic' adaptation of *Great Expectations*. The particular part of the film analysed was the opening, up to the scene in the graveyard and Pip's run home. The lesson focused intently on a very short scene and had very clearly defined stages:

- Pupils listened to the music without image (television SCREEN turned away) and were invited to speculate on the genre and/or specific narrative features which they expected to accompany this music; responses were discussed.

- Pupils listened to the music whilst watching the opening credits to the film and speculated on how the narrative might begin; responses were discussed.

- Pupils then watched (without sound) the opening sequence up to the appearance of the face of Magwitch and speculated on the characters they could see and on narrative development; responses were discussed.

- Pupils made notes of their observations and speculation.

- The results of the observations were discussed.

- The opening scene was watched with sound and discussed.

With the exception of that part of the lesson which involved note-taking, this was primarily a whole-class discussion led by the teacher. Jane stood near the television throughout the lesson, managing the question and answer session and sometimes writing key ideas on the blackboard. She clearly knew the film very well and had high expectations of the pupils' ability to manage film analysis in this way. Though her main role was to manage the questions and answers, she also responded to pupil answers and to the on-screen images as viewer or reader, i.e. she gave the impression of discovering alongside the pupils.

Pupil response

This was an activity which the pupils clearly enjoyed; they were enthused by the 'guessing' element inherent in it. Virtually all pupils were involved in the discussion at some stage. Two or three boys were particularly keen to contribute, and it was necessary for Jane to manage this in order that everyone could contribute. The note-taking and subsequent discussion was important in that it allowed the more reticent pupils at the back of the class to collect their thoughts before making a contribution; Jane commented that these quieter pupils contributed more in this lesson than they were accustomed to. There was certainly a sense that the pupils were working with a medium with which they were familiar and comfortable; from some there was even a sense of expertise. It would be difficult to imagine this particular group of lower-achieving pupils showing similar enthusiasm or expertise if they were doing an equivalent analysis of a print-based text.

When listening to the music without image the pupils were particularly alert to the sort of narrative which might follow such (light, orchestral) music; one pupil suspected it might be Disney, another recognised 'old-classic film' connotations. One pupil, with obvious prior experience of Media teaching techniques, suspected a bluff, assuming that pupils might eventually see the opposite of what they were predicting, i.e. 'sound' connotations of the past, alongside visual connotations of the future. (He prefaced his comment with, 'I bet this turns out to be...')

The film credits themselves were given close visual examination, with Jane encouraging pupils to 'look at the fonts'. In relation to *Media Language*, both pupil and teacher referred (appropriately given the lesson the previous day) to 'shot'. At one point, Jane referred to a 'point of view' shot and observed that the camera was 'looking down on' the image of the book. One pupil referred to 'action shot', another to camera movement, 'it's a zoom-in isn't it?' One pupil was conscious of the effect of lighting, commenting on the face of Magwitch in terms of 'dark side, light side'. Another pupil spontaneously made a connection with a Susan Hill novel (*Woman in Black*) that the class had recently read.

The discussion throughout remained closely focused on the lesson aims (image and sound). At times the discussion was intense with pupils competing to express a viewpoint; it was quite clear that Jane's analytical approach to Media teaching was motivating for these pupils.

As an example of pupil response and media learning, there follows a summary of the main points made by one pupil in the writing activity which (later) arose out of this unit of work. The extract provides clear evidence of the way in which learning about *Media Language* has been absorbed: in the majority of cases, the pupil's references to *Media Language* suggest that the terminology has been understood. For example, though some references to 'shot' are merely descriptive, the pupil often goes on to comment on the implications of the shot for the point of view that is offered.

The pupil made reference to:

- the use of sound/music, including the creation of 'jolly' and 'dramatic' music via 'solo instruments like the flute'

- the use of sound/the human voice to suggest, from the 'formal and very posh way' that the man speaks, that the film is old; the use of 'the boy's screams' to 'take over the other noises in the background'

- the use of graphics/fonts to produce a 'more classical look' compared to the 'plain' fonts for 'titles of the jobs like film director'

- the use of a variety of shots, including 'long-shot', 'pan', 'fade-in', 'cut-back' 'close-up', 'extreme close-up', 'mid-shot', 'high-angle reaction shot'

- the manipulation of point of view, including the fact that 'the camera is behind the boy makes it seem like there is someone behind him getting ready to pounce'; 'a low-angle shot which shows us what it looks like from the boy's position'; a 'low-angle shot which makes it (the tree) look threatening', and a shot in which 'the tree is framed by a dark, gloomy sky which makes it look very scary'

- the use of cultural objects, or features of the landscape, including 'gibbets' to 'make you feel uneasy' and 'make you think of death'; and 'a gloomy sky threatening, and a tiny figure against a big landscape'

- the pathetic fallacy: 'we see the boy close up as if the wind is directing its noise at him'; 'it makes you feel the trees are closing in on him'

- the use of editing including the way the director 'builds up tension to the last few shots' and the way this build-up of 'pace' and of tension 'makes it more exciting'.

Media concepts and media learning

That this lesson was a 'Media' lesson rather than an 'English' lesson is evident from the fact that the teacher never referred to the fact that this film is based on a 'classic' English novel. It was chosen because it is a striking opening sequence per se rather than a striking opening sequence of a film adaptation of literature. Indeed, though it is likely that the origin of the film would emerge in later lessons, Jane regards the film's origins as not significant in this context. However, for Jane, the concepts central to the lesson are to do with the construction of a text and are equally applicable to study of literary texts. (Jane's concern was as much with 'authorial intention' as with the particular devices used). Indeed, when discussing *Media Language* one pupil asked 'Do producers think of these things?' very much in the doubting tone that pupils sometimes use when asked by the teacher to appreciate the literary devices in a poem.

> **Language**: this was clearly the central concept in this lesson and wide-ranging in its scope. Reference was made to sound and music, graphics, a variety of camera shots, the significance of cultural objects and aspects of editing.

> **Agencies/Institutions**: although not directly addressed in this lesson, it is clear that in future lessons would take account of the packaging and marketing of the film.

> **Categories**: this was not central to the lesson, but the activity involving interpretation of music encouraged exploration of music associated with specific *genres*.

> **Representation**: other than the two specific characters in the opening section of the narrative, no particular representations were considered.

> **Technologies**: this concept did not feature strongly in this lesson, though some aspects of film and television technologies were implicit in discussions of lighting and shot; television and video technology were used.

Main characteristics of the lesson

Though the focus of analysis and discussion was the opening of David Lean's film *Great Expectations*, the lesson inclined very strongly to Media rather than literary issues. The teacher wanted pupils to understand the relationship between sound and music, and to grasp the ways in which a film's impact on the viewer is created.

Although the analysis of the film was class-based and strongly teacher-led, the teacher encouraged individual response by severely disrupting the flow of the film narrative. That is, pupils listened without image and watched without sound. At intervals during the lesson they took individual notes to record personal observation and analysis.

An implied text, but absent from the lesson, was, of course, Dickens' *Great Expectations*. However, this was very clearly not a lesson centred on the 'film of the book'. The disruption of viewing described above emphasised for the pupils that 'text' can take the form of moving image and sound. Though discussion of the film in this lesson was decontextualised, it was the teacher's intention, in later lessons, to consider the context in which such a film might be 'sold' to the public through a focus on marketing and packaging.

Agencies was, therefore, likely to be addressed at a later date. In this lesson, although *Media Categories* was implicit in much of the discussion, the emphasis was very strongly on *Media Language*. In particular, there was discussion of the connotations of sound, music, light and camera shot. That this was significant in the pupils' understanding was evident in the written work which followed. In one such written piece, a pupil made reference to the connotations of music, the human voice, graphics, shot, point of view, and cultural objects including landscape.

There was no practical media activity within this lesson. Technology used included the television and VCR.

JOAN
School: Urban girls' comprehensive

Teacher background
Joan teaches only English and is head of department. She has been teaching for 25 years. She has always included aspects of Media work in her teaching, but has consciously and explicitly addressed Media for about ten years. The impetus for this Media work came initially from the original National Curriculum documents and subsequent related developments. However, she was also encouraged in the early days of Media Education by pupils' enjoyment of Media work and their natural interest in the media, particularly magazines and films.

Teacher attitude to Media Education

Joan's approach to Media Education is essentially analytical; as a typical successful lesson she cites a comparison between a cartoon and a film version of *Twelfth Night*. Indeed, comparison between two media versions of a text exemplifies Joan's approach. However, she is also concerned that pupils' own analytical skills are used to resource their creative Media work. She suggests that she, herself, is not skilled enough.

Aims, concepts, approach to teaching

Joan's main aim is to encourage pupils to understand the techniques used in the media to achieve certain effects in order that the pupils can use such effects in their own production. She insists that it is not her intention to make children defensive about the media by, for example, teaching them about the ways in which advertising lies to its audience. She offers a very lucid account of what, for her, Media Education is about. She wishes pupils to 'understand techniques used to achieve certain effects on an audience and to utilise these techniques when they themselves are involved in media production. I don't strongly believe that Media Education is for teaching kids to watch out for lying adverts. I think it is for giving them the where-withal to reach a public audience when they need to, and to recognise the techniques that each separate piece of media may use to reach its audience, and to be able to evaluate successfully how it does it.'

She feels that the girls respond well to media work, and are happy watching, listening to and making video and radio productions. In relation to practical media work, she believes that understanding of the process is more important than the quality of the work itself.

Joan suggests that her personal views about society do not significantly influence her approach to Media Education. She does want the girls she teaches to develop a 'critical eye', to have the ability to step back to consider what they are watching or reading. She is initially reluctant to use the term 'empower', but is essentially concerned that pupils are given some sort of ability to participate on equal terms in the media. However, she suggests her main driving force and influence is the Media syllabus: the need for more Media expertise and the need to address the syllabus (and related concepts and language) are what drives Joan in her teaching of Media.

Concepts are very important to the way that Joan approaches Media. She has developed a mnemonic to help herself, other teachers and pupils to remember the concepts: Aunt Pru Sucks Lemons (A: *audience*; P: *purpose* and *presentation*; S: *style* and *selection*; L: *language* and *layout*). These concepts are explicitly used by teachers and pupils to inform the way in which texts of all types are discussed. The BFI 'Key Concepts' are clearly informing this learning structure but have been adapted so that they integrate 'Media' and 'English' approaches to textual analysis. Most of these concepts, she feels, work equally well for both disciplines, though style, essentially a literary notion, needs more adaptation when applied to Media texts (she feels it is connected with issues like pace and editing). In relation to Media concepts, Joan is happiest addressing *Language*; she feels she is more comfortable with the language of print-based texts. Her own approach to English in general has become more analytical, partly as a consequence of the Media developments described above.

Information Technology is increasingly used as a tool within English. For example, teachers will book the IT suite when they wish all pupils to have access to word processors, and those pupils who choose to produce a media text for their coursework will frequently use computer graphics; much of this type of work, however, is done at home. In addition, teachers are just beginning to get to grips with the Internet – used most recently in order to find out more about a film version of *Romeo and Juliet*. But new technologies in general and the Internet in particular remain as tools within English and have not yet become the focus of study.

Joan is not averse to teaching about *Institutions* or *Agencies* when the issues arise, but feels that the English curriculum offers little or no encouragement to deal with these issues; in any case, Joan feels them to be more appropriately covered within Media Studies and believes that the teacher of Media within English should pay more attention to *language* and text than to *Institutions*.

Joan is confident about the future of Media Education and sees it flourishing over the next ten years, simply because it is so important.

Context: the school

Media is seen by the department as representing a fairly significant element of the English syllabus (approximately one fifth of the coursework; but taking into account the practice of media skills necessary to prepare for the non-fiction examination, Joan reckons that Media probably takes about one quarter of Key Stage 4 curriculum time). The amount of time currently spent on Media is higher than that. The department has a detailed written Media policy outlining the Media 'strand' of the English curriculum from years 7 to 11. This policy distinguishes between non-fiction (assessed in the examination) and media (assessed in coursework).

The existence of a GCSE Media syllabus in the school is significant for the teaching of Media within English. The three teachers who run the very successful Media Studies course (in existence for a number of years and producing the school's best GCSE results) also teach within the English department. This confident Media department has a strong conceptual approach to Media and consciously encourages pupils to talk in terms of Media concepts. The area of *Institutions* is regarded by the teacher responsible for Media Studies as particularly important and not problematic to teach. Such knowledge, and to a degree the approach and expertise, feeds back into the English curriculum.

Though the school has no Media policy, it does have a cross-curricular approach to literacy, and in this Joan recognises some Media elements, particularly in Expressive Arts and in the History department's requirement that pupils write in newspaper form.

In relation to commercial resources, Jane and the department are most likely to use materials produced by NATE and by the English and Media Centre. Two publications to which she made specific reference were *The Advertising Pack* (Grahame, 1993) and a study pack to support the book and film *Gulliver's Travels* – both products of the English and Media Centre.

Joan does not recall Media being mentioned in the verbal or written feedback arising out of the school's OFSTED inspection. However, the department were asked Media-related questions by the inspector and had been conscious of the need to 'keep Media in the limelight' during inspection.

Context: INSET

Joan has not recently attended any external Media INSET. However, her professional development in relation to Media is maintained in two ways. Firstly, she finds that reading the detailed materials produced by the English and Media centre forces her to reflect on her own Media understanding. Secondly, the teacher responsible for Media Studies in the school is regarded as the English department's own adviser. Given the experience of Media teaching of the relevant teacher, this is a significant contribution to Joan's INSET. (In addition, encouraged by Joan, Joan's Media colleagues often go themselves on Media courses, so the advice and support they offer is up to date. These courses included reference to Media within English; one teacher has recently been on two Media courses.

Context: the syllabus

The English syllabus is that offered by the NEAB. The department has always worked with NEAB and did not seriously consider moving away from it when the new 1998 syllabuses were published. However, the NEAB's treatment of Media and its positioning of it within coursework was a positive factor in staying with the Board. Joan regards the effect of the new NEAB syllabus as having sharpened up the study of Media, moving teaching from the more descriptive (as it used to be) to the more analytical (as it now is). These changes she views positively though she sees them as being more demanding intellectually. She interprets the syllabus as requiring pupils to understand specific concepts and to use explicit media terminology. She exemplifies the change in the demands of the Media curriculum over the years by describing a typical 'women in advertising' project: originally, she says, this may have been a fairly descriptive project, tending towards the use of anecdotes, but now it would need to be far more analytical. Such analysis is she feels, though intellectually demanding, still more accessible for many pupils than literature

Joan defines the difference between media and non-fiction in relation to the different sort of texts which they imply, and particularly to the specific examination exemplars provided for non-fiction by the Examination Board. Typically, she comments with some irony, non-fiction texts have been about 'cosmetic dentistry and garden walls'. Sometimes, she says, the non-fiction exemplars will obviously be non-fiction, but others will be more media-related, like a news article on 'smacking children'. Ultimately, for Joan, the difference is to do with audience; if the audience is in the 'public domain', then the study, she feels, is media-related rather than non-fiction.

THE LESSON: READING THE NEWS – WOMEN IN WORK
Teacher: Joan

The class
This is a mixed ability group of 18 girls; the group has partly been constituted with reference to behavioural management criteria. It has been together as a unit since September.

Lesson aims
The lesson had two main aims. One was purely pragmatic and related to the coursework assignment which the pupils were engaged in: Joan felt that the drafts on this to date (related to work experience) did not reflect enough of

the pupils' own views. Secondly, in order to help develop their 'voice', she wanted to draw their attention to the appropriate language for textual and media analysis, and encourage them to use the terminology to which they had been introduced. She wanted them to go beyond references to 'good and bad' and to develop greater fluency and independence in expressing their opinions. The Media concept most relevant to this lesson is, therefore, *Media Language*, and in particular, the language appropriate to analysis of news; she was very aware that the syllabus demands use of appropriate terminology.

As a preliminary to work experience, the girls were considering how women are treated in the world of work. In particular, they had looked at a video about firewomen and discussed and analysed the video techniques. They had also begun to analyse two newspaper articles; they had worked in pairs and presented some of their views on sugar paper in a cut-and-paste exercise (in order to improve their vocabulary). In the lesson the previous day the girls had already been involved in a discussion of the two articles.

The lesson was focused on enhancing the quality of that discussion. Also, the perceived need to improve pupils' ability to deal adequately with the written assignment was central to this lesson. It was Joan's intention to develop the pupils' analytical vocabulary. She says that the syllabus 'demands' specific reference to media features like 'long-shot', 'focus'. etc. In this newspaper-related work, she intended to develop pupils' media vocabulary and understanding of concepts via a game that she devised: pupils would be given on a piece of paper one of four letters from the mnemonic 'Aunt Pru Sucks Lemons'. Each pupil would be expected to use her own letter to refer to the relevant analytical concept (e.g. a pupil receiving A would need to talk about the news article in terms of *Audience*). Joan also felt that other relevant vocabulary items such as stereotypical and equal opportunities were needed.

At strategic points during the lesson and at the end of the lesson, Joan reminded the pupils of the lesson aims. She drew attention to the high quality of their observations and the language which they used to express it; she exhorted them to record such observations in similar language when they came to write their assignment. In addition, at the end of the lesson pupils were reminded that, though they now were greatly critical of the *Sun,* they had indeed laughed **with** the article when they first read it.

Content and teacher approach

Resources used were photocopies of the two articles related to women in work: 'HO-HO HOSE BOYS GET FIREGIRL BLAZING' from the *Sun*; and 'BUILDING A SECURE FUTURE', from a local paper. The local paper article offered a positive perspective on a young girl who decided to enter the traditionally male-dominated building trade; it told of the girl's success and the friendly treatment she received from her male colleagues. The *Sun* article, however, described the sexual harassment received by a girl who worked in the equally male-dominated fire service; the article was sympathetic to the men who harass the girl and made light of her distress. Each article was accompanied by an A3 sheet of specific handwritten advice from the teacher. The advice took the form of a paragraph-by-para-graph essay 'model' with an element of cloze built in. The model offered a structure for the writing and picked out significant features of the text for analysis. For example, 'The purpose of the photo is to show Lynn as 2M.' Each paragraph illustrated a different element in the mnemonic and pupils were reminded of this by the appropriate capital letter (A, P, S or L) written in a circle next to the start of a paragraph.

The lesson took the form of a whole-class discussion. After the *Sun* article had again been read aloud, the teacher drew the vast majority of the girls into the debate. Because of the girls' animated response, and because of the high quality of the discussion, Joan decided to ignore her original intention to move on to the letter game, and instead stayed with the discussion throughout. She drew attention to what the pupils already knew from their previous discussion and gave credit to every contribution made. At one stage, in response to pupil 'requests', she re-enacted a mock faint which she had performed the previous day. On that occasion she had pretended to faint with shock at the very acute observation of one particular pupil (that *Sun* articles are as they are because editors fail in their responsibility to curb what reporters say). The teacher talked in terms of the reporter as the 'writer', placing as much emphasis on the individual who composed the piece as on the publication in which it appeared.

Pupil response

The discussion confirmed Joan's impression that pupils enjoy analysis. They were always interested and usually animated. For these pupils, the representation of women in the *Sun* was a serious issue. Though one or two pupils expressed dissident opinions (accepted by the teacher as entirely valid), most were happy to take the interpretation suggested by the support material and by the line of questioning. However, though the teacher had a clear intention to lead pupils to a particular understanding of the two texts, the pupils' own anecdotal evidence suggested that at least some of them already harboured an antagonistic view of the *Sun*. One particular pupil repeatedly made reference to her own anxiety to divert the attention of her six year-old brother from the pictures of naked women on page 3 of the *Sun*. Though reference was made to the positive features of the local paper, most of the discussion, and nearly all of the animated discussion, arose from hostility to the *Sun*.

Discussion ranged widely. The following examples illustrate the sort of comments which pupils were making about the *Sun* article, often from their own initiative, sometimes in response to teacher prompting:

- Humorous, punning headline and subheading

- Careless spelling in the *Sun* of 'Lyn(n)' proved the writer's lack of respect for the girl

- Lyn(n) was likely to be described in disparaging terms (e.g. 'Rookie firewoman'); in contrast to the men, referred to positively as 'firemen', or non-judgementally and alliteratively, as the 'frolicking four'

- Undermining of the girl's position by use of the word 'claims' applied to her point of view

- Unflattering picture of girl deliberately chosen so as to suggest that her unattractiveness would not have induced men to sexually harass her ('Lynn is no raving beauty')

- Internal contradictions in the logic of the article: men claim their behaviour (eg. dropping their trousers) was a traditional initiation ceremony – difficult to imagine the firemen behaving in this way to a new male recruit.

The help sheet meant that pupils' attention was drawn to the following analytical concepts:

- the target *audience* for the local paper, and its likely appeal to women

- the target (male) *audience* for the *Sun* article

- the celebratory, positive *purpose* of the local article

- the *purpose* of the Sun article to support the male perspective

- the relaxed and friendly *style* of the local reporter

- the humorous and accessible *style* of the *Sun* article

- specific examples of the casual, cheerful *language* used in the local article

- the 'humorous', casual *language* used by the *Sun*

The class discussion began, as the lesson objectives required, with an emphasis on newspaper *language*. However, as the discussion developed, and as the girls became involved in the discussion as individuals, as real (indignant) readers rather than simply as pupils, the debate focused ever more strongly on *Representation*. Interestingly, this is not one of the concepts included in the mnemonic. Joan sees it as a difficult concept to make the focus of a lesson, and would prefer that it arises, in this way, via a discussion of *Language*.

Media concepts and Media learning

Representation: though this was not explicitly part of the aims of the lesson, as suggested above, the way in which women are represented in the world of work and within differing newspapers was at the core of the analysis.

Language: the intention had been to help pupils rehearse their understanding of some general media concepts and terms; the discussion, however, focused more on specifically verbal/ lexical and semantic choices made in journalistic writing.

Audience: there was much talk of how different audiences, such as men, women and young children, might respond to the Sun article; audience was a prominent notion in the pupils' own discussion.

Agencies/Institutions: this was touched on in relation to the respective roles of reporter and editor and in judgements about where the responsibility for tone and content might lie.

Categories: newspaper articles were the only category of writing considered, though the significance of the particular newspaper (tabloid or local) was clearly central.

Technologies: this concept did not feature in the lesson.

Main characteristics of the lesson

The main intention of the lesson was to help pupils develop their ability to use appropriate media terminology in their analysis of media texts. A narrower aim was to develop such ability specifically in relation to two particular newspaper reports, leading towards a piece of analytical writing. This analysis was to take place in the context of pupil rehearsal of basic concepts of textual analysis, namely *audience, purpose, presentation, style, selection, language* and *lay-out*.

The whole of the lesson was led from the front by the teacher, who strove to bring as many girls as possible into the debate. There were significant moments in the lesson when individual girls related their analysis of the *Sun* article to their own experience as females living amongst families where males read tabloids. On these occasions, the girls would tend to speak at length, with some passion about their experiences.

The texts considered were photocopies of two newspaper reports, one from the *Sun* and one from a local newspaper. The photocopies did not contain other elements of the pages from which the extracts had been taken, but context was very important. For example, that the *Sun* was a tabloid with a very particular view on women was always a part of the discussion. Another context was the world of work: both reports offered different perspectives of women at work, significant because the girls were about to embark on their own work experience.

In that media concepts per se were a focus of the lesson, a number of them were obviously addressed, with *Media Language* particularly prominent. However, the concept which was at the heart of most of the discussion was that of *Representation*, particularly, as suggested above, of the representation of women. Interestingly, this concept did not feature in the aims of the lesson, but was one that the teacher was happy to let develop.

No practical media activity featured in the lesson, and information and communication technologies were not used.

Group 2

Mary: Urban boys' school
Brian: Coastal comprehensive
Ros: Girls' grammar school

In the first lesson in this group, Mary encouraged her boys to understand their own self-image in relation to the often negative representation of males in newspaper headlines. Brian was also concerned with representation in newspaper headlines, in this case, representation of young people on holiday. His focus was on the ways in which visual and verbal representation combine to persuade the reader to a particular point of view. Ros took a very broad position, exploring advertising within a Communication Studies model of media, to consider how advertisers seek to exploit the weaknesses of consumers.

MARY
School   Urban boys' school

Teacher background
Mary teaches mainly English, and some Drama (about 15 per cent of her timetable). Mary would like to see Drama separate from English and more 'skills-based'. Another significant interest of Mary's is working with children with Special Educational Needs. Mary had been teaching English for five years, all in her current school, having done her PGCE in English at Southampton University. As part of that PGCE, Media Education was a significant element, though she would have liked to have taken it further with more 'hands-on' experience, 'because there's so much you can do with interpreting visual media'.

When Mary began teaching, Media Education was not part of her curriculum because, 'we were so exam-orientated here and media was not part of the exam'; though Mary did 'surreptitiously' and independently introduce small elements of Media into her own teaching. Mary has always had a strong personal interest in Media, in 'film, television, papers, magazines... I'm a critical reader... and within the family... we deconstruct everything'. As a consequence, when Media did more explicitly enter the curriculum Mary took to it naturally.

Teacher attitude to Media Education
In teaching Media, Mary has two guiding principles: she likes to 'go straight for the controversial', and to 'link it with kids' experience of media

as well'. For example (in this boys' school) she might look at (as in the observed lesson) 'images of males within written and visual Media'. She would typically take such images and 'challenge, and provoke and embarrass', especially now that she feels that the examination has given her licence to do more Media work. For Mary, successful Media teaching is when pupils take analysis further and 'recreate... if they can imitate images or words – that is enjoyable.' She feels that this approach makes pupils less intimidated than they otherwise might be when doing straightforward analysis. What is important is 'imitating the models' which the teacher offers.

In practical work, she feels that understanding of the process is more important than the quality of the work produced. This is borne out in her comments in relation to her approach to Media teaching: she offers pupils opportunity to imitate processes in order to make the learning 'fun', to lessen the impact of potentially intimidating analysis.

Aims, concepts, approach to teaching

In the long term, Mary hopes that pupils will be 'better able to critically evaluate the Media around them'. She also feels that they are not currently always able to distinguish clearly between different types of media (e.g. newspapers and books) and would like them to develop such an ability. She strongly believes that Media Education should help to judge what represents quality in the media. However, she also wants them 'to get a lot of fun out of it.'

Mary' own teaching is influenced by her own views about society and the media. She feels that the media are 'a very powerful force and lead a lot of kids into trouble... or if not trouble, into something other than what they are... American. I don't like that, I think that's wrong.' Also, her family background has inclined her to be quite political, to take an interest in media and current affairs.

Mary feels that the pupils don't always respond positively to analysis. 'They don't feel safe putting forward opinions... to do with taking risks.' But in literature study they are more forthcoming: 'It's printed... more familiar... they are on familiar territory.' 'Sometimes they don't understand the differences between criticising and analysing.' As a teacher she is, if anything, happier when analysing visual images. In a way, she feels it impresses the pupils: 'You can bring so much out of nothing and I think they find that a bit like a magic trick.' She would typically enjoy giving pupils tasks which involved sequencing images.

The BFI 'Signpost Questions' are not part of Mary's framework for addressing media; though they would have been part of her PGCE at Southampton they have since not been significant in her teaching. Instead, she relies on a list of appropriate terminology – designed as a revision guide – supplied by a consortium of local schools. The emphasis in the guide is on verbal language and rhetoric. Terms/concepts in the guide include *style, tone, bias, values, argument* and *effect*.

Institutions is not in any way part of Mary's agenda. She is unfamiliar with it as a media concept but she feels that it does not in any case sound attractive, and should only be introduced if 'pupils wish to know' about it.

Technologies do not figure significantly in Mary's Media teaching. She is most likely to use television and video; however, where she uses a video camera it is likely to be related to Drama or Literature rather than to Media Education. Similarly, word processing and desktop publishing are more likely to feature in English in general as a tool rather than specifically in a Media context. The Internet is available in the school but Mary has not used it yet; CD-ROM is not available, though teachers have had training in it.

Mary is not optimistic about the future of Media Education. Twice in the last few weeks she has seen articles denouncing the position of Media Education within the curriculum. She feels that its survival will ultimately depend on its position within the GCSE framework – if it is part of that framework, part of the syllabus, it will survive. If not, it won't.

Context: the school

This is an all-boys school. Mary has the impression from her head of department that Media Education should occupy very little of the English curriculum, 'just a few lessons', accompanied by appropriate revision close to the examination. However, she notes that it has recently been written into the departmental policy that there should be a little Media at Key Stage 3 – awareness of it seems to be demanded by the Key Stage 3 tests. In general, the Media teaching is examination-driven.

The teacher who is second-in-department is currently writing the Media element of the department's curriculum document: 'We sat down... a whole department meeting, sat down and discussed the content for each year group and that's just being revised at the moment.' In year 7, for example, the emphasis will be on words related to advertisements; later at Key Stage 3 the curriculum will incorporate some use of previous Key Stage 3 test material which is seen to have a significant media content.

There is no obvious source of media expertise on which Mary can draw – neither internally or externally: 'I wouldn't know where to start.' She is not, for example, aware of materials offered by Film Education. Any media resources Mary has are self-produced. There are no commonly available resources which are specifically for Media within the school. Elsewhere in the school, Mary suspects that some media study takes place within the 'peer training' programme as part of drugs education. This is run by the Science department. There is no particular school policy which addresses Media.

Context: INSET

During the years that Mary has been with the department there has been no significant Media Education INSET. The emphasis in Mary' own INSET has been on courses related to children with Special Educational Needs, partly because this is a special interest of Mary's, and partly because the department benefits from having someone who has such expertise.

Context: the syllabus

The SEG English syllabus is used; that is, it has currently been reintroduced. The department has changed syllabuses twice since Mary has been at the school. Originally the department chose SEG, then turned momentarily to MEG, but turned back to SEG. Though Media might have been part of the general discussion that informed such choices, Mary feels that the main criteria guiding syllabus choice would have been the 'prescribed texts'. She feels that there was in the department a perception that Media would not 'throw up any problems'. In reality, however, Mary feels the opposite has been true, 'because in our results the language grade has been depressed in contrast with the literature'. There is now a general feeling in the department that they have not put enough 'time and effort into studying media'.

The Media examination (MEG, sat in June 1998, but since abandoned) is based, thematically, on pre-release materials, but pupils are actually tested on unseen materials. Mary feels, however, that the department's focus for the examination was too much on the writing, on the ability to construct a 'tight argumentative essay'. Mary would prefer a focus on the 'analysis and... terms you are going to use'; her perceptions are supported by the weighting in the examination: 20 per cent on reading and 10 per cent on writing. In short, Mary feels that the GCSE examination does give Media a focus, but that, at present, that focus is not being interpreted appropriately.

MEG makes no particular distinction between non-fiction and media texts, describing them within one inclusive syllabus definition, and one inclusive, examination. Though the Board makes little distinction, Mary feels that there are 'natural boundaries'.

Mary was not at the school during its first OFSTED inspection, though she is fairly sure that no significant mention was made of Media Education.

THE LESSON: IMAGES OF MEN IN THE NEWS
Teacher: Mary

The class
This is a large class, 31 pupils and a top set in year 10. GCSE grades expected range between A and C. Mary describes the pupils as reluctant to speak, lacking in confidence, especially in Media.

Lesson aims
That this is a top set in an all-boys school is, for Mary significant. She was concerned about the image the boys in this class have of themselves in this male environment. In particular, this top set, Mary felt, needed to have a more positive image of themselves. Jokingly, she describes this as 'standing up for the wimp'. Mary feels that there is a problem with boys' image in the school in general: 'I think that the toughies get recognition and the very ordinary kid doesn't.' She wanted to connect the boys' images of themselves with the images of males in society and show that, 'these images are not coming from nowhere... they are created'. The boys 'needed to come to terms with that'. Mary wanted the class to 'provoke the idea that images of males in the media, the written media, are often inappropriate... can be violent, can be quite traditional in some ways as well'.

The general focus was on snippets from newspaper headlines extracted over the past three weeks. These extracts carry negative connotations of the male in society. Her specific focus was to invite pupils to consider 'alternative nouns', and also to focus on actual jobs that men do in order to provide an alternative, positive view of men. 'I think there's a very narrow focus of what is reported anyway, about men in particular... hopefully they'll see that.' She wanted pupils to become more familiar with the type of terminology she has introduced them to, namely, 'tone, expression, image'. Media terminology she sees as important so that the pupils can use it appropriately in the examination. In addition she feels such terminology can be a key to 'exploring all sorts of things... especially at college'.

While the emphasis in the lesson observed was on verbal texts, in the previous lesson the class had already looked at images of men in the visual media (three advertisements that Mary had herself recorded from television). One advertisement for a steam cleaner showed a man as 'a bit of a buffoon... wimpy and incompetent'. The second, more confusing, was for a computer game; the intended audience was unclear until the very end. The third was 'for Scots Porridge Oats... hilarious... a man in a kilt doing a Marilyn Monroe over an air-vent... a bit hunky and a bit muscular'. At the end of that lesson the boys had been asked to write one paragraph from 'an alien just tuned into terrestrial TV'. The task was, following the discussion of the advertisements, to 'describe what a man is'.

The written outcome of the lesson would be an article for a girls' magazine giving an alternative representation of males, using a writing 'scaffold' – see below. The whole task would last approximately another three lessons plus homework. Before the writing she envisaged a group presentation. 'If they speak they'll be much better placed to actually write it.'

Content: teacher approach and pupil response

The main focus of the study was a set of 'snippets' from newspaper headlines, all of which relate to men, and all of which in some way have negative or violent connotations.

Resources

The examples (photocopied in collage style on to an A3 sheet and distributed to each pupil) included:

RHODES BATTERS DELIA
STRAW'S ATTACK
RACISTS
THUGS FACE TOUGHER SENTENCING
PERSIAN TO PACK PUNCH
MoD CHILD PORN BEAST IS JAILED
HAVE THE POLICE GONE SOFT
HARD-RUNNER
DANGER MEN RELEASED AS PART OF PEACE PACT
BERGKAMP BACK BLOW

BUSMEN IN STRIKE OVER YOB ATTACKS
3 MONTHS FOR JURY SEX PEST
SLEAZY: MATT DILLON PLAYS THE RATHER UNSAVOURY
PRIVATE EYE

Also, pupils were given an A3 sheet to support the written outcome of this particular unit of work, a 'framework' for writing an 'Argumentative Article, Men in the Media (Humour)'. The framework included:

Title
Impact opening statement (list three negatives)
Current Stereotypes of Men (which?)
Which sources: magazines/newspapers TV/films
Alternative male roles to mention plus possible photos
Constructive advice – how men should be viewed
Conclusion – what lasting impression of men/boys will be presented?
Describe what a real male could be doing or saying at the present moment.'

Stage 1: identifying themes – negative imagery (20 minutes)
The teacher distributed the collage of headlines and outlined the task for pupils to complete in pairs: 'I want you to find anything that strikes you – that all these headlines of different kinds have in common.'

Group 1 (2 pairs)
This group soon identified a common theme: 'Top ones all to do with violence', quoting as evidence, 'verbal attack', 'batter'.

Group 2 (2 pairs)
This group also identified a common theme: 'it's all about kids getting murdered... it's all about sex.' Other suggestions included: 'All bad words... batters, attacks, racist.' One pupil tried to take the discussion in a different direction: 'I think it's where there's like a double meaning' – perhaps noting some of the puns in the headlines. They became curious about some of the stories which originally followed the headlines, 'What happened to Delia then?' (*Rhodes batters Delia*). Another pupil quickly noted that, as well as violence, 'it's all got men in it... it's got to be about men... it's all about men hurting people.' The group then 'tried out' most of the headlines to see to what degree each one fitted the theory about men and violence.

Stage 2: finding nouns with positive connotations (10 minutes)
The teacher brought the class back together to collect opinions. One pupil suggested 'violence'. That they were 'male-orientated' was also confirmed. One pupil wanted to clarify the nature of the violence and suggested 'abuse.' The teacher tried to draw from the pupils a personal as well as an analytical response, asking, 'Is there anything you find offensive?' 'Racists' was sug-

gested. The teacher then tried to narrow the selection of words and isolate nouns which identified men. Again pupils worked in groups.

Group 3

This group was tentative at first. The pupils were most confident about, 'hard-runner' and 'porn-beast', but one boy offered 'battered.' 'Attack' (as in *Straw's attack*) was offered but rejected because the others believed it to be a verb, suggesting that to be a noun it would need to be 'attackers.' The teacher arrived at this group just as they were grappling with 'danger men', unsure whether to note 'men' or 'danger men.' The teacher agreed with them that 'danger men' written as it was, produced a 'new' word.

The teacher framed the whole-class discussion that followed by reminding the class of the male 'focus or bias'. She suggested to them, 'These nouns – we need to explore what they are on their own because... I think you'll get a very different view of male representation through that.'

One pupil (in a different group from the one attended by the teacher) began by suggesting 'danger men'. The teacher again agreed that effectively, by using the two words in this way, a new noun had been formed. A similar clarification followed pupils' offering of '[child] porn beast', 'sex pest' and 'hard-runner'. Though the teacher had only specified nouns, virtually all the offerings in this section, in fact, included, 'compound' nouns, with, in typical newspaper fashion, a noun used as a premodifier in front of another noun. An exception was the hyphenated 'hard-runner'. The teacher asked the class for a personal response to the use of this type of word: 'Do you think this is a good thing or a bad thing?... is it a dangerous thing... is it a problem?' The teacher also suggested that words or names are sometimes (unfairly) associated with specific groups of people. 'There's an association here – not spoken but it's there.'

The teacher took a clear moral position: 'These representations are not good, but what can we do, what other names could we have to describe men?' That, in fact, was the pupils' next task: 'Find as many nouns, names, titles that you could use to label a man... alternative names.' As a starter the teacher offered 'husband', and reminded the class that the names needed to be 'positive or neutral.'

The pupils again moved into groups. One group, understanding the principle but uncertain about the grammar, suggested, 'intelligent, confident, powerful, commanding'. Another group, rather more confident grammatically, noted, 'king, father, businessman, gay, policeman'. The choice of 'gay' as a noun and as a positive image passed without comment. In a third group one pupil offered 'alcoholic', and a debate as to whether this carried positive or negative connotations ensued; that *alcoholic* could refer to male or female wasn't discussed. Another in the group suggested, 'I think we should put down *milkman*.'

After group discussion the teacher began another whole-class summary by calling for examples which were exclusively male. When 'granddad' and 'brother' were offered the teacher commented, 'They tend to be familial names so far.'

The teacher then moved on to ask for nouns which 'need not be exclusively male'. Suggestions included, 'politician', 'doctor', 'lover' and 'judge'. The teacher pointed out that these words were now describing 'the things they do... their jobs... instead of all the negative things'. Reinforcing the moral position established earlier the teacher suggested, 'Isn't that better?' Trying to put the issue in context, the teacher suggested that, when used in a sentence, a name could still be given negative connotations, as in '*Judge* caught punching girl'; but, she suggested, that was better than, for example, '*Monster* caught punching girl.' She also suggested that, by using words like 'thugs', we are 'dehumanising them [men]'.

Stage 3: *a framework for writing (20 minutes)*
The teacher issued the 'scaffolding' for the writing. The described aim was to show boys and men in a positive light, but in a humorous way, to show 'we're not monsters, we're not bullies, what we are is human... you're going to explain what a current stereotype of a man is, and you're going to link it to the work we did yesterday.' She encouraged the boys to think in terms of visual as well as verbal images: 'Think what photos you would put in – remember the angle of that girl we saw in the picture before.' The teacher spent some minutes reinforcing the point that the aim was to describe stereotypes, but then to offer better, more positive images instead. The work was to begin with the selection of a title for the piece of writing.

Picking up on the teacher's earlier hint that there was a need to show that not all men were 'men behaving badly', a number of boys wrote, as their title, 'Men behaving kindly' or 'Men behaving not so badly'. Looking for an opening statement containing three negative statements (as suggested in the scaffolding) one group used the headline extracts and chose, 'thugs, beasts, sex pests', another chose, 'sex, drugs, rock and roll.' Invited by the next element of the scaffolding to offer alternative 'male roles' one group suggested, 'child-care' (as an alternative to a 'hard' image), 'cooking' in order to counter notions of male incompetence in the home, and 'community service' to counter associations of abusiveness.

After group work, using the scaffolding, the teacher asked the class to share some of the headlines they had written, e.g. 'Men Behaving Nicely', 'The Truth About Men', 'Men Behaving Kindly', 'Men Behaving Not So Badly'.

The teacher focused next on the opening statement. One group offered, 'Is your man a sex crazy, bad-mannered, emotionally challenged guy?' With the lesson coming to an end, the teacher suggested that the task for the next lesson was to continue to challenge the 'many stereotypes for men'.

Media concepts and Media learning

Representation: this, very clearly, was the focus of the lesson. Not only was negative male representation the subject for the analysis, but seeking alternative, positive male representations was just as important. In addition, the focus of the lesson was, in the teacher's mind, specifically and directly related to the way in which this particular group of boys feels about male representation. The teacher sees the boys in this class as males who behave atypically for the community in which they are learning.

Language: this related very specifically to lexical choices made in headlines and to the range of nouns which describe males, in positive and negative ways. Though the examples analysed all came from headlines, the particular features of newspaper headlines (in terms of headline conventions) were not a focus of the lesson. The previous lesson with which this lesson connected had, of course, considered the connotations of the male (visual) image, focusing particularly on stereotypical roles.

Categories: newspapers were the chosen genre, and the teacher was keen to consider ways in which lexical selection in headlines influences reader's perceptions of male roles and male behaviour. Other features of the newspaper genre and other genres were not considered.

Agencies/Institutions: as implied by the teacher's attitude to *Institutions*, the particular agencies involved in creating the language of the headlines were not considered; the teacher was more concerned to look at the language *per se* than the context in which it was produced. The teacher's aim was to help the boys have a more positive image of themselves. In this situation, knowing the contexts in which negative images of males are produced was not particularly significant.

Audience: the emphasis was on the pupils as audience rather than considering the possible responses of other audiences. Pupils were invited to respond personally as readers.

Technologies: this concept was not addressed in the lesson.

Main characteristics of the lesson

To a degree, the aims of this lesson went beyond the prescribed curriculum. That is, the teacher sought to help boys connect self-image with published images of males in society. More specifically, she wanted the boys to understand that many traditional images of males are 'inappropriate'. The focus was on image in the sense of representation achieved through linguistic choices – the nouns by which men are known. Visual image had been addressed in a previous lesson.

For much of the lesson pupils worked in groups, exploring their own personal and collective responses to the linguistic ways in which men are represented. In this sense, a good deal of the responsibility for learning was handed over to the pupils. By contrast, when the teacher did intervene, she was likely to adopt a clear, sometimes moral position, and encourage the pupils to share that position.

The texts considered were print-based, confined to words and phrases extracted from headlines, and taken exclusively from newspapers. The extracts were photocopied and pasted in such a way that they were considered in isolation from the presentational context in which they first appeared. The teacher's concern involved the ideological connotations of masculinity through the lexical choices that we all make. Newspaper headlines provided the source of such choices but were not necessarily the focus.

The lesson was very strongly about *Representations* of masculinity. The *Media Language* addressed was exclusively that of lexis, allied to word class, in particular nouns and adjectives. These two concepts were the main organising principles of the lesson. *Institutional* issues such as whether a given headline was produced by tabloid or broadsheet were not significant. *Audience* became relevant in the practical activity which followed.

The practical activity centred on the production of a written text, an article for a girls' magazine which offered an alternative, positive representation of masculinity. The text was scaffolded by a frame provided by the teacher. No information or communication technologies featured in the lesson.

BRIAN
School   Coastal comprehensive

Teacher background
Brian has been teaching for 20 years and teaches mainly English. He also teaches on the GNVQ Advanced Leisure and Tourism course. This course contains much Media Education, focusing as it does on marketing and customer service; the course makes significant use of video resources as well as requiring Media analysis. Brian's work with GNVQ does have spin-offs within his English teaching, providing him with ideas and resources. He used to be head of English in his current school, but now occupies the role of senior teacher, with a timetable of 20 periods a week out of 40. Because of his experience and his limited timetable, much of Brian's teaching is related to examination preparation, either for GCSE or GNVQ. In addition, Brian is responsible for Personal and Social Education in the school which tackles issue like censorship and representations of gender.

In his previous school there was little development of Media Education, so Brian estimates his Media teaching experience to be about ten years, co-inciding with the time in his present post. Brian's arrival at the school as head of English coincided also with the introduction of the National Curriculum, leading him to review the departmental curriculum to take more account of Media Education, 'mainly – at the time because resources were fairly limited – to do with written material, newspapers more than anything.' Since that time, the interest (for Brian and the department) in Media Education has 'ebbed and flowed'. Brian recalls various 'fashions' in education, of which oral work was one example.

But, regardless of fashion, Brian's particular interest in English remains within Literature teaching: 'I'm particularly interested in Literature ... where my strengths lie... and I suppose upper school really.'

Teacher attitude to Media Education
As an example of particularly successful Media teaching Brian offers a unit of work involving a series of advertisements (taped by the technician). The advertisements were analysed to consider their 'messages... in terms of morals... lifestyles... sexual images'. Although he found the analysis fascinating he was careful to allow pupils a personal response: he had, in fact, begun with the 'face value' of the advertisements, i.e. the enjoyment that pupils found in them. Another feature of this successful project was the pupils' unfamiliarity with the three-year-old advertisements. This un-

familiarity, Brian feels, allowed some necessary distance between the pupils and the advertisements.

Brian points to his lack of specific training in Media and the consequence that he tends to look at it 'through Literature eyes... you're analysing something in the same way that you might analyse a poem.'

Aims, concepts, approach to teaching

Brian's long-term aim for his pupils is that they learn to look at things critically, 'to have an awareness of the ways in which they can be influenced by the media... that they're aware of the pressures brought to bear on them to behave in certain ways, to think in certain ways, to accept certain values.' As an example he quotes an interview he once saw with a representative of MTV, the music channel, who said of young people, 'We don't influence them, we own them.' He feels it would be optimistic to assume that young people can learn to resist such pressures but at least they might realise that 'such pressures are there'.

However, Brian also wishes pupils to learn some appreciation of the media, something of 'the craft of media... the construction of language.. the way things are put together... it's just an interesting area.' He believes that Media Education should help pupils to judge what represents quality in the media. An area of Media Education that Brian is likely to avoid is radio, which he feels to be less accessible than other media.

Brian feels that pupils respond to his teaching of Media as they do to his teaching of other areas of the curriculum: some respond positively, some don't. In each aspect of English what is more important to Brian is the teacher's own interest in and enthusiasm for the subject.

Brian speculates that key concepts in Media Education might be to do with *'form, bias, structure, language'*. He regards *image* as especially important because the visual can be so influential. Brian doesn't see *Representation* as a concept especially important to Media Education within English, other than in the sense that English is always inevitably concerned with 'how all sorts of things are represented'. However, Brian points out that the lesson to be observed does look at the way certain people are represented. He feels that *Institutions* as an issue is potentially interesting (for example in relation to bias or to tabloid and broadsheet ownership) but does not feel that the curriculum requires him to tackle it: it is 'not prescriptive'. He feels that, because of the teacher's own bias, the issue of Institutions can be problematic when it moves into political areas. He is more likely to deal with the idea that large corporations can have influence than to address any specific institutions.

Technologies, Brian says, don't figure significantly in his Media teaching within English, partly because access to computers is difficult. The school has five computer suites, three of which are equipped with PCs that are completely booked up. They once had individual computers in classrooms, but those have since been removed because they were thought to be ineffective. Although there is a requirement that in each of years 7, 8 and 9 pupils produce at least one piece of computer-generated work, in general, Brian feels, most of that type of work is done at home. Access to the Internet is available through one computer in the library, but mainly via the five computers allocated to the sixth form. The school has five much-used video cameras. Brian is more likely to use one of these in GNVQ or in his Literature teaching than within Media teaching. Desktop publishing does not feature as part of the English syllabus, but does feature as part of the IT syllabus. In any case, in practical media work, Brian feels that understanding of the process is more important than the quality of the work produced.

Brian sees Media Education surviving, because 'media is part of people's lives', though he feels, 'it might eventually be less related to the written word'. However, he sees some conflict currently between the way that teachers are so geared towards the written word and the examination syllabus ('You can't avoid that') and the media experiences that children have. This would include their experience of television and easier access to technologies like the Internet. He doesn't see any way in which the conflict is likely to be resolved.

Brian sees no significant difference in the approach of boys and girls to media and/or technology, 'not now... years ago it was very marked... boys were very dominant in their use of technology.' But the school has specifically addressed such issues. The school spent a lot of time looking at how it might have created, albeit unwittingly, a culture where technology is seen as mainly for boys. As one example, Brian recalls that a girls-only IT club was set up.

Context: the school

Brian estimates that in Year 10, Media work would take no more than 5 per cent of the English curriculum, because in Year 10 the focus is on getting through the Literature requirement. Also, in Year 10 the Media work takes place in an 'induction' unit. 'The first year we've done it like this... we've actually had a series of issues, topics and skills that we felt we needed to deal with before we get on to the main body of GCSE.' However, the pattern may vary with other teachers; one colleague, for example, makes use of an inconvenient single English lesson by making Media the focus of it, taking the Media proportion of that teacher's curriculum up to about 20 per cent. However, in Year 11 the amount of Media work builds up (possibly to around 30 per cent) as a consequence of preparing pupils for the examinations. All of the department will at some time this term address the induction unit (as described above) including the Media element of it.

The department maintains a folder of work representative of the National Curriculum, and Media work is part of that. There is flexibility in the lower school curriculum, but the Key Stage 4 curriculum is more constrained. 'It's obviously going to be just the written word ... the skills that they need are to do with the language, to do with summarising ... it's to do with the way things are presented, looking at headlines and pictures.. a very limited nature.' Though Brian describes Media Education as a small part of the whole curriculum, he points out that two other members of the department have a particular interest in it, and there has been a departmental working party looking into it. The working party is still in progress and has produced some resources.

The departmental syllabus is described in terms of topics that have to be done and skills that have to be covered. There are resources available for those things to be done, but there are no specific, common units of work. 'The way in which you deal with it is totally up to the teacher, which is very different from schools in this area'; Brian suggests that it is more common for other departments to follow a set pattern and prescribed units of work.

Outside the English curriculum, another course, 'a form of Media Studies... a sort of film studies', is offered through the option system and run by the Drama department; however, not enough pupils selected it this year to make it viable. Though there is no specific whole-school policy on Media Education it is mentioned in a number of policies, 'to do with multi-cultural, multi-racial... looking at the way we present images of other cultures... gender as well.' Also, it exists within Personal and Social Education (looking at censorship).

There is no particular media 'expert' or expertise to draw on, though Brian believes that his head of department did address Media as part of her original degree, and there is one other (young) teacher who has a great enthusiasm for Media teaching, though no special training in it.

As one example of 'commercially' produced Media resources used by the department Brian cites *TV Friend or Foe?* which deals with issues and images on television – a BBC Schools Programme video tape. Other than that, ideas will appear in *Oxford Secondary English* which the department uses at Key Stages 3 and 4.

As far as Brian can recall, in their inspection almost four years ago, OFSTED made no specific reference to Media Education.

Context: INSET
During recent years there has been no Media Education INSET for anyone in the department. Brian has not been on any Media INSET in recent years other than one course which was not actually described as Media but turned out to have a significant Media element in it.

Context: the syllabus
The English syllabus chosen is MEG, the department having switched two years ago from London EDEXCEL. MEG is seen generally as a more straightforward syllabus – 'old style Lit Crit... straight down the line... easy to interpret questions and syllabus'. The MEG syllabus was discussed in relation to its Media approach and Media specimen papers. These were seen, like the rest of the syllabus, to be fairly straightforward. But Media was not a significant, discrete factor in the choice. The MEG Media examination will typically contain an article or series of articles based around a theme. The examination is related to pre-release materials, but the actual media texts on which pupils are examined are unseen.

The change of syllabus has had an impact on the perception of and approach to Media in the department. Prior to taking up the MEG syllabus, the curriculum was 'not so obviously media-based.' That is, the London syllabus was seen to be dealing more generally with non-fiction, rather than media specifically. However, it should be noted that the London syllabus to which Brian refers was part of the previous GCSE regime – where reading experiences were less specifically defined. Also, Brian points out, recent Key Stage 3 English tests have 'gone down that [Media] road.' This, he feels, has heightened awareness of media at Key Stage 3. In addition, he feels that pupils in recent years with this Key Stage 3 media experience are now more likely to come into year 10 already talking about issues like bias, or fact and opinion. Hence Media is now seen as more prominent than it was.

Any distinctions between the study of non-fiction and media texts in examination terms are of little significance in relation to the MEG English syllabus, for MEG produces a paper called 'media and non-fiction texts' and makes no distinction between them. The syllabus says that 'the texts [non fiction *and* media] will be chosen from a range including newspapers and magazines, advertising material, leaflets and handouts, letters, journals, biographies and travel literature'. It adds: 'Where layout, graphics and photographs are an intrinsic part of the text candidates will be expected to comment on them and their relationship to the written content.'

THE LESSON: PERSUASION IN THE NEWS IMAGES AND WORDS
Teacher: Brian

The class
The class consisted of 31 pupils in the top English set in year 10. Most of the pupils were girls; the eight boys sat together.

Lesson aims
The teacher first and foremost wanted the pupils to understand the power of (newspaper) language, to consider how particular words encourage a particular interpretation of an issue and of an image. The lesson focused on two articles from the *Daily Mail* and *Mail on Sunday* published in late August about Ibiza and the Vice-Consul's decision to resign because of the behaviour of British holidaymakers. The focus was on two images ('a rave... people having fun') and a 'raunchy' news photograph of Kylie Minogue. The question that the teacher wanted to pose to the class was whether or not the images were likely to be read positively or negatively. The emphasis was also on the ways in which the associated verbal text (headlines and the article itself) influenced how the image is read. In a broader context, as part of the year 10 induction programme, this lesson cued pupils into the sort of language study they would be asked to do in relation to the GCSE syllabus.

The outcome of the study would be the production of a summary of the main points of the analysis, followed by 'some sort of comparison between what's written in one article and what's written in another'. Finally, pupils would produce a particular form of persuasive, argumentative writing in which, for example, they might be called on to defend Ibiza as a holiday resort.

This particular lesson had no specific connection with previous lessons because it is the first lesson in this particular induction unit. It introduced pupils in year 10 to study of the media. Of course, there are more general connections with study of media texts in year 9, as described earlier.

Content and teacher approach; pupil response

The materials include two photocopies (one per pupil) of two images and four newspaper articles from the *Daily Mail* or *Mail on Sunday*. The articles included:

'Ashamed to be British' by Jason Lewis
'Tour firms defend 'animals' of Ibiza' – by Kathy Moran
'Playboys' Playground faces bankruptcy' from Ed Owen (an insert into the above article)
'How did the British turn Ibiza into the Gomorrah of the Med?' by Frank Barrett

Also considered was the strapline which acted as the caption for the image under discussion:

'OPERATORS SAY ISLAND IS FAMILY RESORT AFTER VICE-CONSUL'S ATTACK.'

The main image (the 'rave') featured a large number of young people in close proximity, obviously involved in some celebration. The Kylie Minogue image was less clear, but again appeared to involve young people in some sort of party/dance atmosphere.

The teacher was particularly interested in the *Mail*'s perspective on the rave incident. He feels that the *Mail* has 'clearly decided that it's up to them to make the tour operators pay... the tour operators are to blame.' Also interesting to the teacher were references to the resignation of the Vice-Consul which, the teacher suggests, 'has nothing to do with the article at all'. The teacher pointed out that there was implied criticism of the Vice-Consul's right to be critical of the morals of others when he himself was not 'whiter than white'. It was this reference to the Vice-Consul's divorce that the teacher felt to be irrelevant.

The lesson had three clear stages: consideration of the image; consideration of words to anchor the image; consideration of the whole text.

Stage 1: connotations of the image (15 minutes)

The teacher began by offering the pupils the two images which were the focus of the study, and inviting them in pairs to 'try to decide words that you would use to describe these pictures... descriptive words about what is going on... sort of atmosphere in the pictures... single descriptive words, rather than, **it's a party**.' (At this stage, the original verbal text was withheld from the pupils). After a minute or two in pairs the teacher clarified the focus: 'I want you... to try and decide not just what's happening... but the atmosphere... what those pictures are telling you.' From one pair-discussion, words noted on paper included 'party, not behaving well, wet, looks like it's raining'. In response to prompting from the teacher this pair added 'out of control... they're obviously clubbing'. They tried to clarify where the scene might be set, 'they're not out in the streets, they're in a night-club... they're young adults?' Pointing to the Kylie Minogue image they noted from her gestures, 'She's grinning.. dancing... put in brackets next to it, 'dirty dancing.'' Words and phrases offered by other pairs included 'loud music, crowded atmosphere, good atmosphere, getting on with each other, friends, celebrity, lively, joyful, entertaining, wet and wild, enjoyment, together, rain, hot, music, alcohol-induced'.

The teacher drew the class together to collect responses, concentrating the discussion on the first picture (the Ibiza rave). Going round the class and asking individuals produced, in addition to those suggestions above, 'exciting, proud, sweaty, atmospheric, wild, active, flirty, crazy, energetic, giddy, happy, loud, relaxed.'

Stage 2: headlines: selecting words to anchor the image (20 minutes)

The teacher then invited pupils to consider that the picture (the rave) was to be put into 'any old article' and try to think of a headline that 'sums up that picture'. In particular, the teacher invited them to consider whether the picture's impact was broadly positive ('supposed to make you think of good things') or negative ('supposed to make you think of bad things'). Again, after a moment or two the teacher felt the need to clarify the focus: 'What do I mean by a positive or negative picture? Somebody give me an example of what I mean.' One pupil, Alan, suggested teenage drug-taking as an example of negative. Gareth offered, as a positive interpretation, that it could be a picture of young people who had just passed their A levels. A girl offered the suggestion that the picture might be part of an advertisement trying to draw young people to a particular club. The teacher having clarified the focus, pupils then returned to the task.

After brief pair-discussion, pupils as individuals were invited to write a headline to accompany the first image. Exemplifying one of the difficulties of teaching about news, one pupil (very quietly) pointed out that she recognised the image and could connect it with the Ibiza story, but the general thrust of the lesson was unaffected.

After about three minutes, the teacher invited pupils to suggest some headlines. These included:

TEENAGER DIES AFTER DRUG-INDUCED COMA
PEOPLE PARTY HARD AS NEW CLUB OPENS
TEENAGER TRAGEDY OF THE KILLER TABLET
RECORD HIGH – STUDENTS GRADES FLY
MAD MAYHEM AS STUDENTS PASS 'A' LEVELS
YOUTHS YELL AS EXAM RESULT ARE IN
BOOZY PARTIES RUIN HOLIDAY DESTINATION
A LEVELS ON THE UP
CRAZY PARTY GANG GOERS CELEBRATE A LEVEL
SUCCESS
FLIRTY KIDS GO WILD AT CLUB
COOL CLUB OPENS WITH MAJOR FUNKY PARTY
NEW CLUB OPENS WITH WET AND WILD PARTY
WILD WET PARTY ENDS POP STARS WORLD TOUR
NEXT GENERATION GO WILD
SCHOOL LEAVERS OUT OF CONTROL
DRUG FREE FUN FOUND IN NEW CLUB
STUDENTS SWEAT IN WONDERFUL WET IBIZA
IBIZA RAVERS GO MAD

The last two, probably but not inevitably, were offered by pupils who recognised the original news story. The teacher extracted some language points from the examples offered. He commented variously on the use of *rhyme*, *alliteration* and *rhythm* in the headlines. He explored briefly the mixed message implied in the headline, 'MAD MAYHEM AS STUDENTS PASS A LEVELS', the first part having negative connotations and the second part positive connotations. Indeed his main concern in reflecting on the examples was to consider the degree to which the headlines contained positive or negative values. As another example, he explored one pupil's use of the word *flirty,* drawing from others suggestions that this implied, *over-friendly*, *in a sexual way*, and seductive. However, in both of these examples he deliberately avoided offering a 'right answer' to the interpretations.

The teacher pointed out that, despite the pupil references to it, the image contained no evidence of drugs. One girl suggested that the common association of such images with drugs was *stereotyping* of young people simply because they were having a good time.

Though the main discussion centred around the Ibiza image, the teacher did summarise responses to the other (Kylie Minogue) image. Some pupils identified Kylie Minogue.

The teacher now introduced the strapline or caption which had accompanied the image: 'OPERATORS SAY ISLAND IS FAMILY RESORT AFTER VICE-CONSUL'S ATTACK.' (From the cut-and-paste photocopy given to the pupils it was not possible to tell the exact relationship between these words, the image, and the article that had originally accompanied the Ibiza picture.) Copies of the article were distributed to each pupil. The teacher read out the strapline. (The headline for the article itself was, 'Tour firms defend 'animals' of Ibiza.' This headline was also available to the pupils on the sheet but was not the focus of the discussion.)

The teacher asked pupils in pairs to consider, 'What information do you get from that headline?' and then focused the pair discussion for a moment on the phrase 'Vice-Consul's attack'. One pupils suggested, 'some sort of criticism...'. The subsequent task was for the pupils to pick out what they thought were 'important words in that article... words that are deliberately there to cause an effect, in the same way that 'mayhem'... may have caused an effect on us'.

Stage 3: the article: selection of emotive, judgmental (and negative) vocabulary (25 minutes)

At this stage the teacher moved towards consideration of the article itself, distributing a photocopy to each group. The teacher altered the working pattern by forming groups of three or four pupils. One pupil in each group was required to read the article aloud to the group. The group then were to select from the article significant words or phrases that stood out.

The work of two groups is offered below as examples of responses:

Group 1

This group selected the following phrases to mark with a highlighter: *rushed, animals, young Britons, drug overdoses, crime, proud, these degenerates, out of control, oafishness, I'd like to gas the lot of them, unrivalled, fun-loving party atmosphere*. This group tended to select phrases without much accompanying discussion or disagreement. Interestingly, in this group the discussion moved slightly off-task as the pupils brought their own experience as consumers and readers of news to bear. For example, one girl offered the example of her own gran who had recently had a very successful holiday in Ibiza and had found no evidence of unruly behaviour from young people. That is, they reacted directly to the news story and its relationship with their own lives.

Group 2

This group responded differently: in selecting words they would sometimes clarify or justify their choice, or would offer support to another group member for having chosen an appropriate word. Sometimes the word or phrase would have positive or negative connotations; sometimes the justification for the choice of word would be clear, sometimes a half-formed understanding, and sometimes the word would be selected without comment as if the significance was apparent to everyone. This group immediately selected *defend* and accused as being significant. Other comments included:

> 'There is also an emphasis on young.'
> 'Behaving like animals is a good one.'
> 'I think one of the top five holiday resorts, that's like emphasising it.'
> 'Fun-loving... hit-back... accusation.'
> 'Hang on a minute, they said fifty-one as if it was old.'
> 'Deeply ashamed... of the drunken sexual excesses.'
> 'What does degenerate mean?' – one pupil sought clarification
> 'Out of control... and young people again.'
> 'I would like to gas them... that is like the whole thing.'
> 'Families... and older people, jet set resort.'
> 'Exclusive... dance capital... unrivalled dance-capital.. fun-loving, young women.'
> 'Claimed to have slept with 40... claimed is a good one.'
> 'Three months increasingly weary.... implied it's not just something that happened for about a month then they go away, do you know what I mean?'

> 'Other influences, who have pushed this party image... I think pushed is a good one.'
> 'Vibrant youth culture, very few complaints.'

At the end of their trawl through the text the teacher came to this particular group and tried to help them understand the significance of some of their choices. For example, recalling how words like *mayhem, animals*, and *attacks* can carry significant negative connotations, he suggested that their last choice 'very few complaints' was, by contrast, less significant, 'not got the same sort of depth to it as those others... not heavy words'. Though pupils offered some justification, the teacher, while acknowledging the logic of their selection, wanted to drive home the significance of particular emotive or judgmental words: 'You're right in terms of the facts... that's good, but in terms of the language, I don't think that's terribly strong.' He pointed out more 'successful' choices like *'accused, defend, deeply ashamed, sexual excesses* – these are very heavy aren't they?.. but there's a lot in there I think that aren't.' When the teacher left, this group (of girls) remained jealously possessive of most of their choices, 'I think we're right... it's a matter of opinion isn't it... he's quite obsessed with short words.'

After the discussion the teacher again drew the class together. Pursuing the notion of words or phrases which have particularly emotive or judgemental connotations, he asked the class to select from their lists six words or phrases which 'carried the most meaning... that cause you to react in a certain way'. He then gave the groups a few minutes to make their choice.

Group 2 (see above) made their choice:
'Deeply ashamed, degenerate – is that something like degrading?' 'Drunken sexual excesses.' When one pupil suggested 'genuine, fun-loving party atmosphere' she was contradicted by another pupil who suggested, 'No... because the article is really negative, like, and you're trying to pick up negative words.' Interestingly, although the group had earlier resisted the teacher's intervention, they had now clarified for themselves the specific nature of the task and come to an important understanding about the article.

The teacher brought the class together and invited one selection per group from the following Crit:

> animals
> I would like to gas the lot of them
> in pursuit of sun, sex and sangria [invited by the teacher to comment on this phrase one boy volunteered 'the power of three', bringing to bear discussion of rhetoric from a previous lesson.]
> out of control
> exclusive jet-set
> drunken sexual excesses
> oafishly
> degenerates
> dragging us through the mud

The teacher summarised the learning that had taken place during the lesson. He indicated that they had discussed negative and positive associations carried by the image but that, without the headlines that went with it, it was not really possible to tell whether the image was in fact positive or negative. He then reviewed the discussion of the headline, hinting that the references in it to 'family resort' deliberately contradicted what was actually in the picture... 'basically implying it's not true'. In reviewing the selection of words he drew from the class a suggestion that most words chosen were negative or critical.

In pointing to how this work would develop, the teacher suggested that they would next look at how 'the article was put together', to see what it had to say about 'Ibiza itself... about young people... or about the tour operators'. In this last comment he was beginning to move towards his expressed aim to help pupils to see the particular angle that the Mail had adopted (see aims). As yet, he was deliberately withholding this element from the pupils, tackling the analysis in a clear step-by-step process.

Media concepts and media learning

The teacher deliberately chose not to make clear at the beginning of this lesson (and series of lessons) the objectives of the study; withholding knowledge of the context of the image was an important strategy. As a consequence of this approach, learning about specific media concepts was often implicit rather than explicit.

> **Language**: this was very clearly the main focus of the lesson. In this context, language mainly refers to the lexical choices made by the journalist. Consideration of image was of course, also central. The emphasis here was on cultural codes and the connotations which they bring. That is, the discussion focused more on, say, body language, dress, setting, and facial expression than on light, camera angle, or perspective. Strongly implicit in the discussion of image was, of course, the notion of *anchorage*, that the meaning of the image does not become fixed until the reader is guided by the words associated with it. Though anchorage was a principle strongly implicit in the lesson, it was not referred to specifically or explicitly as a media concept.

> **Representation**: both in the consideration of the image and in the selection of lexical choices, *Representation* was at the heart of the lesson. In particular, there was much discussion of how young people were being represented and whether this representation was fair. Also, the subject of the article itself was, of course the (mis)representation of

the holiday resort by those who, according to the article, give a bad name to that resort. And, in the lessons to come, the teacher intended to consider specifically the way in which the newspaper itself chose to represent this particular story, i.e. the way in which the story of the perceived misbehaviour of the young people is to be represented as a story about the tour operators' *misrepresentation* of the holiday resort, Ibiza.

Agencies/Institutions: as with *Categories*, consideration of newspaper ownership and political or ideological slant were likely to feature in later discussion of how and why this particular newspaper or group of newspapers chose to represent this particular story. Also, in this lesson, no significance was attached to fact that the articles appeared in the *Mail* or the *Mail on Sunday*.

Categories: of course, the newspaper text was the focus for the lesson. However, in that the nature of the image and the text was gradually revealed to pupils, the ways in which this newspaper text connects with other newspaper texts, or other types of text was not a feature of the lesson. Also, the focus of this lesson was a lead story. Other materials which the teacher has collected, and which are to be studied later, include editorial and feature writing. In this way, some categories *within* the newspaper genre would be considered.

Audience: emphasis in the lesson was on the pupils as *Audience*; a personal response was sought. The teacher chose not to consider explicitly how the image or text might be perceived by audiences outside this particular classroom.

Technologies: this concept was not addressed in the lesson.

Main characteristics of the lesson

The teacher wanted pupils to understand the power of the visual and verbal language of newspapers. In particular, he wanted them to see how the meaning of a visual (newspaper) image is constrained by the verbal language which accompanies it.

This was a very structured, carefully staged lesson. Each stage had a very specific learning focus. Various textual elements were withheld from the pupils until the teacher felt that revealing those elements would have the greatest impact on learning. Thus, though pupils were allowed ample space and opportunity to develop their own interpretation of words and pictures, the teacher's control over the progress of the lesson and ultimate interpretation of the text was secure.

The texts included various extracts from newspapers, either in the form of image or of image plus verbal text. Context was important in a number of ways. For example, the ambiguous social context of one 'party-goers' photograph appeared to open up the possible range of interpretations of the image. Also, the presentational context of words in relation to image was seen to be significant. The particular newspaper or type of newspaper from which words and images were taken was less significant in the context of this lesson.

Media Language and *Representation* were at the heart of the lesson. The most significant element of Media Language was the notion of *anchorage*, the way in which words can constrain or influence the reading of the cultural codes (body language, clothes etc.) in a given image. In this way, pupils considered how holiday-makers in general and young holiday-makers in particular are represented.

Practical work, other than creating headlines to accompany the given image, was not a significant feature of this lesson. However, some form of persuasive writing was to be one outcome of this project. No information or media technologies were used in this lesson.

ROS

School: Girls' grammar school

Teacher background
Ros began teaching 20 years ago, in the school where she is now. Though now head of English, she was originally head of Careers, teaching English alongside it. Careers, she feels, gave her a particular experience of media: 'I was there at the time they were changing from the written word to using computers... I went on the local radio as head of Careers a couple of times giving advice.' Four to five years ago she was appointed head of English. In addition, Ros had taught a GCSE Communication Studies course to sixth-form pupils for about five years. This gave her a particular background in and outlook on the mass media. Also in the Communications course Ros tended to use video cameras and overhead projectors as aids to supporting oral presentations and the development of communication skills. The course stopped when a particular group of students (needing an extra GCSE) stopped attending the school. Her interest in Communications Studies is still with her, but she sees a conflict between this interest and the new curriculum constraints of Media within English: 'I get very interested in newspapers. it's something the kids enjoy doing, but it's a question of how much time you can spend on it in the curriculum mainstream.'

Ros has been teaching Media within English 'in one form or another' for most of that 20 years. Her early memories of it include use of film and projectors. She first recalls Media 'as a separate title' or 'a separate strand' when it became part of the GCSE syllabuses linked to the National Curriculum. She enjoys doing the Media element of the course, having gained confidence from her Communication Studies experience, though she has some concern about the particular expectations of the Media element in the current EDEXCEL GCSE syllabus.

Teacher attitude to Media Education

Her particular focus on teaching about media is 'upon the words' – but not always the written word. For example, one unit of work currently used in year 9 is taken from the English and Media Centre's *Advertising Pack* (Grahame, 1993). With her colleagues, Ros strives to keep the Media course wider than the requirements of their MEG syllabus: 'We wanted to teach mass media as mass media, looking at TV, video... even though in the exam room we're not going to get a video.' Her most successful lessons would typically include pupils in 'group or pair work, learning new concepts and producing something for themselves.'

Aims, concepts, approach to teaching

In the long term, Ros wishes that pupils become 'alert and understanding when looking at the media... that they are not fooled... that they question things and understand what's going on... people can accept what they see as truth because it's in print or on TV; I want them to be aware, to think about it... I want people to be questioning, to be selective in something like TV which seems to dominate so many lives.' She believes that Media Education should help pupils to judge what represents quality in the media.

The pupils, she feels, because of the high profile of the media see the study of it as enjoyable... 'they like making up their own adverts.' She suspects that pupils see the analysis element of Media Education as 'more like hard work' compared to the 'playing around' of production.

Despite her background in Communication Studies, *Purpose* would now be the most important concept for Ros. The BFI 'Signpost Questions' were not influential in determining Ros's view of Media Education; she was not particularly aware of them. For Ros, *Audience* and *Purpose* are more important concepts, notions that are in tune with the syllabus view of media. (The EDEXCEL GCSE English syllabus advises teachers that 'candidates should be encouraged to read media texts in the light of the following statement: Media texts are constructed *by writers, for particular readers, for particular purposes.*')

The concept of *Institutions* also currently plays little part in Ros's English teaching, although it used to be a prominent concept when she was doing Communication Studies. Also, her careers experience led her to deal in a practical way with a range of organisations. However, she feels that she might even have steered away from *Institutions* as an issue, afraid of bringing too much of Communication Studies into English teaching. Also, she feels that that kind of focus is more likely to crop up at sixth-form level in the English (language and literature) syllabus which the department runs. She sees little scope or encouragement within the GCSE English syllabus for dealing with issues of *Institution*. In general, she feels that the teacher of Media within English should pay more attention to language and text, and less attention to media institutions. There are no particular concepts or topics which Ros tries to avoid, though she is conscious of having to cut down on things like TV and radio advertising because they are unlikely to appear in the present syllabus.

Because of Ros's past experience in Communication Studies and in Careers, she is happy with the use of technology, though in a production rather than an analytical sense. Word processing figures significantly in the English curriculum (Ros herself is a user). Ros's colleagues are likely to take pupils into the computer room, though she herself has less confidence in using information technology in relation to English teaching. Word processing within English is seen as a curriculum opportunity rather than a requirement. That is, teachers may opt to use it but are not obliged to by the syllabus. Similarly, the video camera is seen as an effective tool, more likely to be used as part of an oral presentation than specifically within the context of Media Education ('unlike Communication Studies where I would get them all making a film.') Elsewhere in the curriculum all pupils do a short course in IT though Ros is unsure of the course content. Pupils do use computers to retrieve information (eg. for Shakespeare) but not specifically for media and they do not specifically consider the issue of information retrieval. The school has access to the Internet but it has not yet figured in the English curriculum.

Ros feels that her Media teaching influences her approach to English. She describes it as an overlap – 'analysis and enjoyment of the visual and the verbal.' Ros is optimistic about the future of Media Education though she does not necessarily see its future within English. She does, however feel that the issues connected with the Media are too important to be squeezed out altogether from the curriculum.

Given that this is a single-sex school, Ros feels unable to comment on girls' response to technology in particular or to media in general. That is, she has no experience of teaching boys and, therefore, has nothing with which to compare the response of girls. In the recent GCSE examinations (June 1998) the girls did better in Literature than they did in Media, partly, Ros feels, because the teachers themselves are probably more confident in their Literature teaching.

Context: the school

The year 10 syllabus is currently being redesigned; the Media content is scheduled as approximately 15 hours in year 10 and 12 hours in year 11. But Ros sees this as a minimal description since she feels that Media has significant overlaps with other areas. For example, there are connections with mainstream English in the work on persuasive language and on the non-fiction element of the syllabus, and 'much of the poetry terminology comes into Media as well'. The department has worked more collaboratively in recent years and the syllabus, ('something we reached by common consensus') as well as the Media element within it, has been accepted by all departmental members. Consequently, although there are no rigorous checks on how individual teachers follow the syllabus, Ros is confident that similar things are done, within a similar timescale – 'Co-operative ownership rather than me imposing it'. In general, because of constraints on time, the Media Education at Key Stage 3 is broader than the department can offer at Key Stage 4, influenced significantly as it is by the GCSE examinations.

The department syllabus describes Media provision in each year in terms of core provision. For example, for year 10 it describes *core resources; core assignments* ('analysis of a leaflet; produce a leaflet – one subject [but for] two audiences; compare and contrast the same story in different newspapers'); and Speaking and Listening ('persuasive speech; formal debate; analysis of TV advertisement; role-play – advertising agency to a company, balloon debate').

There is no specific Media taught in the school outside English, but Ros recognises that, since the advent of the National Curriculum, activities such as designing advertisements and writing newspaper reports are done quite widely. In the early days Ros did expect some adverse reaction from children because of repetition of these media activities, but she has not found that to be the case. Her most recent experience of cross-curricular media is when an outside agency visited in connection with TEC. The agency led a careers lesson and invited pupils to create a TV advertisement and present it to the class (Ros sat in on the lesson).

The most likely outside agency to supply support in media is the Examination Board, who offered an INSET day in media related to the new syllabus. Ros still receives media material from Film Education, though this is largely a hangover from the Communication Studies era; the Film Education material is not much used now, unless it relates to a novel which is part of the English syllabus.

Within the English department there are two or three teachers with a particular enthusiasm for Media, but no particular expertise.

One of the commercially produced resources used by the department is *The Advertising Pack* (Grahame, 1993) produced by The English and Media Centre. This is currently used in year 9, though the department is considering it as a possible year 10 resource. Key Stage 3 pupils also use media resources within general English course books (Collins). Teachers also make use of Susan Davies' book *Argument and Persuasion*.

The OFSTED inspection made no reference to Media Education – praise for the oral work stood out more than anything else in the report.

Context: INSET
Apart from the GCSE Board's one-day support offered in relation to the new Media syllabus, there has been no recent Media INSET for Ros or her department. However, much INSET time within the school has been devoted to the development of the new GCSE syllabus, of which the Media element is a significant part. Any INSET, consequently, has been generated entirely within the department, and has come from the shared experiences and enthusiasms of department members as they sought to establish a curriculum to meet the demands of the new GCSE.

Context: the syllabus
The department choice of syllabus was London (EDEXCEL). This Board is very specific about its attitude to Media Education in English. For example, it makes clear that the syllabus will not 'presuppose knowledge of a specialist Media Studies vocabulary, although candidates will be expected to understand certain media terms which are in general use'. It goes on to offer a glossary of such terms. They include:

NEWSPAPERS: tabloid, broadsheet, national daily, Sunday, regional daily, local evening

MEDIA TERMS: editorial/leader, news articles, feature articles, headline, caption, subheading

ADVERTISEMENTS: small ads, display ads, billboards, posters, mailshots, leaflets

MAGAZINES: general readership, specialist readership.

The EDEXCEL syllabus also makes clear that there are limited expectations in relation to production: 'Candidates are advised to use their time in the examination wisely, focusing on the written content of their answers not the layout and design.' But some significance is accorded to layout and design in relation to the analysis of texts: 'Candidates... may be expected to comment on the ways in which communicative effectiveness may be enhanced by particular features of layout and design.'

Media Education and Diverse Cultures were two particular areas of concern when the department chose its new GCSE syllabus two years ago. The department thoroughly evaluated all syllabuses before it came to its decision. In general, it was felt more important to have Diverse Cultures in the coursework, allowing the department more freedom of choice; this left Media in the examination. However, the choice was not unanimous, with two teachers favouring Media in coursework as offered by NEAB. The EDEXCEL syllabus seemed to the department to be effectively structured without being dogmatic. Also, Ros resisted the NEAB free anthology, the main selling point of NEAB's syllabus: it was felt to be inappropriate for the pupils in this school who needed expanded wider reading.

The new syllabus has had the effect of worrying the teachers about whether or not they are tackling Media appropriately. Initially, they had difficulty applying the marking scheme in the specimen papers offered by the Board – an assessment issue. However, the overall impact has been to increase the amount of Media being tackled. 'It's a high priority because it's a whole exam paper.' (EDEXCEL's other terminal examination in English requires response to the non-fiction and poetry material in its pre-release anthology.)

One significant difference for Ros between non-fiction and media relates to assessment methods: with EDEXCEL, non-fiction is assessed on the basis of an anthology of pre-released material (a mixture of diaries, newspaper extracts, autobiographies); Media is assessed via an unseen text in the examination. But Ros feels that the techniques of analysis are essentially the same. The non-fiction teaching is an area which Ros considers weaker, requiring the building up of resources which the school currently lacks (e.g. collections of letters, diary extracts). Also questions on the non-fiction are, says Ros, 'very imaginative... Zlata's diary... very much 'imagine yourself and how would you feel?'... so the response requested from the pupils is different on non-fiction... When we teach non-fiction we teach them how to write in different formats – diaries, letters,... whereas with the media our focus is upon analysing the techniques used and producing examples of media.' Ros's interpretation of the EDEXCEL syllabus sees non-fiction broadly as a writing issue and Media broadly as a reading issue.

THE LESSON: WHAT IS MEDIA?:
AN INTRODUCTORY LESSON
Teacher: Ros

The class
A year 10 mixed ability group of 22 girls within the context of a girls' grammar school. The class has, until today's lesson, being working on an autobiographical theme as part of the teacher's objective to get to know this (new) class better.

Lesson aims
Ros aimed to introduce Media in a number of different ways. She wanted the pupils to:

- understand how the word *media* is used 'what the media are... examples of different forms of media'

- understand some basic concepts, 'begin to use concepts like *Audience*... getting a *message* across... what sort of message, the fact that there can be an underlying one'

- consider advertising within media, 'how adverts work.'

She expected this early look at Media to be quite superficial but the lesson (one that Ros has used successfully in the past) would end with the production and annotation of a very brief advertisement.

The aims were, inevitably, not specifically linked to previous learning in year 10 – this was a 'new' class recently engaged in an autobiographical theme. However, the department syllabus ensures that pupils have studied newspaper photographs and news headlines earlier in the school. In year 9 the emphasis will have been on TV advertising. Ros has long-term aims for this class which relate to the understanding of emotive language, for example in the news. But, despite the emphasis on language, there was still a sociological/communication studies element to Ros's Media aims for her year 10 class. She would, at some time, get the pupils to 'watch different version of the news and do comparisons of running order of the news on TV getting them to talk about news values'.

The work from this lesson would develop in the future specifically in relation to advertisements, with pupils bringing in advertisements and constructing examples of their own.

Content and teacher approach

This lesson had, as the aims above suggest, three main elements. The first involved discussion, albeit at a fairly superficial level, of those things which make up the media. Then the lesson narrowed to focus on some elements of advertising, including where advertisements might be seen, and significant features which might make them successful (see resources below). The third element involved pupils, mainly in pairs, producing very quickly a draft of a light-hearted advertisement in which they try to 'sell' English lessons. The focus in this activity was on the verbal language used; the intention, after the lesson, was for the pupils to return to their advertisements (written on A3 sheets) and note their persuasive langauge features.

There were two main resources used, both A4 sheets. The first, entitled *Why Do Advertisements Work?* looked, with cartoons and headline messages, at some of the communication principles which inform advertising. These included:

Use of language (supported by a cartoon which reads 'We have cheap dresses for fat old ladies' as an unlikely alternative to 'We specialise in inexpensive dresses for the mature fuller figure').

Exploitation of Weakness including:

- avarice – products that are sold as bargains or with free gifts
- gluttony – advertisements that appeal to your greed for food or drink
- envy – advertisements that suggest you need a product to make you happy
- pride – the advertisements dwell on how exclusive and superior the product is

- sloth – advertisements that offer ease, comfort and plenty of leisure time

- sex appeal – ... but often the pretty girl or handsome boy has little or nothing to do with the product

Exploitation of people's fears including:

- personal success – a lot of advertisements promise success in love, in friendship, in business

- conformity – many people hate to be different and gain pleasure from being the same

- security – advertisements of this kind offer a cosy, safe life, secure from disasters. Advertisers for insurance tend to push this aspect

- identification – advertisers may use a well-known figure in their advertisements

- respect – scientists, doctors, nurses etc. may be used... to give a product credibility

- maternal/paternal love – suggest that the mother/father who really cares for their child buys this product

- health – these advertisements often show before and after pictures. They create a fear of an illness and then offer a cure.

Appeal to humour

Double Meaning

The other resource focused on rhetorical devices (to be related to the verbal language in advertising) which 'write or speak powerfully or persuasively'. They included the naming of the device in italics, followed by a single sentence or phrase defining that device; the devices listed were: *rhetorical questions, addressing people directly, repetition, antithesis, alliteration, slogans, comparisons, bribes or threats, emotive vocabulary, deliberate exaggeration, assertion of opinion.*

Stage 1: *(20 minutes)*

Ros began by explaining how, according to the pupils' curriculum chart, Media appears twice, once in year 10 and once in year 11. She suggested that they would be dealing with *rhetoric* and the concepts of persuasive writing as used in advertising, linked to oral work in speeches. ('You keep coming back to persuasive language.') She also alerted pupils to the end point of the course, the time when Media would feature as 50 per cent of the written examination in English that the pupils would encounter, 'which is why we are giving it quite a bit of focus'.

The teacher began by making explicit what pupils already know about media. Apart from television as one mass communication medium, pupils offered, as others: non-fiction books, newspaper, radio, Internet, magazines, leaflets, posters, and word of mouth. Of these, non-fiction books and word of mouth needed some clarification since they did not obviously fit in with the commercial mass media which the teacher wanted to focus on: 'You're focusing on media there as equalling information, facts, yes?' She also explained how a medium was 'a way of getting a message across', and 'word of mouth is the medium for gossip or rumour'. To the above list, in order to prepare for the second stage of the lesson, the teacher added advertisements. She also clarified the grammar of the word – 'medium singular and media plural'. Pupils jotted down the list of media into their files and added to it others that they could think of.

As part of the context setting, the teacher underlined a number of features of mass media, the first being their scale: 'Usually when you're talking about media you're talking on a mass level.' In her explanation she included notions of *message, sender* and *receiver*. She then briefly elaborated on this communications model: 'You're all used to communicating with each other... by look, by glance, by gesture... On a simple level you can talk about a TV station sending out an episode of *EastEnders* with you being the receivers in your sitting room.' In preparation for the work on advertising the teacher chose to distinguish between main media messages and 'underlying messages'. Staying with *EastEnders* as her example of a message sent, she developed the notion of underlying messages in terms of *moral issues* such as conflict in relationships and AIDS.

The teacher pointed out (by reference to the availability of viewing figures in the *Radio Times*) that with so many watching a programme such as *EastEnders*, '*eventually* it's going to rub off on some of them – the attitudes the ideas, they're all going to be exposed to the same message.' But she did not imply passive reception on the part of the audience: ('They may not agree with the message.') Ros did not pursue with the girls what that particular message might be.

Stage 2: (20 minutes)
The teacher asked the pupils to write down where they had seen or heard any advertisements during the course of the day. After about three minutes

the teacher listed pupils' suggestions on the board, clarifying, for example, the impact of school uniform on the capacity of clothes to carry 'advertisements'. The teacher also introduced the notion of the logo, 'a symbol or a name that triggers memories of that company'. To make the category as inclusive as possible the teacher encouraged pupils to think of Radio 4 as *advertising* programmes which are later to be broadcast. She also cited advertisements for local companies on local radio. The teacher was keen to get pupils to see themselves as the audience for advertisements. She pointed out to the pupils, 'You've already been exposed to a large number of advertisements since you woke up.. be aware that they form part of your day without your even realising it.'

The teacher then moved on to advertising costs, exploring at a very general level with pupils the length of a given advertisement and its cost implications: 'They're incredibly expensive...'. She then continued the theme of pupils as audience; the purpose of introducing cost as an issue was to indicate to the pupils that advertisement do work: 'You've got to realise that they only pay those costs if they know that it's worthwhile.' In this wide-ranging overview, the teacher pointed out that some advertisements are intended not to sell a product, but 'to boost the public image of a company... so you think well of them'. Pupils were then asked to jot down specific advertisements that they could remember.

Narrowing the focus still further, the teacher invited pupils to consider, in relation to those advertisements recalled to mind, 'What is it about them that makes you remember them?... how are they actually setting out to make an impact?' Again Ros reminded pupils that advertisements are effective, that they do work. In discussing types of technique, the teacher encouraged pupils to recall similar work lower down the school. She listed on the board pupils' suggestions and then moved from whole-class to pair work to continue these suggestions. When food advertising was suggested by a pupil, the teacher pointed out the importance of colour and lighting to make food attractive. This process of whole-class discussion plus very brief pair work characterised this part of the lesson. At this point the teacher distributed the resources. She offered them as summary or confirmation of ideas already raised; she suggested they would 'add to the good ideas' about advertising techniques which pupils had already listed.

The teacher elaborated on the 'seven (deadly) sins' origin of the *Exploitation of weakness* section of the first resource. She gave examples of each and asked pupils to imagine an advertisement using each form of exploitation, e.g. 'Envy – there used to be a lot of advertisements around cosmetics and deodorants for example suggesting you need that product to be very successful.' Next, the teacher addressed the other elements from one of the A4 sheets, of *exploitation* of *people's fears*. In order to illustrate a particular verbal technique (the use of 'ambiguity' – referred to in the resources as *double meaning*), the teacher pointed to a classroom poster already on the wall. The poster appealed for donations to a charity, and highlighted *I can* – being a pun on *one can*, the suggestion for the donation. One other advertising technique very briefly discussed was described as *before and after*.

The teacher then moved on to exemplify briefly two of the features of the second resource, concentrating more on verbal techniques related to *persuasion*. The examples referred to were *rhetorical questions* and *catch phrases*.

Stage 3: (10 minutes)
For the last 10 minutes of the lesson, pupils were invited, as individuals or pairs, to create a draft advertisement that would effectively 'sell' English lessons. The focus was entirely on verbal language: 'You've got to come up with the sort of language that advertisers use...'

The lesson ended with the A3 sheets containing the advertisement pinned up on the board – allowing for annotation and discussion in future lessons, though there was no time to do more than glance at them in this lesson.

Pupil response
Pupils were initially tentative in responding to the teacher's exploration of their media knowledge, but began to suggest examples of media, some of which did not easily fit the mass media commercial model under discussion (one suggested 'non-fiction books' and another 'word of mouth').

When invited to consider the notion of sub-text they were quick to see what might be meant by 'underlying issues', one pupil suggesting 'moral issues', though no specific issues were exemplified.

Pupils were most enthusiastic and animated in relation to the messages in *soaps* (particularly *EastEnders*) and advertisements. In each case a hum of excitement developed as these pupils recalled and recounted to each other their favourite and most prominent television experiences.

The pupils helped the teacher to build up a list of places where one might expect to find advertisements, suggesting bus shelters, side of bus, in assembly, school bags, on clothes, trainers, shop windows, billboards, the radio, notice boards. As suggestions for typical features or techniques of advertisements, pupils offered good-looking people, slogans, using a celebrity and jingles.

When the pupils were asked to create an advertisement, most worked with extraordinary speed to produce a slogan-based advertisement in a very short space of time. Some pupils needed reassurance from the teacher that they were not meant to treat this task with much seriousness, and that they were allowed, in this context, to satirise English lessons, and, indeed to parody advertisements ('free homework with every lesson'). The teacher felt that the still new relationship between teacher and pupils made some pupils doubtful as to the teacher's expectations.

Though the focus on media and advertising techniques had necessarily been broad, this able group showed their ability to produce, almost instinctively, the sort of advertising sloganising which the teacher had in mind. Examples taken from the pupils' A3 sheets included:

stimulate your mind
if you have trouble sleeping...
new understanding and insight
exotic and interesting
professionally taught
express your feelings
if you're not excited now – check for a pulse.

One cynic, possibly speaking for adolescent cynics everywhere, suggested 'an hour a day to learn what you already know'.

Media concepts and Media learning

In one sense, the emphasis in relation to Media was narrowly focused, very specifically addressing verbal language features associated with persuasion. But this rhetorical perspective was situated within a very broad overview of what Media is and what media are. In this sense, albeit superficially, the Media learning dealt with:

Agencies/Institutions: this included a simple communication model outlining who is communicating with whom. It introduced ideas of senders and receivers of messages, with a strong emphasis on the human weaknesses which senders of messages manipulate in order to encourage receivers to accept a given interpretation.

Audience: this element included consideration of the effectiveness of advertisements. The teacher persuaded the pupils that advertisements do work and do have effects.

Categories: in discussing where pupils had seen advertisements they were, implicitly, considering the different *forms* (e.g. notice-board leaflet, clothes label) that media texts can take.

Languages: this element dealt largely with the list of rhetorical devices and pupils' own experiments in rhetoric.

Representation: this was addressed through the final task, albeit with a light, humorous touch, where pupils needed to *represent* English lessons in such a way as to make them appealing.

Technologies: this concept was not addressed in the lesson.

Given the aims of the lesson, and the syllabus context, the annotation of the advertisements might, in future lessons, be more likely to lead inwards towards verbal rhetoric than out towards broader media concepts.

Within this broad Communication Studies context, and within this single lesson, the media concepts described above were implicitly rather than explicitly addressed.

Main characteristics of the lesson
The teacher was mainly concerned to offer pupils a very broad overview of some (mass) media-related issues with particular reference to advertising. Essentially, the approach derived from a Communication Studies model with which the teacher was familiar. There was an emphasis on what advertisers do to consumers: 'exploitation' was the organising feature of the supporting materials used.

There were opportunities within the lesson for pupils to work independently or collaboratively, but the emphasis was on guiding them towards a common understanding of general principles and specific rhetorical devices.

The emphasis was on context rather than text. That is, most textual references, drawn on to exemplify approaches to advertising, came typically from pupils' recall. No specific media text was considered.

Given the breadth of this (introductory) lesson, it is not surprising that virtually all Media concepts were touched on either explicitly (as in *Media Language*), or implicitly (as in *Media Audience*). Also implicit, in the focus on exploitation of consumers, was the notion of *Agencies* (used in the narrower sense of the term, i.e. advertising agencies). In particular, copywriters, though not named as such, were seen as the agents who produced the exploitative messages.

Practical work was an essential ingredient of the lesson. The preparatory discussion offered access to general principles of exploitation and rhetoric, though it is possible that pupils drew as much on their own prior awareness of media slogans. The choice of product to be advertised suggests that, as implied by the teacher, the emphasis in this lesson was on creativity and fun rather than authenticity. No information or communication technologies were used in the practical work.

Group 3

Claire	Semi-rural Comprehensive
Chris	Comprehensive school
Heather	Urban girls' school

The first two lessons dealt specifically with film. Claire, a film enthusiast from her University days, took the pupils through an intense analysis of John Ford's 'classic' Western *The Searchers*. The emphasis was on the director as author (*auteur*), creative force behind the narrative. Chris is also a film enthusiast. His lesson dealt with four approaches to screening Shakespeare. His emphasis was on the way in which Shakespeare is mediated via film and film posters to attract a new and younger audience. Heather, a Media Studies curriculum organiser, used the media representational device, the storyboard, to support her pupils in their analysis of a poem. Media and literature are connected by notions of image, metaphorical and visual.

CLAIRE
School   Semi-rural comprehensive

Teacher background
Claire is in her sixth year of teaching. She gained a B.Ed. Honours degree at Cambridge, but recalls no Media element as part of that course, and in her first year of teaching there was no explicit Media in the English syllabus. Since then, however, she has accumulated a significant amount of Media experience. Claire teaches English up to A level. She is Key Stage 3 co-ordinator for English. In a previous school she also did one year's GCSE Media teaching, introducing and delivering the MEG syllabus. ('I learnt on the hoof, one stage ahead of the students.')

Her time in her current school has coincided with the official introduction of Media Education into the GCSE English syllabus. Given this 'authority' and her own developing confidence, Claire sees her teaching of Media as being part of a natural progression.

Film is something of a passion for Claire. In particular, she enjoys old B movies ('Hollywood as it used to be'). She used to be a member of the film society at Cambridge, with a particular interest in the Indian films of Bollywood.

Teacher attitude to Media Education

Claire asserts, 'As an English teacher first and foremost, I love my Literature... probably my overriding passion.' But Media teaching is also very important to Claire, and she does as much as she can. She suggests that curriculum constraints severely limit the time one can spend on it. In any case, she asserts, 'I wouldn't want to teach Media at the expense of English.'

She recalls one of her most successful lessons as a comparative study of two treatments of the creation scene from *Frankenstein* – one a Kenneth Branagh version and one a BBC version. Analysis included 'props, colour, lighting, facial expressions and body language as well as issues of morality, including good and evil, natural and unnatural birth'.

Claire feels that Media Education should help pupils to judge what represents quality in the media. This view is in keeping with her teaching approach to *The Searchers*, the focus of the lesson observed going beyond the stereotypes to understand the film's 'deeper, darker message'.

Aims, concepts, approach to teaching

Claire feels that her own attitudes to media and society do have an impact on her Media teaching. In particular, her 'interests and enthusiasms' influence the choices she makes in Media teaching. She tries to 'extend and broaden their [the pupils'] knowledge beyond their own world... to historical, social and political levels'. She believes that 'Media enriches the 'world picture' and widens the students' knowledge'.

In the long term she would like her pupils to 'develop an increasing awareness of the different types of media'. She would like them to realise when they encounter any media text that 'there are different layers of interpretation... the relationship to the reader, the writer, the text'. She also is concerned about 'the power of the media... social control, manipulation'. She feels that pupils respond well to Media work, but initially are too ready to expect clear answers to all questions: 'They like to be able to pigeon-hole things.' Claire feels that their usual (domestic) context for responding to the media means that 'they want all the answers given to them [so that they can] relax with what's happening on the screen'. She is concerned that they learn to understand that some questions can be left unanswered.

She sees some difference in girls' response to Media when compared to boys. Girls are, she feels, better at reflective work. She aims in her classes to sit a boy next to a girl where possible in order to encourage exchange of views across gender: 'Boys tend to be analytical, logical and concise... girls more reflective, descriptive, imaginative.'

Claire describes her approach to teaching in general (including teaching Media) as 'structured and very interactive'. She likes pupils to understand clearly the aims and objectives, the core elements of any essay, which means they can 'focus from the start on what they need to do and need to know... rather than going off at a tangent'. The unit of work in the lesson observed typifies Claire's approach.

Claire regrets that in her Media teaching pupils will not often have time to do much practical work. Any practical activities as such are likely to take the form of oral work arising out of media study. 'The nature of our course is such that we have to be very careful not to go over the time.. so you can't go off at too many tangents.' As a consequence, Claire's Media teaching tends to focus on the analytical.

Claire is familiar with the concepts described by BFI's 'Signpost Questions' and uses them readily with pupils in her study of film. She is comfortable with teaching *Institutions* as an issue, but spends little time on it: 'That's partly the difference between teaching Media as part of the English course and Media as a subject in itself.' She points out that shortage of time militates against teaching about *Institutions*, as does the fact that the grade-related assessment criteria do not reward understanding of institutional issues. Claire stresses that she would, when appropriate, address the impact of newspaper ownership on newspaper editorial policy, but not to any great degree – almost entirely because of limitations of time.

Technology does not feature very significantly within Claire's English teaching. Though she will use television and video, and the Internet will be used by individual students, she is unlikely to use video cameras or mixing equipment. Personally she is not confident in her own use of technology, 'because of lack of opportunities to develop the skills'.

Claire feels that studying film treatment of literary texts is one of the most effective forms of Media Education. Given her interest in film this is not, perhaps, surprising. Claire is clear about her view of the process that constitutes watching and responding to film: 'What I'm trying to make them think about is a special marriage between the reader, the writer and the text.' She regards text as encompassing the visual as well as the verbal. However, she recognises the complexities of such a relationship and acknowledges, for example, the collaboration which goes into producing a film. She is also conscious of the shifting nature of the audience for a text, pointing out to pupils that the original audience for *The Searchers* would have had very different responses to Westerns from those of contemporary audiences: 'The audience is from a different time, a time when they used to dislike automatically the Indians and perceived them as heathens, a time when cowboys were automatically seen as heroic.'

In addition, she wishes pupils to understand very specific notions about aspects of *Media Language*, including, *narrative, framing* and *shot*, but is anxious that pupils should not learn to name shots without understanding their 'meaning'.

Claire is very optimistic about the future of Media Education. To support her view she cites the 'growing knowledge and enthusiasm of the teachers', its place within the syllabus in coursework and (via non-fiction) in the examination, and 'the sheer range of resources available'. She is confident that Media is not one of those buzzwords that will pass over.

Context: the school

Media occupies one half-term within the two-year English course, though, for that time, virtually all lessons are devoted to the Media unit. The department works collaboratively, and they 'draw upon each other for ideas and resources'. Each teacher spends a similar length of time on a Media unit. The content of that unit, however, will vary with the teacher's personal choice. A number of advertisement-based themes are popular with some of Claire's colleagues, including the English and Media Centre's *Advertising Pack* (Grahame, 1993).

Media Education is strong within the school: GCSE courses, GCE A level courses, and GNVQ course in Media Studies are offered. Historically, however, these have been run by the Creative and Expressive Arts department, and any Media links with the English department tend to be on an informal basis. The Creative and Expressive Arts department does, however, offer to Claire and her colleagues within English a source of expertise or advice when needed. Such connections are made on an ad hoc and informal basis. But Claire does not have access to any external sources of Media expertise.

Claire says that the department (and, through Creative and Expressive Arts, the school) is very well resourced, 'one of the best that I've seen for a secondary English department'. They have most of the resources from the English and Media Centre as well as a good range of other commercial resources. In recent years the department has also produced a number of teaching units, including video resources. In addition, the technological facilities of the Media Studies courses (including an editing suite) are available to teachers within English. In practice, because of curriculum pressures of time, Claire and her English-teaching colleagues are unlikely to make use of such resources.

As far as Claire can recall, OFSTED made no significant mention of Media teaching within English.

Context: INSET

Claire has attended two particularly influential courses. One was a BFI course held at the Waterfront Media Centre at Bristol (concerning connections between Drama and Media) and another was held at the University of Southampton. The latter, Claire attended with some GNVQ students, and it was at this course that she became acquainted with the teaching materials related to John Ford's film, *The Searchers*, the focus of the lesson observed. Also, NEAB led some INSET on their new GCSE syllabus, including Media teaching.

Context: the syllabus

Two years ago, the department thoroughly reviewed all the new GCSE English syllabuses available to them and chose NEAB. The Board's treatment of Media was not the most significant factor in that choice; rather, NEAB was chosen because of the poetry and the literature content. However, NEAB was regarded favourably because it placed Media within coursework. Claire is clear about the impact of the syllabus on Media teaching within English: 'It's complemented and enhanced our teaching methods... and helped us to develop and progress... very positive and very encouraging... The department in general terms find it very exciting.'

Claire is quite clear about differences between the ways in which she defines media texts and non-fiction texts. (The NEAB offers Media in coursework, but non-fiction in a terminal examination.) For her, the difference is related to range: Media Education would 'entail a greater range of the medium ... advertising, film, TV, broadcasting whereas the non-fiction part of the examination is all about leaflets, pamphlets, magazine articles, layout, subheadings, language presentational devices... those kind of textual features.'

THE LESSON: ANALYSIS OF THE FILM WESTERN *THE SEARCHERS*
Teacher: Claire

The class
This is a large class, 32 pupils, with 2 absent. It is evenly balanced between boys and girls. The class is a broadly banded top set in year 10. Their predicted GCSE grades range from A to D, but most will gain above C.

Background to the lesson
The scheduled lesson (10 November 1998) turned out to be inappropriate for systematic observation because prior circumstances had meant that the teacher needed to use the time for (mainly uninterrupted) viewing of the film narrative. Consequently, evidence from the November lesson is used to provide background to the second lesson, which became the focus of the systematic observation.

The November Lesson
The teacher wanted pupils to realise that, in the film which is the focus of the study, the portrayal of the American West goes beyond stereotypes: in 'The Searchers, there is a deeper message, a darker message... we're looking really at the whole idea of what's called a modern myth.' The piece of written work which would be the outcome of this study would fulfil the requirements of one piece of NEAB English syllabus coursework, 'marked for Media and marked for Writing'. The class was working towards their essay title, 'How is the film *The Searchers* by John Ford unique for its genre?' Each week (over a period of four to five weeks) the pupils would study a different aspect of the film in detail. Those aspects included *framing, props, costume* and *dialogue and Technicolor.*

Viewing of the narrative was to be done largely without teacher intervention so that she did not excessively influence the pupils' first response to the film. This unit of work was this class's first experience of film study. Prior to this lesson, the class had watched a commentary on the film by John Ford and the actors – originally produced with the aim of publicising *The Searchers*. They had also considered the nature of *genre*, in particular, the Western. The teacher aimed to show the class that this film is 'not about stereotypes, but about something deeper'. As part of that discussion about stereotypes, the class discussed 'protagonists and antagonists, hero and heroine'.

The teacher tried to frame the viewing of the film so that, although intervention was to be very low key, the pupils were not 'just watching'. The questions framing the viewing were: 'What do we learn about the setting? What are our first impressions of the strengths and weaknesses of the two main characters? What do we learn about the storyline?'

The teacher began the viewing by focusing the attention of the class on the part of the film where they had last left off: 'The family have all been slaughtered.' She reminded pupils of the significance of certain visual clues, including 'Martha's blue dress'. She advised the pupils of the need to understand the 'horror and impact of what happened.' The class then viewed the film, taking notes as they did so. The pupils were encouraged to organise their notes under the main headings: *character, story line, location*. In addition, the teacher occasionally intervened, without disrupting the flow of the narrative, and suggested to the pupils:

> Ethan has knowledge of Indian culture...
> Note how the set is changing within the search...
> Why are they separating... who is the third one?
> Think about how the atmosphere is changing and why.
> The title is *The Searchers*. Who searches for what?
> Look at the time of year shown and changes in the season.

When the lesson closed the teacher encouraged pupils to organise their notes at home, and suggested that 'using Internet and Encarta', they find more information about John Ford and The Searchers. Pupils remained quietly attentive throughout the lesson, taking notes as suggested. Below is a selection of the comments made by some pupils in their notes; most of these comments appeared to help the pupil/viewer establish character and plot.

> It was a stereotype when the girls hysterically screamed
> Ethan wants to go off alone
> Rangers separated – Ethan can't stand authority
> Ethan started to get angry
> Ethan is now searching for love
> Colour – bright yellows/greens/blues/dark red
> Ethan wants to give orders

Marty is shy around women
Ethan has found something – Debbie's dress
Marty gives up relationship to go after Ethan

Lesson aims

In the second lesson on 8 December, and in this section of the unit of work, the teacher's aim was to develop within pupils an understanding of Ethan, the John Wayne character, as an example of 'The hero who does not fit.' Between the first and second lessons, pupils had covered, in considerable detail the significance of the title; the portrayal of the settlers; the portrayal of the army; and the issue of racism.

To support the pupils in their understanding of their progress through the unit, the teacher issued to each pupil a photocopy of a closely written summary, taking in all of the main points. As an introduction to the lesson the teacher reviewed some of the main elements of that summary. Under 'the significance of the title', pupils were asked to consider:

- How is the theme of the hunter and the hunted shown?

- How is the film like the quest for the holy grail?

- How can this be described as a story of revenge?

Under 'racism', pupils were asked to analyse the scene very carefully, thinking about dialogue, camera shots... and consider, 'How has Martin's lack of kin and his ethnic background become a motif for mockery throughout the film?'

In relation to the focus on the film's hero, pupils were reminded, 'to use and analyse... specific aspects of the film... close-up shots, long shots, framing, colour, sounds, props etc.'

Content, teacher approach and pupil response

Stage 1: *Review of progress to date (10 minutes)*

Referring to the essay check list/prompt sheet, the teacher reviewed progress in the unit to date. Introducing the theme of this lesson, 'The hero who does not fit', the teacher stressed that this element of the essay on *The Searchers* was likely to be a significant criterion in determining who achieved an A or A• for the essay because 'it's this area that John Ford is really concentrating on... the whole idea of the hero and the anti-hero'. (For A• in writing, Claire suggests, students need to be able to express complex ideas, arguments and subtleties of meaning.) She reminded pupils that they were to be examined on their ability to 'understand the audience and the purpose... the media languages of visual images, dialogue, dramatic devices, the type of camera shots, the angles... the way the director, John Ford... is trying to make us think and react'.

This part, like the rest of the lesson, was conducted as a teacher-led, whole-class analysis of a range of still images from the film, all of which involved the portrayal of the hero. The approach was partly motivated by the fact that many pupils, the next day, were to be out of school; the teacher felt the need to make good progress this lesson.

Stage 2: Introduction (5 minutes)

Referring to the prompt sheet, the teacher invited pupils to remember which two images best portray the typical Western emergence of the hero from 'the dusty wilderness', and to consider the ways in which the hero is portrayed as an outsider. In this introduction, and throughout the analysis, the teacher made constant reference to the pre-eminence of the director, John Ford, in guiding the response of the viewer. A typical teacher question would begin, 'How does John Ford...?' She referred to '*his* use of shot, *his* use of colour'.

In stressing the nature of the hero as outsider or anti-hero, the teacher offered pupils the terms, *antagonist* and *protagonist*. Throughout both lessons the teacher encouraged pupils to engage with complex vocabulary and concepts; for example, she asked pupils to research, during the week, the meaning of *neurotic* and *psychotic*, and to consider in the lesson the meaning of *enigmatic*. Before the class began its shot-by-shot analysis of the hero, the teacher once again reminded pupils of the need to refer to specific camera shots, underlining: 'You know all this now – you're getting good at it.'

Stage 3: Shot-by-shot analysis (40 minutes)

Shot 1: *the emergence of Ethan (John Wayne) from the wilderness, in the distance, as he moves towards his family home*
The question asked of this frame was how and why John Ford brought Ethan 'from the wilderness to domestic bliss'. A boy suggested, 'He's coming alone'. Another suggested that we don't see his face. A third pupil pointed out that in most Western films we would typically see the town that the hero approaches.

The teacher asked, 'Who is he? Where is he coming from? What is he doing? What kind of shot does John Ford use?'

When a pupil suggested 'long shot' the teacher reminded the class that it is not enough to describe a shot: one must also comment on its significance. In this scene, other elements discussed included the symbolism of an Indian blanket ('reliance, trading, marriage and unity').

Shot 2: *the greeting between Ethan (John Wayne) and his brother*

The teacher asked, 'What didn't they do?' Pupils pointed out the absence of a hug, and the way in which the brothers appeared to be 'separate', 'not relaxed.' The teacher stressed that the film would never provide an answer as to why these brothers weren't close; it was up to the pupils to interpret the relationship. One pupil volunteered a comparison between the way in which women might greet each other in similar circumstances, leading to a comment from the teacher on the role of men in Western films, 'the issue of masculinity'.

The teacher also invited the class to consider the choices that the actors, under the guidance of the director, might have made in order to convey some sense of masculinity and/or tension between characters. She then drew attention to another cultural sign within the image, the fact that the cowboy carried not a gun but a sabre. This and the fact that he wore a grey coat led to a brief summary from the teacher of the role of the mercenary after the Civil War, and how Ethan might have earned a living this way. Typically, the teacher posed to the class a question about Ethan's coat, a question which, again typically, she was careful not to close down or to answer for the pupils. 'Does that mean he fought for the South, i.e. he supported slavery... or did he fight for the Union, the law, and did he kill somebody for their coat, or what?'

Shots 3/4: *Ethan and the family – including lifting a young girl in an embrace*

Pupils were most keen to raise the question of Ethan's relationship with his brother's wife Martha, and whether this might be the cause of family unease. Again the teacher stressed that such a relationship is 'something we can't prove', but might be something that 'John Ford is suggesting'. In response to the family images, a pupil suggested how it showed that 'Ethan had a good heart'.

Shot 5: *Ethan's response to Marty, referred to later by Ethan as 'half-breed'*

At this point the teacher drew attention to the 'racist issue' described on their prompt sheet. She invited the pupils to consider how the hero, Ethan, treated Marty, reminding them that 'John Ford is trying to show us a more complex hero'. When Ethan referred directly to Marty as 'a half-breed', the teacher pointed out the racist connotations of the term and the significance of describing Marty as 'one-eighth Cherokee'. For a while, this led to discussion between teacher and pupils as to what genetic mix constituted a given race.

Shots 6/7: *Ethan gives his niece a doll as a present and his nephew a sabre*

The teacher here guided a discussion as to the significance of the doll, which later became 'a dramatic device for finding her [his niece]'; 'Why', the teacher asked, 'would John Ford use something so emotive as a doll?' A girl said that it suggested being feminine. A boy commented upon how Ethan gave his sabre away, almost, the teacher added 'as if he were ashamed'.

In addition, the teacher drew out from the class the significance of Ethan having the place of honour by the fireplace. A boy drew the discussion back to the relationship between Ethan and his brother's wife. He, and other pupils, were very keen to resolve this question. But the teacher stressed, 'He (John Ford) doesn't give us the answer.' Using question-and-answer, the teacher led the pupils to consider, via body language, implied tensions in the relationships of the characters.

Shot 8: *Ethan pays for his stay*

The teacher asked pupils to consider the source of Ethan's money – likely to be his employment as a mercenary.

The lesson closed with the teacher inviting the pupils to review their checklist to see the progress they had made towards answering the question posed in the essay.

Media concepts and Media learning

Audience: the teacher pointed out how an earlier audience might have a different interpretation of this film. In this lesson, notions of *audience* were mainly acknowledged via the discussion of the role of the director John Ford. That is, the teacher guided the class to consider those themes and ideas in the film that the director might have wanted the audience to perceive. Consequently, the discussion centred on the impact of given directorial choices on the audience.

Language: throughout this unit of work, in spoken and written form, there was great emphasis on a wide range of film codes, including *camera shots, colour, light, sound, dialogue, acting, and props.* There was early discussion of a long shot and the fact that the viewer is not allowed to see the stranger's face as he approaches. Thereafter, most of the discussion related to cultural signs including *the wilderness, blanket, sabre, doll, the coat, body movements,* and *eye contacts.* In addition, there was much discussion of narrative development, with particular emphasis on character relationships and how these were conveyed by the actors.

Representation: this was another concept central to the whole unit. Apart from the issue of how the director of the Western represents his ideas to his audience, there was also consideration of how *race, masculinity,* and *family relationships* were represented.

Categories: of course, the particular category of the Western was the central motivation for this unit of work. Most of the discussion related to the Western genre and implied general knowledge of other films within this genre. That is, the emphasis (as expressed in the essay title) was on what makes this a Western different from or typical of other Westerns rather than what makes the Western different from other film genres.

Agencies/Institutions: the teacher pointed out how, in film-making, the director is actually one member of a team. Such relationships were not a significant element in this lesson. The main agent discussed was the director. Ideologies were considered as part of the social and historical context in which the film was set. The particular emphasis was on the institutions of the American West rather than on the institutions which constitute the film industry or the film's production context. As an example, the check list invited pupils to consider the role of the Church in the American West, 'The Reverend goes as far as to yell 'Hallelujah!' when fighting the Indians. Why is this surprising? What does this show?'

Technologies: this concept was not addressed in the lesson; video and television technologies were used.

Main characteristics of the lesson (s)

The teacher's aims were focused very firmly on the Western film, *The Searchers*. In general, she wanted pupils to understand that the film's portrayal of the American West went beyond the usual stereotypes. In particular, she wanted the pupils to come to understand John Wayne's character, Ethan, as a 'hero who does not fit'.

In the first lesson the teacher was concerned to avoid allowing her own interpretation of the film to determine the way in which pupils would view and understand it. This meant little intervention from the teacher beyond a number of questions to frame the viewing. In the second lesson (well after the viewing) the teacher was much more concerned that pupils should share her particular and very detailed understanding of the film. Thus the lesson took the form of a teacher-led, whole-class analysis. In the discussion all pupil responses were allowed and valued, but essentially interpreted by the teacher so that they supported in some way the analysis which she wanted the pupils to grasp. Yet the teacher was also keen that pupils should learn to tolerate ambiguities and uncertainties in film narrative and should understand that analysis would still leave some questions unanswered.

The entire focus of the two lessons, and of the half-term unit of work, was the film, *The Searchers*. Elements of the text analysed included narrative, historical perspective, representation of race and gender. Film codes included camera shots, colour, dialogue, performance and direction. Cultural codes analysed included body language and artefacts (props).

As suggested above, there was significant emphasis on *Media Language* and *Representation*. The *Media Category* analysed was obviously the Western. However, there was at least as much attention to *Media Agencies* as to *genre*, in that much of the discussion privileged the particular choices made by the film's director. In film study terms, the approach drew on *auteur theory* rather than *genre theory*.

Technologies used by the teacher included the VCR and television. There was no practical work involved.

CHRIS

School: Comprehensive school

Teacher background

Chris teaches mainly English, with about one fifth of his timetable occupied with Drama. He is in his third year of teaching after doing his PGCE at Nottingham University. Media was a part of that PGCE, but not a significant element in it, and didn't make a great impression. Chris has always had a strong personal interest in film and it is largely from this that his interest in media work has developed. When he took up his present post he found a department in which Media was very clearly inscribed into the English curriculum ('a lot of Media emphasis from Key Stage 3 to Key Stage 4') and a GCSE syllabus which demanded media awareness ('You need to become conversant with media terms and media techniques'). His natural interest in media and film developed within this context.

Chris runs a Film Studies group in extra-curricular time. As well as viewing selected films, this also typically involves viewing with a particular focus, for example, concentrating on a particular film genre or on the work of a particular director.

In terms of Media, Chris regards himself as mainly self-taught. He is a keen advocate and practitioner of Media Education but feels that literature is at the heart of most of his English teaching. But, although he thoroughly enjoys the Media element of the curriculum, this is not the area in which he feels he is strongest; he expresses a need for more Media INSET.

Teacher attitude to Media Education

For Chris, Literature is central to his teaching and much of the Media work that Chris does will arise out of some study of Literature. For example, consideration of the way that men and women are represented in love poetry might, typically, be followed by a study of the representation of men and women in the media, perhaps 'looking at an article which considered cultural stereotypes'. Often, study of literary texts will be combined with study of magazines and magazine articles. As one example of particularly successful Media teaching Chris describes how some work on war poetry was followed by a study of the attitudes to war reflected in the television series, *Blackadder*. 'The way they'd been stereotyped... certain themes that came out of the poetry and the insensitivity of the generals and officers were actually reflected in that.' That work was followed up by studying the same theme in contemporary news, and in war letters, culminating in a study of First World War propaganda. He wants pupils to consider 'who's presenting what to whom ... to think about the audience, which is very important'. This reflects his general interest in studying persuasive and rhetorical language. 'I'm particularly interested in using language for specific effects.'

Chris believes that studying film treatment of literary texts is an effective form of Media Education. This is reflected in the lesson observed as part of this research; in particular, the content of the lesson involves the study of publicity material for four film productions of Shakespeare. Also, Chris points out, 'You study the processes, then try and imitate those processes, not necessarily to get the same quality but to actually get an idea of the language processes.'

Aims, concepts, approach to teaching

Chris's enthusiasm for film is balanced by a more defensive approach to media in general, and his own views about the media are reflected in his long-term aims for the pupils. He wishes pupils, through analysis, to understand the ways in which the media are manipulative. He does not want them to have exaggerated respect for the media, but rather to understand that the media are 'not some great important thing' and that they 'very often [have] some persuasive agenda'. He wishes pupils to understand something about the choices which media make in presenting facts, to offer pupils 'a different perspective' and encourage them to 'weigh up evidence'. These broad aims are, he says, reflected in his approach to Media teaching. For example, in order to demonstrate media manipulation he is likely to select for analysis texts which are 'overtly manipulative', in order to exemplify most successfully the methods which are used. As an example he quotes from *Klondyke Kate* (Bleiman *et al.*, 1995) in which there are two very contrasting articles on poverty and homelessness, one by the right-wing critic Tony Parsons, and one by the left-wing journalist, John Pilger.

Pupils, Chris feels, really enjoy media work. Their response is more positive than say, to Shakespeare, and he uses film to enhance Shakespeare study. In general, he feels that though pupils do enjoy practical work, they respond more positively to analysis, largely because pupils are not always able to turn their imaginative ideas into practice and 'sometimes a level of frustration creeps in'.

Chris talks about media concepts at two levels. On one level he feels it important that pupils understand particular media conventions like 'title block' or 'tag-line' (the latter being a significant element in the lesson observed). At a broader level, important concepts for him are those of *audience, producer* and *medium*. Most important of all, he says, is the relationship between *producer* and *audience*: 'Assumptions that the producer makes about the audience, and assumptions that the sophisticated audience makes about the producer, determine how they read the text or how the text is produced.' Media Education for Chris seeks to 'analyse how assumptions are borne out by the text'.

Although Chris probably feels that the teacher of Media within English should pay more attention to the language and text than to media institutions, the concept of *Institutions* is implicit in the Media teaching that Chris does. He does not set out to plan for its inclusion in his teaching, but it is dealt with opportunistically when it is appropriate. As an example he cites Rupert Murdoch's proposed takeover of Manchester United, comparing the presentation of this news item in Murdoch's own newspapers, *The Times* and the *Sun* with, say, the *Mirror*. 'You have to make it clear.' Chris himself raises the issue of *ideology* which he feels is important in media teaching and which he explicitly addresses with pupils.

Chris is a keen user of television technologies. Television and video were at the heart of the lesson observed and, at the end of the project, pupils will have used a video camera to produce a film trailer. He is similarly keen about encouraging pupils to use information technologies. For example, when setting homework, Chris will sometimes offer a helpful web site address. In a recent class debate on the subject of *cloning* some pupils drew materials from the Internet; Chris feels that it was an important element of that work to question the credibility of the source of those materials. But sometimes he and/or pupils encounter significant logistical obstacles. These include too many children making simultaneous demands on the school IT network, and the general slowness of the computers available in the IT suite (the fastest machines, he says, are in the library). The school's CD-ROMs are not networked; in any case, he suspects that CD-ROM is a technology with a limited life span and, with increasing access to the Internet, is becoming, 'less and less useful.'

Chris is optimistic about the future of Media Education over the next ten years. He hopes that the current review of the National Curriculum for English will provide 'more leeway in syllabuses at GCSE' and he sees post-16 developments in GNVQ as a positive sign for Media Education. Chris feels that the case for Media Education in the current technological climate is unarguable. He suggests that you are not addressing what is important 'if you're not using film and resources like the Internet'. Failure to use and address technology will, he argues, produce a 'credibility gap... leaving the kids behind'.

Chris feels that Media Education particularly supports boys. They benefit, he argues, from analysing a process, then imitating that process in a creative task; boys need this supportive framework. Girls, though able to work well in this mode, are equally happy given a much more open-ended task. Media Education, therefore, allows boys to compete on an equal footing with girls.

Context: the school

Media occupies a significant proportion of the GCSE English curriculum in the school, approximately one-sixth. The department works in half-term curriculum units of work, and this term the unit is Media. Consequently, a visit to any English classroom would be likely to reveal some Media work currently in progress. Not all lessons during the half-term are explicitly centred on Media work; some would be related to the separate Literature examination but even where they are not, Media approaches or Media links are likely to be introduced. And where Media is not central, as for example when looking at persuasive writing, Chris is still likely to bring in media texts.

The departmental scheme of work describes Media 'as an essential part of the curriculum at Key Stage 3 ... language devices in persuasive advertisements, within different styles of representation in newspapers and in magazines'. But the Media curriculum is described in fairly broad terms, allowing for individual teacher interpretation. 'You can choose to look at a specific focus on advertisements rather than a specific focus on newspaper language... or on documentaries.' At Key Stage 4, 'as long as you satisfy the absolute requirements of the exam there is certainly scope for doing your own thing'. Teacher interpretation of the scheme of work and consequent use of resources are up to the individual. For example, the materials and approach used by Chris in the lesson observed are very much his own.

Though there is no whole-school policy on Media Education, Chris is confident that it does take place elsewhere in the school curriculum. For example, he cites GNVQ work done in the sixth form in the Communication Studies element, and in the GNVQ modules in Health and Social Care, Tourism and Leisure. In these areas, promotional material will be analysed and the analysis used as a basis for production. (When Chris first came to the school he taught an element of Communication Studies in GNVQ.)

Also, in History, war in the media and the propaganda of war are specifically considered.

Though two members of the English department have MAs in Media or Media-related studies, in general the members of the department share ideas and work collaboratively rather than rely on the 'expertise' of an individual member. The only other outside agency used is Film Education who supplied the material for the work in the lesson observed. The examination preparation booklet provided by SEG, Chris feels, is 'not a real media analysis to be honest...is very word-bound.'

The most prominent commercial resource nominated by Chris is *Klondyke Kate* (Bleiman, 1995). Other than that, most media resources (in terms of teaching ideas) are likely to be found as sections in the general English course books used. Chris regards as more significant the need for individual teachers to collect magazines and other real contemporary media texts to be used as part of the curriculum. In addition, Chris' membership of Film Education ensures that he has access to a wide range of film resources.

As far as Chris can recall, the department's very positive OFSTED report made no significant mention of its approach to or treatment of Media Education.

Context: INSET
During the three years that Chris has been with the department there has been no significant Media Education INSET, though, as mentioned above, two members of the department do have significant expertise in this area. Despite Chris's enthusiasm for film, teaching of film is still the Media area where he seeks support. The school has provisionally agreed that he can attend a Film Education course to be held in the near future, the subject being *Supporting Literacy Through Film*.

Context: the syllabus
The SEG English syllabus was already chosen when Chris arrived at the school. Given freedom to choose for himself he would not select SEG, though 'increasingly there's very little to choose between them'. Though the syllabus was already chosen, there has since been some departmental discussion over whether or not SEG remains the most suitable syllabus. As part of that review, Chris says, the Board's treatment of Media was not a significant factor. Much more important was how the different Boards treated Literature, since the demands of the Literature element of all the syllabuses are seen to drive the curriculum.

Chris outlines two main features of SEG's treatment of Media. On the one hand its very inclusion (as with all Boards) mean that it is strongly written into the curriculum: 'If you've got to satisfy requirements in terms of persuasive language ... then to do that your examples are going to be drawn from a whole range of media texts and media sources ... so the implicit content is quite high.' On the other hand, he suggests, its explicit Media demands are minimal, and poor in terms of range. More important in the syllabus is the way in which the Media analysis acts as a means to produce analytical and argumentative writing. (SEG's pre-release booklet, on which the examination is based, has a section entitled, *Argument in Media Texts.*)

The relevant examination paper contains separate assessment of reading non-fiction and media texts. Chris distinguishes between media and non-fiction largely in terms of the sorts of texts they address (published in the pre-release materials). For example, media texts will include large, wordy magazine articles or advertisements, while non-fiction texts will include travel writing, biographies and autobiographies. Commenting on the SEG examination papers of 1998 Chris adds, with a little irony, 'I'm almost tempted to say you can tell they are media texts because they use photos.') He feels that sometimes pupils are unclear as to the distinction and the impact that distinction might have on their examination preparation. To clarify the distinction he might invite pupils, when studying media texts, to say, 'Let's look at presentational devices... lets look at audiences... let's look at the use of images.' He feels that SEG does not make significant distinctions between media texts and non-fiction texts and feels that 'the media texts are very poorly chosen'.

THE LESSON: SCREENING SHAKESPEARE: ANALYSIS OF FILM POSTERS AND TRAILERS

Teacher: Chris

The class
This is a mixed gender English set (set 4) of 23 pupils in year 10, together as a group since September.

Lesson aims
Chris wanted the class to understand the structure of a film trailer, to analyse its main features in the context of film promotion and to produce, at the end of the study, a film trailer of their own. 'They should understand the structure of a film trailer, the stylistic devices that are in there and be able to employ them.' They should be able to 'put together a film trailer,

script it, direct it' and also be able to understand concepts like 'credit blocks, tag-lines'. The work fits into a set of broader aims in which Chris links prior study of Shakespeare to analysis of film techniques. He sees the work as important in that it reinforces knowledge of Shakespeare's plays: 'They have to... know the plot and characters inside out and also know the themes in order to produce a trailer.' Also, it offered an introduction to Media, with a focus on stylistic devices and media techniques so that when they went on to consider articles and magazines they were already able to look at such things as titles, the positions of images and references to other periodicals. Also, this work provided practice for the SEG examination, in which pupils have to analyse audience and technique. Finally, the scripting and filming work that followed would provide opportunities for oral assessment, 'the ... discussion that's gone into their preparation'.

As in his expressed approach to media work, Chris sought to connect the study of media with the study of literature. The class had already read *Macbeth* and had, within the previous two weeks, compared extracts of different film presentations, for example, a BBC production of the banquet scene from *Macbeth* and the equivalent scene from Roman Polanski's version. In that study the emphasis had been on the opening credit sequences, setting, and genre.

The SEG's assessment in Media requires analysis of a written text in the terminal examination. Consequently, the assessment outcome related to this study of film treatment of Shakespeare would take the form of an analytical piece of writing. The coursework would also fulfil the syllabus requirement to write about Shakespeare. That is, the study would provide the content and the focus for the writing. The unit of work was likely to last for another six lessons, or two weeks.

Content and teacher approach (and pupil response)

The lesson had four distinct elements, and was strongly based on materials produced by Film Education, entitled *Screening Shakepeare* (*Getting the Audience*). The complete unit of work involves consideration in turn of the trailer and publicity poster for *Romeo and Juliet* (Baz Lurhmann), *Looking for Richard* (Al Pacino), *Richard III* (Richard Lancraine) and *Hamlet* (Kenneth Branagh). This particular lesson involved the first half of those elements, that is, study of the trailer and poster for *Romeo and Juliet* and *Looking for Richard*. The materials also included a large number of questions which the teacher might invite the pupil to ask of the text (trailer or poster). These questions are very wide-ranging, and include consideration of cultural codes (like age and body language) as well as conventions related to the particular medium employed (like bullets, graphics, words and tag-line). In the lesson, tag-line was used to refer to the particular phrase at the end (i.e. bottom) of the poster, which for example, in the case of for *Romeo and Juliet*, was 'the greatest love story the world has ever known.' The teacher, however, was clearly very familiar with the materials, and made no explicit reference to the questions on the page. Instead of colour posters he used overhead transparencies which he produced prior to the lesson. Although these were in black and white, he suggested to the pupils that the particular features that he wanted to explore would not be affected by the absence of colour

The video used includes on it trailers of all four films with particular film clips numbered for easy access. Thus, during the lesson, the teacher was easily able to move between overhead projector and video recorder (on opposite sides of the room) drawing pupils' attention to the appropriate technology and text.

The lesson had four clear stages: analysis of the Romeo and Juliet poster; analysis of the *Romeo and Juliet* trailer; analysis of the *Looking for Richard* poster; analysis of the *Looking for Richard* trailer. The whole lesson was conducted as a teacher-led analysis, with most pupils contributing by answering questions which probed the text. They also asked questions and offered interventions of their own. Teacher approach and pupil response are considered together below.

Stage 1: the publicity poster for Romeo and Juliet (15 minutes)

This poster largely features the two main protagonists, but, particularly, the image of the currently very successful Leonardo DiCaprio. The poster combines images of screen action (including a bullet ripping through the poster) with conventional images of love. The teacher first drew attention to its appeal to a young audience. 'Shakespeare wrote this play 400 years ago but you're presented with something quite modern ...this is deliberately aimed at a young audience.' Pupils suggested ways in which that was achieved:

> lots of action – the bloke's got a gun

> they're [the actors shown in the poster] about that age [referring to the image of Romeo kissing Juliet]

In order to draw attention to the way in which different elements of the poster targeted different (young) audiences, the teacher suggested, 'Let's deal in a stereotype here... you reckon the top appeals to men and the one underneath to women.' (The top of the poster contains more images of action, the bottom half of the poster more images of romance.) The teacher also invited pupils to consider the range of emotions in the images and in the words *hope, despair, tragedy, love*. The teacher then turned the discussion of emotions into an investigation of some of the themes in the play/poster.

In order to address the issue of star billing, the teacher used an earlier comment from a pupil: 'Let's come back to what Hilary said, 'you've got to see it because of who's in it.' ... There are more characters in this film than Romeo and Juliet, yet on the posters you only really see *them* ... how are their names presented to you?' He drew the pupils' attention to the small lettering and positioning in the poster of the name 'William Shakespeare' in relation to the larger lettering of 'Leonardo DiCaprio'. He thus implied that the designers of the posters were aiming to draw the audience to the name which would most likely attract them to the film. Responding to a pupil he agreed, 'Right – isn't it that they don't want to associate Leonardo DiCaprio and Claire Danes with boring old Shakespeare?'

In particular, the teacher appeared to wish to draw pupils' attention to some tension between the tag-line, The greatest love story the world has ever known – written in comparatively small lettering – and some of the violent imagery of the poster, including the bullet motif. Agreeing with a pupil, the teacher suggested, 'Right ... the tag-line is not very big because it's not just a love story.' In particular, the teacher was implying a contrast between the small letters referring to love, and the larger, more dominant action images above: 'You've got the bullets, you've got the gun....' Most pupils seemed to accept the point, though one girl did seem to see romance or love more strongly portrayed in its images, pointing out that the image of Juliet 'stands out – Juliet with [angel's] wings.' But the teacher seemed careful not to force the point and, before moving on to the trailer, left the contrast between romantic theme and violent image unresolved, asking the class, 'How many people would or would not be attracted by the poster?'

Stage 2: the trailer for Romeo and Juliet (10 minutes)
The teacher first linked the viewing of the trailer to the pupils' earlier analysis of film, reminding them of their study of Polanski's and Orson Welles's versions of *Macbeth*. The trailer was then treated as the next stage in the selling of *Romeo and Juliet* as the teacher sought to look for links or disjunctions between film and poster. In inviting the pupils to view the

trailer the teacher suggested some framing devices. 'What's the first thing you ever see?' he asked, 'Is it mostly presented as a violent film or a love story? ... Concentrate on the use of stylistic features.... sound effects ... how much of the actual text is used on this trailer..' The teacher also asked, if the trailer backed up the poster or contradicted it?

After the viewing, pupils seemed certain that the action was more dominant in the trailer: 'Masses of violence ... it was basically violence.' After the teacher asked, 'What extra things did you get from the trailer that you didn't get from the poster?' pupils commented on some differences in the medium used, ' visual images', 'not static', 'sound'. One picked up on the contrast between romance and action through the 'love and hate reference'. Another noticed that though the film was modernised the language was not.

The teacher drew attention to the film's tag-line, i.e. 'star-crossed lovers', again pointing out that 'amidst all the violence is a love story.' The teacher also sought to draw connections between the soundtrack (music) and the age group of the intended audience.

Through further question and answer the teacher drew attention to:

- the sound effects (distinguishing between noises produced by gun-fire and noises produced by the storm)
- the setting ('an American setting', following one pupil's sugges-tion that the setting was urban and another's that the setting was Verona)
- the vast number of images seen ('you're assaulted by all the images')
- the order in which the images were seen (referring explicitly to the trailer convention of deliberately disrupting the chronology of the narrative)

The teacher invited pupils to consider the very first image of Romeo, walk-ing across the screen then 'looking at you... at the camera'. A pupil sug-gested that the effect of this gaze was that 'it makes you more involved.' The teacher also explored the music used, suggesting that it makes the pro-duction 'of its time', i.e. the 1990s, and that possibly, in ten years time, new audiences would be less able to connect with the film. One pupil helpfully drew a comparison between the conventions used by the trailer and a pop video. At the heart of discussion of trailer and poster was the tension in the trailer (and, implicitly, in the play) between romance and action. Pupils were left at the end of the trailer with the suggestion that the contrasting values of the film trailer reflected, to a degree at least, the contrasting values of the play.

Stage 3: The poster for Looking for Richard (10 minutes)

A number of contrasts were drawn. Firstly there was a contrast between this poster and the one advertising *Romeo and Juliet*. A pupil suggested that this poster contained fewer visual images and more words; the teacher elaborated, pointing out that the poster contained few images from the play itself. A second contrast was drawn between the star of *Romeo and Juliet* (Leonardo DiCaprio given top billing in large letters) and the star of *Looking for Richard* (actor and director Al Pacino's name appearing second in a horizontally presented list of other star Hollywood names).

But the teacher also drew the attention of the pupils to the central, dominating image in the poster. 'How can you tell, even if I ignore all the text, who is the star of this film?' (The poster features Al Pacino in modern clothes, standing at a New York bus stop, in front of a very big close-up poster on a hoarding of Al Pacino's bearded face and crowned head as Richard III). 'He's in the foreground if you like, and his body language... arms folded... right in the foreground... in a very smug attitude.' Given this lead, one pupil commented on the contrast between the black of the foregrounded character's clothes and the whiteness of the page/city behind him – suggesting that it was as if there was a light source or a spotlight.

A significant element of the image (to which one pupil drew everyone's attention) was that the leg of Al Pacino the actor effectively hid, and took the place of, the third symbol of III. She commented, 'It looks like Richard II... you can't see the third line.'

As in the discussion of the *Romeo and Juliet* poster, the teacher invited discussion of *audience*. He pointed out the function of using quotes from reviews and drew attention to the fact that, in this poster, they came from *Rolling Stone* and *The New York Times*, publications bought by older readers. The teacher invited pupils to identify the tag-line ('400-year-old work in progress') and use it as a springboard for considering the main focus for discussion. This was the tension, not, as in *Romeo* between images of love and images of violence, but between the past and the present, 'a modern New York Street... 400 years old but still relevant, yeah [reinforcing a pupil's comment]... image and text go together... you can't separate them'.

Stage 4: The trailer for Looking for Richard *(10 minutes)*

As with *Romeo and Juliet*, the teacher invited the pupils to consider to what degree the trailer supported the message of the poster: 'Does the trailer back up the fact that Richard III is modern?' The pupils responded after watching the trailer: 'It can't be all modern... It goes all modern, then old.' The teacher drew attention to the music of *Looking for Richard* (identified by pupils as medieval) – different from that of *Romeo and Juliet*. 'It was saying... this is about English history.'

Other themes from the trailer were highlighted by the teacher, including the use of one eccentric English character to argue (stereotypically) that Americans could not be expected to know about Shakespeare. Again, following the pattern of the analysis of *Romeo and Juliet*, the teacher invited the pupils to consider the tag-line of the trailer, 'Now is the winter of our discontent'. In summary, the teacher reviewed the trailer's convention for sequencing images, the conflicting emotions present in the trailer, the use of music, soundtrack and humour. Finally, the teacher alerted the class to the fact that the next day they would repeat the approach of this lesson, but with reference to a different version of *Richard III* and a version of *Macbeth*.

Media concepts and media learning

Given that four media texts were tackled in the lesson, the media learning was necessarily broad. However, a number of specific themes emerged, tackled with more or less equal emphasis:

Audience: particular contrasts were drawn between the youth audience sought by the *Romeo and Juliet* trailer and poster and the older audience sought by *Looking for Richard*. Within the former, there was further discussion of audience in terms of young male and young female, and in the latter in terms of English and American.

Language: this was particularly wide-ranging and included discussion of film conventions such as sound effects; music (modern and medieval); cultural codes such as body language, clothes, cars; graphic techniques including lettering; positioning of text on the page; visual motifs (bullet); and tag-lines.

Representation: of youth and age, of emotions and themes (love and violence; ancient and modern), of cultures (England and America).

Categories: though one genre tackled was obviously 'Shakespeare', there was as much emphasis on the trailer itself as a film form.

Agencies/Institutions: though this was less prominent than any of the media themes above, there was much implicit discussion of the star system, via consideration of the prominence of Leonardo DiCaprio in the *Romeo and Juliet* poster.

Technologies: this concept was not directly addressed in the lesson, though television, video and OHP technologies were used.

Main characteristics of the lesson

Although the aims encompassed knowledge about film structure *and* understanding of literary texts, this lesson strongly favoured film and film promotion. Indeed, the teacher's own enthusiasm for film was evident in the choice of material and in its delivery.

The lesson took the form of a teacher-led, whole-class analysis. Pupils were confident enough to intervene and ask questions where appropriate, but the teacher's position in managing the technology, coupled with the lesson aims, meant that he was inevitably in control of the lesson's progress. However, he was careful, particularly at the end of each stage of the lesson, not to close down the possible range of meanings of a given segment of film or printed text.

Elements of texts studied included print, graphics, layout, still image, moving image, narrative and sound. The moving images came from high quality trailers distributed by Film Education. The still images (the film posters) were black-and-white overhead transparencies taken from the Film Education teacher material. The context in which the films and film posters are received was important in the lesson. That is, *purpose* and *audience* were at the heart of the film study.

Media Language was central to the lesson, as was the notion of different *Audiences* targeted by film clip or poster. In relation to media language the teacher was keen to use explicitly with pupils terms and conventions which would support film and poster analysis. *Institutional* issues, including, for example, relationships between film production, distribution and promotion were not specifically addressed. That is, the emphasis was on the media texts and their impact on potential audiences, rather than on the context of production. However, the star system of modern Hollywood was implicit in much of the discussion.

Although there was no practical element in this lesson, pupil production of film trailers was an intended outcome of the unit of work. Technologies used in this lesson included television, VCR, and overhead projector.

HEATHER

School: Urban girls' school

Teacher background

Heather teaches mainly English but also has a responsibility for a GCSE Media Studies course; she produces schemes of work and resources for the other two teachers involved. The syllabus has been running for two years.

Heather is in her third year of teaching. She did her PGCE at Southampton. Prior to that she had done an MA in Women's Studies. As part of that MA Heather did quite a lot of work on television and popular culture. The English teaching job that Heather applied for (her current post) happened to include Media Studies.

This combination of past experience and available post meant that Heather found herself in a position where she was becoming increasingly involved in Media Education. Developing her own resources and using BFI or Film Education materials has been part of that development. Heather never went out to seek a teaching career in Media Education. However, she acknowledges that she was never likely to pursue a career, for example, in English and Drama, the latter being an area where she feels less confident.

Teacher attitude to Media Education

Heather does not really favour one element of English over another. She enjoys 'poetry analysis with top sets' as much as media projects based on 'relevant and more modern stuff'. As implied above, she is more comfortable with Media Education than with Drama, though her attitude to Media within the English curriculum as compared to GCSE Media Studies is very different (see below). She does try to squeeze into her English teaching as much Media work as she can but, she says, 'we've got to get results at the end of the day.' The pressure, she feels, comes both from the need to 'plough through' the Literature element of the syllabus, and from the need to give appropriate emphasis to language and analytical skills.

Personally, Heather enjoys film though she never teaches about radio, a medium in which she feels far less confident.

Aims, concepts, approach to teaching

In describing her approach to teaching about Media, Heather outlines some strategies within Media Studies: 'I start off with basic skills like analysing images.' The rest of the course is divided into modules, covering, for example, film, advertising, soap opera, pop music. 'I tend to do a bit of theory and then a bit of practical.' She finds it difficult to define her approach to Media within English because, she feels, 'It's... limited... the approach that our department has, and I think it's the approach of most departments who teach NEAB, is – you do the coursework, it takes six weeks and that's it...' Heather's implicit criticism does not specifically relate to Media but rather describes her attitude to the GCSE English syllabus *per se*: 'It's exactly the same with Shakespeare... you do the Shakespeare in six weeks and that's it.'

Heather doesn't see Media Education as a defence for pupils against the media. In the long-term she wishes pupils to be analytical and to enjoy Media work: 'I don't think there's any more than that to it really.' At first she suggests that her personal views about media and society do not particularly influence her teaching. Those views, however, include the notion that there exists a great deal of cultural snobbery. 'My personal view... is that all media and all culture is equally relevant...' She acknowledges that this might have some impact on what she deals with in the classroom, for example, 'We talk at length about *Home and Away*'. This inclusiveness applies to English as well as Media. She clearly resists any notion that Media Education should help pupils to judge what represents quality in the media. She includes popular culture in the curriculum simply for the enjoyment that it offers.

Heather is familiar with the BFI 'Signpost Questions' in Media Education. (She immediately offers *audience, representation*, and *language* as three examples.) Of these, in English, Representation will be used a great deal, in that 'in English you tend to look at ... character... how a character is represented. In Media Studies it tends to be more audience based... possibly Language as well.' In *Language* she includes 'film language' though, she suggests that in English there isn't much opportunity to deal with it.

Heather feels that within English the issue of *Institutions*, 'hasn't raised its head – hardly at all'. But within Media Studies she feels it to be very important. This would include, 'censorship, control,...all the institutions that deal with that... looking at news ownership.... in English I've never touched on anything like that.'

Again, within English, *Technologies* have very limited significance. 'We don't use cameras in English, we don't do any kind of practical stuff.' The only time cameras have featured in English has been to film Drama work. Within Media Studies Heather and the pupils will use cameras and the Internet. The Internet when used is likely to be used as a resource rather than becoming the focus of analysis itself. Heather is very clear about her contrasting approaches to Media Studies and to Media within English. Aside from some Key Stage 3 work filming an advertisement, Heather can recall very little of this type of practical activity within English. 'You just don't have time to do that with the pressures of GCSE.'

Resources available to Heather include Film Education materials, and materials from the English and Media Centre (including *The Advertising Pack* and the *News Pack* (Grahame, 1993; 1995). Heather has quite a good selection of film on video.

Context: the school

This is a girls' school. Media Studies is also taught as a discrete syllabus and has been running for two years. Three teachers are involved, one of them being Heather, who, as the person responsible for the syllabus, prepares appropriate materials and schemes of work. There are three Media groups currently running, two in year 11 and one in year 10

Though Heather feels that she would typically spend about six weeks at Key Stage 4 looking at Media work within English (much of it film-related) and another two weeks looking at newspapers, she still regards this as a small proportion of her teaching time, 'less than 10 per cent... it's very low on the list of priorities when you look at the exam requirements.' This proportion, she suggests, is probably common in the department since all coursework pieces tend to be done separately. The teachers tend to do the same things: 'I did a piece on *Independence Day* and promotion of it... and so on, and because I did it lots of other people did it.' Though Heather is also responsible for the discrete GCSE Media syllabus, her Media role in the English department (providing ideas and resources for other teachers) is unofficial. The *Independence Day* unit of work had involved looking at trailers for the film and how the 'images presented by the trailers bring out the key things'. Heather produced, in relation to this unit, a proforma to guide pupils' observation of the trailers, and an essay plan. Another piece of Media work commonly done by the department is a study of Levi Jeans advertisements from *The Advertising Pack* (Grahame, 1993). Typically, in response to such work, the pupils will be asked to do straightforward analysis which Heather regards as 'safer' for the pupils, more likely than creative approaches to Media to produce successful coursework.

Some teachers in the department lack confidence in teaching Media and are happy to take ideas and advice from Heather. Within the overall agreed departmental approach teachers are free 'to teach their own thing'; common approaches in Media result from some teacher insecurity, but essentially, each teacher is responsible for her own group and 'whatever's on the syllabus, we've got to provide it... I think it's fair to say that in English, Media is still something that everybody is getting used to the idea of, and it's taking a long time.'

Heather is clearly the member of the English department whose expertise is most drawn on by others. She doesn't really have much contact with anyone else who teaches Media Studies, other than via her attendance at official GCSE Media Studies support meetings (SEG), and feels herself to be 'quite isolated'. Heather has received no examination-based (NEAB) support in the context of Media within English. However, she has had recent and relevant INSET (see below).

Context: INSET

Heather has been on two training courses, including 'a good course that the BFI ran' at the South Bank in the summer of 1998. She attended the course with both Media Studies and Media within English in mind. She knows of no other teacher in the department who has received INSET with a Media focus. Heather has, in a limited way, provided INSET for other teachers, 'giving out resources, talking people through it in meetings, ...on INSET days with the department'.

Context: the syllabus

In its choice of examination syllabus the department has moved from MEG to NEAB. A significant factor in that choice, Heather feels, was the provision by NEAB of a free anthology, 'more choice, less resources to buy'. But Heather was not herself party to the decision about syllabus choice. She does not remember NEAB's treatment of Media Education as being a significant factor in the discussion when the decision was made.

Heather feels that the new syllabus has made teachers think more carefully about 'what we actually do... MEG's syllabus was far more traditional... criticism-based. The NEAB one means we have to pay more attention to audience and that kind of thing.' Heather also points to the NEAB non-fiction examination as one containing 'media-based texts... kids do need to know some media terminology to write well about it.' So, when Heather talks about the Media element of the English curriculum she also has in mind 'non-fiction'. (Heather points out that the non-fiction examination paper will typically ask for pupils to comment on layout.) She distinguishes between Media and non-fiction in terms of the format of the text: non-fiction might, she suggests, include autobiography, but adds that 'if it's a leaflet, newspaper, magazine article, something like that...then you could use some kind of Media knowledge to describe and write about it... even if it's as limited as talking about headlines, bullet points, use of images.' Thus Heather expects Media knowledge to be applied to some of the texts in the non-fiction examination. The Media element examined in the coursework allows study of a wider range, including 'film and soap opera if you want'.

Heather was in the school when the department received its OFSTED inspection. She recalls that OFSTED commented (in relation to a Media Studies lesson) on the good Media resources, though, at the time, only Heather was teaching Media Studies and only with one class. But she recalls no OFSTED reference to Media Education within English.

THE LESSON: FROM POEM TO FILM – STORYBOARDING
Teacher: Heather

The class
The is a top set of 24 girls in year 11, many of whom are expected to get A and A* at GCSE. In some ways, Heather feels, this leads her to spend perhaps too much time on things like literary criticism and analysis – because a great deal is expected from these girls. With a lower group, Heather feels she might be inclined to use more Media. A number of pupils in the class are also members of Heather's GCSE Media Studies group.

Lesson aims
It should be noted here that Heather had considered teaching a lesson connected with film. However, she felt it important to continue with the natural progress of her scheme of work, which currently focuses on the NEAB Literature anthology. As a consequence, the Media Education in this lesson was part of that prepared programme.

Heather's main aim was to prepare the poem for understanding in preparation for the examination. In terms of the Media content she wanted the pupils to concentrate on 'the images in the poem and produce a visual account of the poem.'

Prior to this lesson the class had just started on poetry analysis related to study of the NEAB anthology. The area was 'fresh' to the class. With regard to Media this class had, in year 10, watched four films and done a comparative piece of coursework on them – the focus in the four films (Stargate, The Fifth Element, Blade Runner and Judge Dread) was 'characterisation, theme and motif.' The class, therefore, were familiar with film and with the use of the storyboards which Heather intended to use in the lesson. Heather saw this particular poem as a good one to build Media work into because 'it reads like a song.' The focus would be on the images in the poetry and the interpretation of them. Heather saw Media work here as a way into verbal, literary language.

At the end of this particular poetry study the girls would probably be invited to do a presentation to their peers based on their storyboards, justifying their choice of images. Heather feels that, from her perspective, using storyboard doesn't constitute a 'Media' lesson, but is the sort of thing one might do in the context of Media within English.

Content, teacher approach and pupil response

The focus of the lesson was *Limbo*, by Edward Kamau Braithwaite, taken from the *Other Cultures and Traditions* section of NEAB's Literature anthology. The poem offers images of a journey on board a slave ship, 'the dark deck is slavery' interspersed with a rhythmical dance image as a refrain, 'limbo like me.' Two sets of images and ideas and two distinct rhythms converge and diverge throughout the poem.

Stage 1: *exploration of the poem – main images and ideas (30 minutes)*
The teacher began by outlining the source of the poem and its connection to the pupils' GCSE syllabus. She also outlined for them the task: to consider the ideas and images in the poem, and to imagine that the poem was a pop song or a children's song and consider how it might be filmed. She then played to them an audio recording of a reading of the poem by the poet himself.

The teacher began by exploring general impressions about the poem's content. One pupil was called on to demonstrate the limbo dance to the rest of the class. Particular images were explored, 'Stick is the whip... what might that mean?' In particular, the teacher wanted the pupils to see the two main themes or ideas which were being combined; the image of the stick as the whip, she suggested, drew the two threads together. The idea was considered of 'limbo' as a place between heaven and hell, a state of nothingness. She then asked the pupils to consider 'this metaphor between dance and slavery, and try and work it out.' Supporting questions were written on the board. These included:

- Which line describes the dance being done?

- Are there two voices in the poem?

- Why might the poet have chosen a song-like style to tackle such a serious subject?

- How would you interpret the title?

The teacher encouraged the pupils to work 'in pairs or in small groups... to start discussing and writing notes...'

Group 1

They began by discussing the use of typography (italics) to separate one part of the poem (one voice) from the other. One pupil said she liked the expression of serious ideas in a 'song-like way'. In clarifying the significance of the title the group talked about the connotations of *limbo*. As well as carrying associations of dance, and a place between heaven and hell, one pupil suggested 'It could be the place between... slavery and freedom.' Another pupil voiced a regular concern of pupils analysing texts, 'Maybe we're reading too much into it.' At one stage in the discussion a pupil wanted clarification from the teacher: 'What kind of video are we going to make?' On being told that the storyboard would not actually be turned into a video, with good humour but evident disappointment the pupil said, 'That's not fair.' This group quietly continued their (gentle) rebellion... 'I want to make a video – Media people did.'

Having answered the questions set, the group was keen to discuss the video theme: 'Do a rap version of it... do a singing version.' The teacher called the class together to compare responses to the questions in order that pupils could clarify their annotation of the text. The teacher accepted and noted pupil responses and added further explanation, e.g. 'Some of them [the lines] are metaphorical... to do with the slavery... and add that dark tone.' The teacher then explored the possibility of there being 'two voices' in the poem, but she was careful to leave options open, for pupils to have their own reading in this respect.

In considering the song-like quality of the poem, the teacher pointed out the poet's personal liking for Calypso music. Clarifying a pupil's comment that the song-like quality might relate to slaves' historical connection with song the teacher, commented, 'Often in slavery, groups of people who spoke different languages were all mixed in...', and suggested that song and rhythm were very important in this context. Again she was careful not to suggest that her views could not be challenged, having prefaced the previous remark with, 'I don't know a great deal about it but...' She added that song was 'to do with the oral tradition'. The teacher also clarified inter-pretations of *limbo*, suggesting that it implied a kind of 'living death'. In order to support the pupils' annotation of the text the teacher offered other observations, e.g.:

- the existence of the refrain

- the analogy between successfully moving under the limbo stick to the other side and the sea voyage

- the use of repetition in the poem

- parallels between the slavery whip and the limbo stick

- the association of the positive element of the poem with the image of the sun rising

- the reader's uncertainty about the fate of the slave

- the connection between the visual associations of shape and the movement of the dance

Stage 2: *adaptation of the poem for video – teacher advice (10 minutes)*
The options for storyboarding the poem were clarified and ranged from a pop video to a 'slot on *Blue Peter* you want to provide a bit of film for'. The teacher reminded the pupils, therefore, to 'think about [your] audience first of all'. Referring to some of the pitfalls in storyboarding, the teacher warned, 'It's an easy thing to do badly... but a difficult thing to do well.' Briefly, the teacher outlined some of the characteristics of pop videos, in-cluding the tendency of the earliest videos to 'tell a story.' But now, she sug-gested, it was common to have 'a sequence of images'; videos by Madonna and Robbie Williams were offered as examples. The teacher encouraged pupils to choose specifically between narrative or simply 'disjointed images' associated with the poem, suggesting that, for example, narrative might better suit the *Blue Peter* audience.

She then offered some specific advice to the pupils. The first concerned choice of shot. She warned of the dangers of too much 'mid-shot...very boring to look at.' For variety of shot she encouraged pupils to 'zoom in or pan across'. The teacher clarified on the board what was meant by each type of shot. In exemplifying the use of such shots the teacher suggested that pupils might wish to start by panning across the scene or 'start really close up and pull back, pull back, pull back...' She pointed out that drawing skills were not necessary because each image was to be accompanied by a verbal description of the shot. She also invited pupils to write the lines of the poem alongside the appropriate image, possibly accompanied by choice of music.

Stage 3: pupil response (40 minutes)

Some pupils worked in pairs, others individually. Given that the nature of the task was essentially doing rather than talking, the following evidence of pupil response was gathered via conversations with pupils and reference to the work in progress.

Pupil pair 1 decided early on to 'zoom in' on the ship and have no music but silence and natural sounds, including waves. The decision was also taken to opt for a narrative approach with action/drama.

Pupil 2 decided to eschew the narrative in favour of something 'not literal...obscure.' She decided to set the images in the seventies because she was 'obsessed with the seventies... gold... glitzy... very bizarre I know'. She was determined to include images of glitter and glamour. Her clear intention was to provide a contrast between two very different sets of images. The seventies images, she suggested, would be used to convey happiness and cheerfulness. The first image she described as a dark one, consisting of a chain going across the screen: it would zoom slowly into close-up and we would see 'the chain pulled taut.' Then 'it cuts very quickly to a seventies disco scene with a glittery chain going across... funky baselines in the background.' She talked of the 'juxtaposition of bright cheerful stuff instead of having the darkness all the way through'.

Pupil pair 3 wanted to adopt an American theme, 'black rappers... in a rap video', to link ideas of slavery with images of black rappers. Rap rhythms were to be used to help distinguish between the two voices (those words in italics, those not in italics). They opted for a narrative approach with 'black connotations...sort of trendy to talk about your African roots if you're in America.' At this stage of the planning they were opting for a narrative, but were not yet clear what form this would take.

Pupil 4 was keen to begin with a long distance shot, 'a boat in the distance... and it's night-time... the boat lit by moonlight' and then move closer and closer to reveal the suffering. She wanted to show images of two sides of the boat (representing the contrasting images in the poem) by having a figure dive under the boat and come up the other side.

Under the water the diver would be suffocating (reflecting the feelings of drowning and suffocation in the poem).

Pupil 5 had a clear sense of what was to be in the frame: as in a typical holiday brochure, one would see a tropical beach hotel, an empty room after a party – quiet apart from the sound of crickets. The viewer would see a boy looking out to sea, and the eye would be drawn back and forth between the shore and the boat. (This pupil was also a Media Studies pupil with a great deal of previous storyboarding experience). The main perspective was of the boy looking out to sea as a boat was leaving. There would be no narrative connection between the boy and the boat.

Pupil 6 had a clear sense of narrative and chronology, 'following the storyline'. The storyboard would show a ship coming in; we would see contrasts of dark and light; a man (possibly the poet) watching the ship come in; the ship would be 'swallowed by darkness.'

Pupil 7 wanted to show experiences on the ship in terms of contrasting, good and bad sides. The narrative would begin with happy images, the slaves lying on the floor. The emotions would alternate between happiness and grimness or sadness, 'getting worse and worse.' This (Media Studies) student also had a clear sense of the sound she wanted to accompany the image – happiness conveyed via the limbo music and sadness via 'a drum beating or monotone'. The storyboard began with long shot and then moved straight to close-up.

Pupil 8 concentrated on the refrain, and the need to have a 'dancing' image repeated in the storyboard. The first picture was a long shot of the ship approaching. She did not intend to convey the whole narrative, 'just a part of it'. That is, she intended to move from opening to closing, but selecting only particular narrative fragments.

Pupil 9 had a sense of her intended audience, 'national poetry day, or something like that... a real-life kind of drama.' She was clear about the sound to accompany the images – including African voices in chorus, quietly humming. This pupil offered probably the most literal of the interpretations.

Pupil 10 was going to employ 'a chant... two different atmospheres.' This was to be contrasted with 'a party kind of scene'. A happy ending was planned.

Throughout, the teacher circulated amongst the pupils offering advice. She suggested variously to the pupils:

- describe the image before attempting to draw it
- one could repeat an image – possibly in relation to the chorus
- just because the poem has images of slavery, this does not mean that the storyboard should reflect that
- it might be useful to have monosyllabic sounds accompanying fast-moving images.

The lesson ended with advice from the teacher about some other ongoing coursework, and an expressed intention to continue next lesson with the storyboards.

Media concepts and Media learning

Language: at the heart of this lesson was a clear intention to connect the verbal imagery of the poem with the film/video language of the storyboard. A significant concept which pupils applied to both film and poem was that of *juxtaposition* – of mood, idea, and image. Indeed *juxtaposition* was a term volunteered by several pupils. However, the most obvious connection was the reference to *image*, so that it might simultaneously mean the poet's representation of slavery and the pupil's visual framing of an element of the poem. Teacher and pupil made reference to a number of different elements of film language including, *narrative, shot, pan, zoom, focus*. They also briefly considered ways in which sound might anchor image and guide interpretation of the visual.

Representation: in one sense *Representation* was central to the lesson in that the pupils' task was to *re-present* the poem's central images in the form of a film or video. In addition, the poem, and consequently many of the storyboards, were dependent on the representation of slavery. The emphasis was on *how* slavery was represented in practical (linguistic and visual) terms, rather than on a critical evaluation of such representations.

Audience: the teacher did invite pupils to consider audience (a *Blue Peter* audience was offered as an example). The idea of *Audience* seemed implicitly to influence what pupils were doing, though, at this early stage of storyboard planning, audience was not often made explicit.

Categories: other than, of course, the poem, the genres considered were the pop video or short film (documentary?) slot on a children's programme such as *Blue Peter*.

Agencies/Institutions: as implied in the teacher's comments about institutions, the professional, social and economic context of Media production were not intended to be a part of this English lesson.

Technologies: this concept did not feature in the lesson; audio technology was used.

Main characteristics of the lesson

The main aim for this lesson was to support pupils in their understanding of the poem *Limbo*, by Edward Kamau Braithwaite. The poem was part of NEAB's literary anthology which the pupils were studying for a terminal examination. The Media element of this lesson was the use of storyboarding as a means by which understanding of the poem could be enhanced.

While the lesson focused on certain themes and features of the written text, the teacher led the class through an understanding of its salient features. During this whole-class stage the teacher was concerned not to close down or deny any alternative interpretations. In the second half of the lesson, where the Media approach was introduced, pupils were very much responsible for their own interpretation of images, both literary and visual.

Three different texts featured in the lesson: the poem (a copy in each anthology), an audio version of the poem, and the storyboard produced by individuals or pairs of pupils. The context for the study was the 'Other Cultures and Traditions' section of the anthology from which this poem was taken.

Though issues of *Representation, Audience* and *Category* were touched on, the focus was very clearly on the ways in which the (mainly) visual *Media Language* could be employed in order to interpret metaphor and meaning in poetry. That is, the lesson hinged on the relationship between literary and visual image.

Practical work, in the sense of drafting for a media production, was obviously an essential element of this lesson. Unusually, however, for a teacher with a very strong leaning towards Media Studies, there was to be no realisation of the storyboard narrative in terms of video production: time and syllabus constraints were seen as obstacles by the teacher.

References

Bazalgette, C. (Ed.) (1989) *Primary Media Education: A Curriculum Statement* London: BFI

Bazalgette, C. (1999) *Sabre-Tooth Tigers and Polar Bears* <http://mediaed.org.uk/posted_documents/Sabretooth.html> (June 1, 2001)

Barratt, A. J. B. (1998) *Audit of Media in English* London: BFI

Bleimann, B. Broadbent, S. and Simons, M. (Eds.) (1995) *Klondyke Kate and other non-fiction* London: English and Media Centre

Bowker, J. (Ed.) (1991) *Secondary Media Education: A Curriculum Statement* London: BFI

British Film Institute (1999) *Making Movies Matter: Report of the Film Education Working Group* London: BFI

Brown, J. *et al.* (1990) *Developing English for TVEI* Leeds: Leeds University

Brown, S. and Visocchi, P. (1991) *Hurdles and Incentives: Introducing Media Education into Primary and Secondary Schools* Edinburgh: Scottish Council for Research in Education

Buckingham, D. (1990a) *Watching Media Learning* London: Falmer

Buckingham, D. (1990b) English and Media Studies: Making the Difference *English Magazine* 23, pp. 8-12

Buckingham, D. (1990c) English and Media Studies: Getting Together *English Magazine* 24, pp. 20-23

Buckingham, D. (1993a) *Children Talking Television* London: Falmer

Buckingham, D. (Ed.) (1993b) *Reading Audiences: Young People and the Media* Manchester: Manchester University Press

Buckingham, D. and Sefton-Green, J. (Eds.) (1994) *Cultural Studies Goes to School: Reading and Teaching Popular Media* London: Taylor and Francis

Buckingham, D., Grahame, J. and Sefton-Green, J. (1995) *Making Media: Practical Production in Media Education* London: English and Media Centre

Buckingham, D. (Ed.) (1998) *Teaching Popular Culture: Beyond Radical Pedagogy* London: University College

Buckingham, D and Jones, K. (2000) Modest Proposals and Cultural Creativity *The English and Media Magazine* 41, Spring, pp. 11-16

Burn, A. (1998) The Robot in the Cornfield: Media Arts Across the Curriculum *The English and Media Magazine* 39, Autumn, pp. 27-32

Butts, D. (1986) *Media Education in Scottish Secondary Schools: A Research Study 1983-86* Stirling: University of Stirling

Cohen, L. and Manion, L. (1994) *Research Methods in Education* London: Routledge

Cooper, G. and Hart, A. (1991) *Understanding the Media* London: BBC/Routledge

Davies, C. (1996) *English, Language and Education* Buckingham: Open University Press

Department of Education and Science (1989) *English for Ages 5-16* York: National Curriculum Council (The Cox Report)

Department for Education (1990) *English in the National Curriculum, No.2* London: HMSO

Department for Education (1993) *English for Ages 5-16* London: HMSO

Department for Education (1995) *English in the National Curriculum* London: HMSO

Dickson, P. (1994) *A Survey of Media Education in Schools and Colleges* London: BFI

Goodwyn, A. and Findlay, A. (1997) *Media Education and Mother Tongue Teaching: Conflict or Convergence?* Paper delivered at Southern Media Education Research Group Symposium at the European Conference on Educational Research, Frankfurt

Grahame J. (1993) *The Advertising Pack* London: English and Media Centre

Grahame, J. (1995) *The News Pack* London: English and Media Centre

Graddol, D. (1994) The Visual Accomplishment of Factuality in Graddol, D. and Boyd-Barrett, O. (Eds.) *Media Texts: Authors and Readers* Clevedon: Multilingual Matters, pp. 136-160

Hall, S. and Whannel, P. (1964) *The Popular Arts* London: Hutchinson

Hart, A. (1992) Mis-reading English: Media, English and the Secondary Curriculum *The English and Media Magazine* 26, pp. 43-6

Hart, A. (Ed.) (1998) *Teaching the Media: International Perspectives* New Jersey: Lawrence Erlbaum

Hart, A. and Benson, T. (1993) *Media in the Classroom: English Teachers Teaching Media* Southampton: Southampton Media Education Group

Hughes, J. (2000) The Global Marketplace: Making Sense of the Future in Fawcett, D. (Compiler) *e-britannia* Luton: University of Luton Press pp. 7 and 23-42

Lankshear, A.J. (1993) The Use of Focus Groups in a Study of Attitudes to Student Nurse Assessment *Journal of Advanced Nursing* 18, pp. 1986-1989

Learmonth, J. and Sayer, M. (1996) *A Review of Good Practice in Media Education* London: BFI

Leavis, F. R. and Thompson, D. (1933) *Culture and Environment* London: Chatto and Windus

Livingstone, S. and Bovill, M. (1999) *Young People, New Media (Summary Report of the Research Project: Children, Young People and the Changing Media Environment)* London: London School of Economics

Masterman, L. (1980) *Teaching About Television* London: Macmillan

Murdock, G. and Phelps, G. (1973) *Mass Media and the Secondary School* Basingstoke: Macmillan

Media Education Wales (1996) *Review and Evaluation of Media Education in Wales* Cardiff: Media Education Wales

Qualifications and Curriculum Authority (1999) *English: The National Curriculum for England* London: DfEE, QCA

Richards, C. (1998) Beyond Classroom Culture in Buckingham, D. (Ed.) *Teaching Popular Culture: Beyond Radical Pedagogy* London: University College, pp. 132-152

Schools Curriculum and Assessment Authority (1995) *GCSE Regulations and Criteria* London: SCAA

Tobin, J. (2000) *Good Guys Don't Wear Hats* Stoke-on-Trent: Trentham

Tweddle, S., Adams, A., Clarke, S. *et al.* (1997) *English for Tomorrow* Buckingham: Open University Press

Twitchin, R. and Bazalgette, C. (Eds.) (1988) *Media Education Survey Report* London: BFI/NFER; New Edition (1994)

Wilson, V. (1997) Focus Groups: A Useful Qualitative Method for Educational Research? *Educational Research Journal* 23/2, pp. 209-224

The Authors

Dr. Andrew Hart is Senior Lecturer in Education at the Research and Graduate School of Education, University of Southampton, where he teaches Media Studies on the MA(Ed) course and directs the Research Training Programme. He has published widely on Media Education and has worked closely with teachers as Director of the Southampton Media Education Group (winner of the British Film Institute's Paddy Whannel Award for innovation in Media Education), as Director of the Southern Media Education Research Network and of the Media Education Centre. He has worked for SCAA and QCA as a specialist consultant on Media curricula and examinations. He is currently UK moderator of the *World Network for Media Education* and Editor of the *International Journal of Media Education.* Recent publications include *Understanding the Media* (Routledge, 1991), *Developing Media in English* (Hodder, 1995) and *Teaching the Media: International Perspectives* (LEA, 1998).

Dr Alun Hicks is Research Fellow at the Centre for Media Education, where he has carried out research for this project and for the Distance Learning Project. He was previously a secondary school teacher, Head of English and Advisory Teacher for Dorset LEA. He is an OFSTED Inspector and educational consultant who has worked extensively for QCA. He has published articles on Media teaching, historical fiction and story telling, including a chapter in *Making 'The Real World'* (Hart, 1988) on televisual presentation of science. He is External Moderator for the PGCE course in English at the University of Exeter and is currently completing a PhD at the University of Southampton on teaching about newspapers in secondary education in the UK.

Education Centre

Aims and Activities

Launched in 1996 and based in the *Research and Graduate School of Education, the Media Education Centre* has grown out of regional, national and international activities in the study of the media over the last decade. It will consolidate and extend the work of the *Southampton Media Education Group* and the *Southern Media Education Research Network* with Media researchers and practitioners both regionally and nationally. Internationally, Centre staff have established links with other European and world-wide work on Media through research and conference activities and through an extensive list of publications.

The *Media Education Centre* is a cross-faculty initiative linking Education, Arts and Social Science postgraduate work. Through its programme of seminars, conferences and publications, the Centre will act as a catalyst for new developments, as a forum for debate and as a mechanism for research collaboration. Postgraduate taught and research courses (including Distance Learning options) are also offered through the Research and Graduate School of Education.

Key features

* a forum for discussion about Media Education practice

* a source of current information and ideas about Media teaching

* an opportunity to meet professionals from the Media industries

* a well stocked Resource Bank of materials on free loan

* access to high-quality courses

* a means of evaluating and improving practice in Media Education through research and development work

Index